EURIPIDES

THE COMPLETE PLAYS
VOLUME IV

OTHER SMITH AND KRAUS TRANSLATIONS
BY CARL R. MUELLER

Aeschylus, *The Complete Plays, Vol. I*
Aeschylus, *The Complete Plays, Vol. II*

Johann Wolfgang von Goethe, *Faust, Part One* and *Part Two*

Heinrich von Kleist, *Three Major Plays*

Luigi Pirandello, *Three Major Plays*

Arthur Schnitzler, *Four Major Plays*

Sophokles, *The Complete Plays*

August Strindberg, *Five Major Plays, Vol. I*
August Strindberg, *Five Major Plays, Vol. II*

Frank Wedekind, *Four Major Plays, Vol. I*
Frank Wedekind, *Four Major Plays, Vol. II*

EURIPIDES

THE COMPLETE PLAYS
VOLUME IV

PHOENICIAN WOMEN
ORESTÊS
BAKKHAI
IPHIGENEIA IN AULIS
RHESOS

Translated by Carl R. Mueller

GREAT TRANSLATIONS SERIES

A Smith and Kraus Book

A Smith and Kraus Book
Published by Smith and Kraus, Inc.
177 Lyme Road, Hanover, NH 03755
www.smithkraus.com
© 2005 Carl R. Mueller
All rights reserved.

First Edition: October 2005
10 9 8 7 6 5 4 3 2 1
Manufactured in the United States of America
Cover and Text Design by Julia Hill Gignoux, Freedom Hill Design
Cover Illustration: Artemis. East Frieze of the Parthenon. 432 B.C.E.
Acropolis Museum, Athens.

The Library of Congress Cataloging-in-Publication Data
Euripides.
[Works. English. 2005]
The complete plays / Euripides ; translated by Carl R. Mueller. —1st ed.
v. cm. — (Great translations series)
Contents: v. 1. Alkêstis. Mêdeia. Children of Heraklês. Hippolytos —
v. 2. Andromachê. Hêkabê. Suppliant women. Êlektra. The madness of Heraklês —
v. 3. Trojan women. Iphigeneia in Tauris. Ion. Helen. Cyclops —
v. 4. Phoenician women. Orestês. Bakkhai. Iphigeneia in Aulis. Rhesos.
ISBN 1-57525-300-3 pbk (v. 1) ISBN 1-57525-433-6 cloth (v.1) —
ISBN 1-57525-321-6 pbk (v. 2) ISBN 1-57525-434-4 cloth (v.2) —
ISBN 1-57525-358-5 pbk (v. 3) ISBN 1-57525-435-2 cloth (v.3) —
ISBN 1-57525-374-7 pbk (v. 4) ISBN 1-57525-436-0 cloth (v.4)
1. Euripides—Translations into English. 2. Greek drama (Tragedy)—Translations into English. 3. Mythology, Greek—Drama. I. Mueller, Carl Richard. II. Title.
III. Great translations for actors series
PA3975.A1 2005
882'.01--dc22   2005051719

CONTENTS

Euripides and the Athenian Theater of His Time 1

The Plays 13

A Note on the Translation 33

PHOENICIAN WOMEN 39

ORESTÊS 101

BAKKHAI 169

IPHIGENEIA IN AULIS 231

RHESOS 291

Glossary 333

Select Bibliography 343

Euripides and the Athenian Theater of His Time

I ᘓ THE LIFE

Of the many tragedians practicing in Athens during the fifth century (note: all dates are BCE), the work of only three of them is extant. Numerous others we know by name, from records, from stone inscriptions recording their victories in dramatic competitions, and from commentary by their contemporaries. Why, then, should the work of only three of these have survived? One answer might be that they represented the cream of the crop; that their plays were popular and received numerous productions after their first appearance in competition in Athens, productions not only in the outlying demes of Athens, but as far away as Sicily and the Athenian colonies that dotted the coast of Asia Minor. These productions would have needed copies of the original manuscript, and the proliferation of such copies gave them a chance of survival that less popular plays would not have had. Additionally, their work was taken up by schools and used as teaching tools for learning the art of rhetoric. This leaves us with the Big Three of the Athenian fifth century: Aeschylus, Sophokles, and Euripides. And little as we know biographically about Aeschylus and Sophokles, we know next to nothing about Euripides.

By the time people came to be interested in the details of his life, it was too late. The documentation was gone; letters to and from him, recollections of friends and family had been swept away by the tide of time, even as early as the age of Aristotle, midway in the fourth century. The majority of references to him remaining from the fifth century are from the Old Comedy tradition of Aristophanes and others. It was part of the art of Old Comedy to be topical. Few public figures escaped lambasting by Old Comedy: politicians, military men, civic leaders, philosophers, poets, playwrights, even the gods. Everyone was a potential target, and they must have loved it; it was part of an open society. Even Sokrates must have laughed at his not-so-flattering representation on Aristophanes' stage. These contemporary references, of course, were not meant to serve posterity as biographical source material, and yet not a few have used them as such.

It is said by some that Euripides, for example, was philosophically inclined and that that inclination served to cast doubt on Greek tragedy's religious basis. He is also said in his dramatic work to have been an antitraditionalist. But, as David Kovacs has pointed out, such imputations most likely rely on the evidence of Old Comedy. And, comedy being comedy, it has as its principal bent the art of exaggeration. If Aristophanes in *Clouds* makes Sokrates appear to be, as Kovacs writes, "a quack scientist and a teacher of dishonest rhetoric," it should be understood as part of the joke that Old Comedy not only had the right but was expected to indulge in. "For a joke to be worth making in Old Comedy, there need only be a slight resemblance between the actual person and his comic representation."

How little need be the resemblance between the comic representation and the individual being referenced is seen in Aristophanes' *Frogs* in which Aeschylus and Euripides are pitted against one another in Hades. The Aeschylus caricature is seen as retrogressive in his grandiloquence, pompous, infatuated with the past, old-fashioned in the extreme, a staunch moralist and a didact, while Euripides is faulted with the infelicity of introducing speaking slaves onto his stage and with allowing for the lowly and conventional. The truth of the matter is that slaves with speaking roles appear first in Aeschylus, and, as Kovacs points out, Orestês' wet nurse even describes her one-time ward's toilet-training, a liberty to which not even Euripides would sink. Kovacs continues:

> The Aristophanic Euripides is as new-fangled as his Aeschylus is old-fashioned. The real Euripides, of course, had made innovations in the tragic art, and on many points of style he stands at the opposite pole to the practice of Aeschylus. It makes comic sense, however, that as the representative of the new manner he should also be given other traits that may not correspond to the real Euripides any more than priggish moralism or exaggerated decorum belonged to the real Aeschylus. Where Aeschylus is pious, he is an atheist. Where Aeschylus champions the heroic and believes in tragic decorum, Euripides is the spokesman for *verismo* and dwells with artistic satisfaction on the ordinary and everyday. It is quite possible that the comic poet has here given himself a great deal of latitude to portray both the tragic poets in ways that do not necessarily correspond to the way they are or are perceived.

Or to put it another way: a major attribute of comedy in all ages is to allow for distortion to activate the risible.

Equally suspect is the tendency of some critics to interpret the plays based on "facts" from unreliable biographical sources and, contrarywise, to see in his plays intellectual and behavioral tendencies of the man himself. Was Euripides an agnostic? Was he a misogynist? If Euripides' purpose in writing *Mêdeia* was to demonstrate the evil of Woman, and if Hippolytos's condemnation of Woman is really the voice of his creator, then by all means. The problem, of course, is that there is no evidence on which to base such theses. No more (indeed far less) than we have for a similar misguided exercise in regard to Shakespeare.

What, then, do we know about Euripides with reasonable certainty? The fact is not much. He is said to have been born on the island of Salamis off the western coast of Greece on the very day of the Battle of Salamis in which Athens finally defeated the Persian Empire under Xerxes. This is doubtful, and most likely an example of remembering a difficult date by shifting it to a date that is easily remembered, as the Battle of Salamis most certainly was. It is safe, however, to say that he was born in the 480s but precisely where is suggested by only one or two bits of stone-engraved evidence, namely that as a boy he participated in a festival to Apollo Delios in Phyla, one of the demes of Athens. Another indisputable fact is that he won the prize in tragedy four times, one of those being posthumous. We know, too, that he first entered the tragic competition at Athens in 455 and that his final entry in the Great Dionysia was probably in 408, after which he left for Macedonia and the court of King Archelaus. It is said he left Athens a bitter man, possibly because he felt unappreciated. The more likely explanation, as has been suggested, is that life in Athens, after a war of more than two decades, a war, moreover, that Athens would soon lose, became too difficult. He died in 406. Athens fell to Sparta in 404.

Richard Rutherford has summarized Euripides' life rather well: "The constant parodies and references to his plays in Aristophanes' comedies are not only satirical criticism but a kind of tribute to a playwright whose work he obviously knew intimately and whose significance was beyond question."

II ∾ THE THEATER AND ITS FORM

One of the fascinating questions in regard to the Athenian theater of the fifth century—used by Aeschylus, Sophokles, and Euripides—is what was it like? Actually we know virtually nothing about it, as little as we know about the origin of Athenian tragedy. What we do know is that the first performances of Athenian tragedy in the mid-sixth century took place in the Agora, the

Athenian market place, a place of general assembly, and that spectators sat on wooden bleachers. Then, around 500, the theatrical performance site was moved to the Sacred Precinct of Dionysos on the south side of the Akropolis. At first spectators may have sat on the natural slope of the hill to watch the performance, an arrangement most likely superceded by wooden bleachers introduced for greater audience comfort. But even this is guesswork, logical as it sounds. From here (or perhaps even before we arrive here), the general public image of the Athenian Theater of Dionysos makes a great and very wrong-headed leap some one hundred and fifty years into the future to the middle of the fourth century and the most esthetically harmonious of all Greek theaters, that at Epidauros. There we have a stone *skênê* building to serve as backing for the action, a building with from one to three doors and fronted by a line of pillars, the *proskênion*; possibly there is a second story to the *skênê* building and a *logeion*, the *skênê's* roof for the appearance of gods and even mortals. We then perhaps see a raised terrace or low stage area in front of the *skênê* where some if not most of the action takes place, and then, in front of all that, the most crucial element of all, a perfectly round and very large orchestra made of pounded earth and circled in stone. And, not least, the vast reaches of a stone auditorium, in Greek the *theatron*.

Certain as that structure may still be at Epidauros, it has no precedent in Athens until the 330s when *stoa, skênê*, and *theatron* were finally finished in stone. There is evidence, however, that the oldest stone *skênê* in Athens dates from sometime between 421 and 415, some thirty-four to forty years after Euripides first ventures into playwriting. And we know that for some years prior to that, the *skênê* was made of wood, torn down at the end of each festival, and rebuilt (perhaps newly designed) the next year. Just when, however, that wooden *skênê* was first introduced is a mystery that may never find an answer, if for no other reason than the fragility of such a structure and/or the fact that it was regularly demolished at the close of each festival. The earliest call in an extant Greek tragedy for a *skênê* of whatever construction comes in 458 for Aeschylus's *Oresteia*. But that is no indication that the *skênê* did not exist earlier in the century, that it could not have been called for by a play that no longer exists. Nonetheless, we can at least say that Euripides' first extant play, *Alkêstis*, in 438, unequivocally calls for one, as do his remaining eighteen extant plays.

As for a raised acting area in front of the *skênê* for *Oresteia*, it is possible, but it is only in the late fifth and early fourth centuries that there is evidence in the form of vase paintings of a low, raised platform for the performance of tragedy, a platform raised about a meter (roughly forty inches) and mounted via a flight of steps in the center, steps suggesting that action was not confined to the platform but spilled out into the orchestra. This, of course, still tells us nothing about the positioning of theatrical action in the earlier period from the late sixth to well into the fifth century, nor is it conclusive evidence that such a raised level actually existed in Athens in the fifth century. Nothing short of archeological evidence could do that, and of that there is none. From a purely practical standpoint, it must be asked what if anything would have been served by such a raised level, especially considering that the action of the play was looked down upon by a steeply raked *theatron* of spectators and that even the first row of seats, the thrones for priests and dignitaries, was itself raised above the ground-level playing area.

It is also not known what the original shape of the early Athenian orchestra might have been, that area where the Chorus sang and danced elaborate choreographies. There are examples of smaller, outlying Attic theaters of the later fifth century, whose orchestras were other than circular. Both Thorikos and Trachones had tiny provincial deme theaters in which the audience was seated on wooden benches in a rectangular arrangement in close proximity to the acting area, which, as well, may have been loosely rectangular, or, even more likely, trapezoidal, with only two sides being parallel. It is possible that the early shape of the theater at Athens was the same, with the exception that it would have been on a much grander scale. Where does all this lead? Not much of anywhere except more speculation. Some scholars maintain, for example, that there is no evidence for a circular orchestra in Athens before the 330s, whereas others argue that the choreography performed by the Chorus required a circular area, and thus there must have been one from the start. In any event, the question for Athens can never be answered because subsequent reconfigurations of the theater have destroyed all archeological evidence.

III ✧ THE MASK

Whatever the layout of the early Athenian Theater of Dionysos, it is a fair guess that to accommodate the numbers of male citizens of that thriving metropolis and many from its outlying demes, not to mention important foreign visitors, the structure could not have been less than sizable. And size brought with it distance from the theatrical event as the eventual *theatron* at Athens in the 330s still demonstrates, rising as it does to touch the fortified walls of the Akropolis some hundreds of feet away. The capacity of the theater has been judged to be somewhere between fifteen and twenty thousand.

Whether distance served as an incentive to the use of masks (some have speculated that they served as a megaphone to project the voice to the farthest rows) is not known, nor is it the most salient reason for the use of the mask, for there are others. There is ample evidence, for example, that in Greece the use of the mask in cult ceremonies was widespread. Adolescent rites of passage, puberty rites, known from Sparta, made use of masks of considerable grotesqueness. And the cult of Dêmêtêr and Dêspoina at Lycosura is known for its use of animal masks. Then, of course, there is the mask used closer to home, in the cult of Dionysos, from which the mask in Greek tragedy most likely derives. Whether amplification had any part in the use of masks on the Athenian stage, they at least gave a greater presence to the actor wearing one, for they were large enough to cover the entire head. Made generally of linen, the fifth-century mask represented types rather than individuals. Perhaps the most compelling reason for them is the need for two and later three actors to act out all the speaking roles.

The rationale might also have been one of economy. Considering that tragedy was a masked entertainment, it was only practical to confine the number of speaking parts in any one scene to three actors, the reason most likely being, as Easterling suggests, to enable the audience to tell "where the voice is coming from," inasmuch as facial movements were obscured by masks. This practical limitation, however, permitted an actor to be double- and perhaps even triple-cast, a practice much used and most often, one must assume, to very good effect. In any case, even though the primary reason for only three actors was very likely a financial consideration, to have a single actor play, for example, the roles of Klytaimnêstra, Êlektra, and Athêna in *Oresteia*, or, in the same play, the roles of Agamemnon and Orestês; or in Euripides' *Bakkhai* Pentheus and his mother Agavê, and in Sophokles' *Women of Trachis* the roles of Dêianeira and Heraklês—each of which possibilities offers resonances that are far-reaching and highly intriguing. One must also not forget that masks were helpful in disguising the male actor who traditionally assumed female roles, women being excluded from theatrical performance. As for the numbers of nonspeaking actors on stage, there was no limit, and exciting stage effects with scores of extras would not have been unusual.

IV ✧ THE CHORUS AND DANCE

Of all the elements of theatrical practice, the importance of the Chorus cannot be overestimated. In Athens especially there was a long tradition (even before tragedy) of an emphasis on the competition of dithyramb choruses that consisted of both song and dance. Even in the days of tragedy, there were separate competitions devoted to the dithyramb in which each of the ten demes of Athens participated. In Aeschylus's day the tragic Chorus numbered twelve, then Sophokles added three more for a total of fifteen. In his *Tragedy in Athens* David Wiles gives a brilliant and convincing exposition of the degree to which the tragic Chorus participated in the theatrical event. He posits (with help from other scholars) that not only was the choreographed movement of the Chorus not in straight lines or highly formalized, as previously thought, but that it was often particularly active. When, for example, the Chorus of Young Theban Women in Aeschylus's *Seven Against Thebes* makes its first entrance, it is anything but sedate; it is disordered in the extreme (choreographed disorder, to be sure), but their terror of the encroaching war outside their city gates is such that it prompts the agitated reentry of Eteoklês who deals harshly with them for their civic disturbance. In Sophokles' *Oedipus at Kolonos* there is a similar entry by the Chorus of Old Men who dart wildly about the orchestra in search of the intruder into the Sacred Grove.

Wiles makes a most insightful deduction when he posits that the subject of each choral ode is acted out by the Chorus in choreographed dance. And even more startling, that during long narrative speeches, such as the Persian Herald's speech in *Persians*, in which he describes the defeat of the Persian forces in the naval battle at Salamis; or the narrative in *Bakkhai* describing the death of Pentheus; or in *Hippolytos*, the bull from the sea; or the sacrifice of Iphigeneia at Aulis. In each of these, the Chorus was actively acting out a choreography that visually complemented the verbal narration. The brilliance of this deduction is staggering in indicating the degree of the participation of the Chorus in Athenian tragedy: they were seldom inactive, and not only did they wear the persona of their first function as Old Men of Kolonos or Young Theban Women, but also served as an abstract or distanced body that acted out the subject of others' narration of which in no event could they have had any foreknowledge. It helps to understand why when Athenians attended the theater at festival times they spoke of going to the "choreography" rather than to the play.

V ∿ MUSIC

Of music in Archaic and Classical Greece we know very little. Some music scores survive, but they are largely fragmentary and date from the Hellenistic period or later. Although the Greeks were knowledgeable about a great many musical instruments, especially from their eastern neighbors, they adopted only two main sorts: stringed instrument (lyre) and wind instrument or pipe (*aulos*), not a flute but sounded with a reed (single and double). In tragedy of the fifth century, the double-pipe *aulos* was the instrument of choice to accompany the musical sections of the dramatic action, though drums may very well also have been employed, as for example in *Bakkhai* where drums are frequently mentioned.

The musical element in the performance of fifth-century tragedy was of primary importance. Every one of the extant tragedies has built into it a number of choral sections (usually five) that cover generally short passages of time and in which the singing and dancing Chorus holds the center of attention in the orchestra. In addition, there are sections in which song is exchanged between characters, as well as an alternation between spoken dialogue and recitative or song, the latter often between a character or characters and the Chorus. As Easterling rightly points out, these sections exist in the same time frame as the scenes of exclusively spoken dialogue. The rationale behind this practice being "to intensify emotion or to give a scene a ritual dimension, as in a shared lament or song of celebration." To what extent music was employed in performance is not known, but it is intriguing to speculate that its role was enormous and went far beyond those sections of the plays that call unequivocally for it.

VI ❧ THE CITY DIONYSIA

What we know about the production of tragedy in Greece is almost totally confined to Attica, though other areas were also active producers. In any event, from the close of the sixth and throughout the fifth century, tragedy was primarily performed as part of the Great or City Dionysia in Athens, though tragedy was also a part of the Rural Dionysia during the winter months when access to Athens was inhibited because of weather. But tragedy was not the sole reason for these festivals. They also scheduled processions, sacrifices in the theater, libations, the parade of war orphans, and the performance of dithyramb and comedy. And as summary, the final day was devoted to a review of the conduct of the festival and to the awarding of prizes.

Three tragedians competed with three plays each plus a satyr play, all chosen by the *archon*, a state official who also appointed the three *chorêgoi* who undertook the expense of equipping and training the choruses, the actors and playwrights being paid for by the state. One judge from each of the ten tribes or demes of Athens was chosen to determine the winners of the competition, and the winning playwright was crowned with a wreath of ivy in the theater. Till about the middle of the fifth century, the three tragedies of each day's performance comprised a trilogy of interconnected plays; eventually each of the three plays had a different subject and were independent of one another, but always there was a satyr play.

And then there was Dionysos.

VII ∾ NOTHING TO DO WITH DIONYSOS?

Dionysos. What had the theater to do with Dionysos, and Dionysos with the theater? How did the two become one and mutually express one another as an indigenous Athenian institution? What is it that is quintessentially associated with Dionysos that makes him the appropriate representative of the art of drama, and in particular of tragedy?

Some scholars believe that, since the subject of the dithyramb chorus was Dionysos, tragedy, developing out of the dithyramb (as Aristotle conjectured), simply took with it its subject. Now, of course, we are less than certain of that succession, especially when one considers, as Herington puts it, the "catholicity of the art form" of tragedy in the subjects it treats; for, though Dionysos plays a significant part as a subject, he has considerable competition. Or is it his otherness that makes him tragedy's apt representative, his transformative aspect (both animate and inanimate), or simply his inability to be pinned down as being either this or that? Some would say that his cult ritual, which existed long before tragedy, possessed aspects that made it prototypical of drama: the use of masks for disguise, ecstatic possession and the capacity to assume alternate personalities, mystic initiation. And then there is wine, discovered by Dionysos, and the wildness of nature, the power of his ambivalent sexuality, his association with dance in partnership with satyrs and maenads. These are only a few of the possibilities that may have led to this inexhaustible god's association with drama. Which it was, of course, we will never know; but a fair guess might be that each of these attributes, and perhaps others, contributed

One thing, however, is certain, that in the early period of tragedy, from the late sixth and well into the fifth century, tragedy was associated with the satyr play, that light send-up of a classical mythological subject. What's more, once tragedy emerged, the same playwrights who wrote the tragedies also wrote the satyr play that culminated the day's dramatic event.

Easterling finds that all three of these forms (dithyramb, satyr play, and tragedy) share one thing: song and dance, and, as she says,

. . . among them it was satyr play that was the most obviously
Dionysiac element, since the chorus of satyrs, far more than any other
choral group, was explicitly and by definition part of the god's entourage, and satyrs of various types, as we have known from vase-
paintings, had been associated with Dionysus well before the dramatic
festivals were established.

The question remains: what made Dionysos the god uniquely suited to
drama? Authentic, testable proof from the time of its formation doesn't exist,
and we have only the extant plays (a small remnant of the total production of
those years) to look to for possibilities.

Perhaps one of the most salient reasons for Dionysos as god of theater is
the mask, for at its core it is the very essence of the Dionysiac, which, ultimately, is escape. But who would think of Greek tragedy as escapist fare, the
means of leaving reality behind? And yet, is it so impossible that tragedy's re-
moval from real life gave the same satisfaction, then as now, albeit of a different kind? Greek tragedy, after all, is filled with Alienation devices. Just as the
Elizabethan playgoer didn't speak the language of Shakespeare's stage in the
street, the diction, the vocabulary, the very syntax of Attic tragedy (not to
mention the emotional manipulation possible through various skillfully applied metric systems) was even more removed from the daily patter of the
Athenian Agora, especially in Aeschylus and Sophokles, though perhaps less
so in Euripides, dramatic dialogue in whatever age never being the argot of
the marketplace.

And as for the mask and its Dionysiac potentialities, it permits an actor
to take on not just one but as many roles as needed in the course of the tragic
trilogy and its culminating satyr play. In the early days of tragedy, there was
one actor, then Aeschylus added a second, and Sophokles a third. No matter
how many actors (one or three), they were required to play as many speaking
roles as the play called for, each time changing masks to assume another character. And since only males were permitted to act, a male would as easily per-
form a female as a male role. Pentheus, for example, in *Bakkhai*, also plays his
mother Agave who at the end enters carrying her son's severed head. In other
cases an actor could play four or even five roles. Furthermore, each of the four
Choruses in a tetralogy would assume another, separate, identity, finally and
inevitably ending up as a band of cavorting and lascivious satyrs. And then,
of course, there is the distancing of the music as well as the elaborate choreography of the Chorus.

So fictive is this convention of masks in the Attic theater that it is as
iconoclastic in regard to everyday reality as is the Epic, anti-illusionist, theater

of Brecht. No Athenian in that Theater of Dionysos could have failed finally to be aware of the game openly and unashamedly being played on him, and he must have relished it, knowing by subtle means, by the timbre of a voice, by delivery, or some other telltale sign that Pentheus was now (in the terrible/ wonderful deception that was theater) his mother carrying his own head. Which doesn't mean that theater couldn't also be the bearer of weighty messages, such as: as you sow, so also shall you reap—a lesson Pentheus learns too late. In any event, an illusion of reality was deliberately broken that said to that vast audience that this is not life as you know it, and besides, there's always the down-and-dirty ribaldry of the satyr play to send you home laughing at its unmediated escapist function, just in case you fell into the trap of taking things a bit too seriously.

One other thing regarding the mask needs saying. As we know from Greek pottery (in particular large *kraters* for the storage of wine), in the cult rituals of Dionysos, the god was frequently "present" in the form of a large suspended or supported mask, suggesting two intriguing possibilities: (1) that he served as an observer, and (2) that he observed the playing out in the ritual of many of his characteristics. It is fascinating to associate that spectatorship of the ritual Dionysos with the fact that at the beginning of every City Dionysia at Athens a large statue of Dionysos was placed dead center in the *theatron* to oversee the day's theatrical representation of himself in the form of mask, transformation, disguise, ecstatic possession, dance (to name only a few), and, in the satyr play, debauchery, drunkenness, and general ribaldry.

And then there was sex.

VIII ⟶ THE ALL-INCLUSIVE GOD

The sexual import of Dionysos and his cult is quite beyond refutation. His most formidable aspect *in absentia* is the giant phallus, a sign of generation and fertility, a ritual instrument that was prominently displayed and carried through the streets in procession on various holidays, as well as ritually sequestered (in small) in a cradlelike enclosure and treated at women's festivals as the product of its fertility, a baby. In small, it was a piece of polished wood looking like nothing so much as a dildo.

As a subject for Attic tragedy, sex cannot be denied; it appears so often as not only a motif but as a catalytic motivational force in one play after another, so significant an element that Attic tragedy could scarcely do without it.

One has only to think of Phaidra and Hippolytos; the Suppliants and their Egyptian suitors; Mêdeia and Jason; Laïos, Oedipus, and Iokastê;

Heraklês and Dêianeira; and Pentheus and Dionysos. In each of these relationships, sex is dark, disruptive, tragic, leading inevitably to the resolution of all problems: count no man happy till he is dead.

Dionysos and death? The Dionysos who gives wine, who causes milk to flow from the earth and honey to spout from his ritual *thyrsos*, who carouses with his satyrs and maenads in the mountains? The answer can only be yes, as much death as freedom, as much death as liberation, as escape, as dissolution, as sex itself—no infrequent carrier of the death motif as rapture in destruction. Death is, after all, the only total escape, the only true liberation from pain and distress and dishonor and fear, the only unalloyed pleasure that ultimately is nothing less than the paradoxical absence of that pleasure in nonbeing.

When we consider how often the death expedient is invoked in Athenian tragedy—and particularly, perhaps, in Euripides—and how often it is the only answer to the dark shadow of sex that enfolds these plays, we come to the realization that the Dionysos situated commandingly dead center in that Athenian theater that bears his name, watching himself onstage in every event that transpires on it, from the playful to the tragic, is not only watching, not merely observing from his place of honor, but, like the gods in various of his plays, directing, manipulating the action and the fate of his characters—like Aphroditê and Artemis in *Hippolytos*, like Athêna in *Aias*, like Dionysos himself in *Bakkhai*. In the end, Dionysos is the god of the theater because Dionysos is Everything, All: light-dark, hot-cold, wet-dry, sound-silence, pleasure-pain, life-death. And if he lures his Athenian audience unsuspectingly into his theater to escape "reality" by raising life to a level that exceeds, indeed transcends, reality, whether by means of language, or dimension, or poetry, or the deceptively *fictive* games he plays with masks and actors playing not only their own characters but others as well, he does so with a smile (he is, after all, known as the "smiling god," though at times demonically, eyes like spiraling pinwheels, tongue hanging lax from languid lips). He knows what they don't know—that it really is life up there on his stage, a mirror of him and of all things, of his all-encompassing fertility (which also includes death). As such there can be no question why he is the god of theater, but most specifically of tragedy, because in the end death is the only answer, and sex, life's greatest pleasure, becomes the catalyst that ultimately leads to death, which is the greatest pleasure of all and has everything to do with Dionysos.

Carl R. Mueller
Department of Theater, School of Theater, Film and Television
University of California, Los Angeles

The Plays

PHOENICIAN WOMEN

I

Phoenician Women is one of the most varied of all Euripides' plays. It is packed with incident as is no other extant Athenian tragedy. It is spacious in its descriptions of places and details of things, suffusing it with so gigantic a sweep that Kitto was inspired to call it not only a cinema but a "very good cinema." An unusual description for a work that ostensibly is meant to be a tragedy inasmuch as tragedies tend to focus inward rather than outward.

The scene is Thebes, in front of the royal palace seen so often on the Athenian stage in its rich proliferation of plays devoted to the myth of the House of Labdakos and its inhabitants: Kadmos, Laïos, Iokastê, Oedipus, Eteoklês, Polyneikês, Antigonê, and Ismênê. The façade is pierced by a single large portal, and its roof will be prominently used in this play. There is also an altar to Apollo near the door. Given the theatrical fame of this palace on the Athenian stage, the audience seated in that Theater of Dionysos around 409 will know it to be ancient, vast, and splendorous. This is, after all, Thebes. Perhaps, from time to time, to reduce the place's expansiveness and provide more of a focus, Euripides mentions the women's quarters, Antigonê's apartment, and the rooms that house the blind Oedipus.

Nonetheless, the playwright outdoes himself with detail, not least regarding the outlying city of Thebes. We are constantly reminded, as Elizabeth Craik notes in her edition of the play, of temples, statues, altars, tombs; of the site where Teiresias carries out his work of divination, the cave where the famous dragon of Thebes slain by Kadmos once lived, and the cliff above it that will figure in one of the play's major incidents. Then, of course, there are the majestic, fabled seven gates piercing the proud fortifications of the walls, and the towers of those walls. And then the natural terrain. From the roof of the palace her old Tutor invites Antigonê to look out: "From here you can survey the plains and the vast encampment of the enemy Argive army beside the waters and streams of Ismênos and Dirkê." And Kithairon, mysterious mountain of the fate of Oedipus.

But this is a war play, Thebes is under siege. And so we hear from the very first scene of military installations, siege works and trenches. "This background," writes Craik, "established early and sustained throughout, gives the play a strong spatial sweep and sense of locale, enhancing the presentation of the current action in the play's imagined territory and fostering visualization of past Theban events."

II

In *Phoenician Women* Euripides introduces a number of moves that must have both surprised and delighted his fifth-century Athenian audience. To begin with, Iokastê, mother and wife of Oedipus, is still alive. When last we heard of her in Sophokles, for example, she had committed suicide when faced with the shame of her fate. And we soon learn that Oedipus, too, blind and ancient, is still in the palace and not out wandering in exile. We learn in due course that when his two sons Eteoklês and Polyneikês learn of their origin as sons as well as brothers of their father/brother, in shame they keep him in captivity in the palace. In turn, for their mistreatment of him, Oedipus puts upon them the curse of mutual fratricide. The brothers agree to rule Thebes in alternate years. Polyneikês, the younger of the two, fearing the curse of Oedipus, goes into voluntary exile. But when the time comes for Eteoklês to cede his throne for a year to Polyneikês, he refuses, and in addition himself exiles his brother. Polyneikês goes to Argos where he marries the daughter of King Adrastos, who helps him in organizing the military expedition known as the Seven Against Thebes. As another surprise, Euripides makes Eteoklês the bad brother and Polyneikês the good, quite the reverse of their natures in Aeschylus's *Seven Against Thebes*. But that element of surprise was expected and much appreciated by the contemporary classical spectator.

III

Much has been made in the course of these play discussions in trying to link up the theme of Euripides' plays with the historical time of their composition, most particularly in regard to their relationship to the ravages of the decades-long Peloponnesian War and the effect it had on the Greek people. One possible date for *Phoenician Women* is around 409, by which time the Peloponnesian War is well into its third decade and things are not going well. Vellacott sums up the situation with particular acuity.

The real significance of this play lies first in the truth it presented to a population which was beginning to feel itself besieged; and secondly in the lucid diagram it offers, to readers of subsequent ages, of the springs of war in the emotional attitudes of men. The play is addressed directly to the citizens of Athens on the one topic which in 409 confronted them afresh every day, especially at the time of the Dionysia, when one more—the twenty-third—summer's military activities were about to begin. The theme is war—the war of the Seven against Thebes; but from the outset Thebes is clearly and deliberately identified with Athens in the minds of the spectators. Iokastê as Prologue tells the listeners that the scene is Thebes, a besieged city, and that the issue of the drama is to be the quarrel between Eteoklês king of Thebes and his brother Polyneikês who has come with a foreign army to attack and destroy the city of his birth. This all too real situation is made almost visible in the prologue to an audience who for several years past have watched from the walls of Athens the movements of Spartan troops, now permanently based at Decelea, an hour's ride to the north.

Tragic as the fall of Athens to Sparta may have been in 404, not too many years off from 409, in many respects Athens created the situation that lead to its defeat. The Peloponnesian War was a battle between brother states over who would dominate the whole of Greece with power, might, wealth, influence, and colonization. By this time there cannot but have been Athenians who questioned both their political and moral stance, as indeed Thucydides did repeatedly in his history of that desperate period.

IV
The text of *Phoenician Women* underwent much interpolation in the centuries after its first performance and therefore is subject to considerable editorial emendation, in particular in its closing section. Every editor and translator must either accept the totality of what tradition has handed down or try in the best way possible to restore it to what each perceives to have been its original form. That is the approach taken here.

◦∾◦

ORESTÊS

I

There are critics, as M. L. West in his edition of the play notes, who maintain that the behavior of Orestês, Êlektra, and Pyladês in the latter portion of Euripides' *Orestês* is a reflection of the general temper of the time as described by Thucydides in his *History of the Peloponnesian War,* a reality which he saw as early as the year of the war's inception in 431. Thucydides writes:

> As a result of these revolutions, there was a general deterioration of character throughout the Greek world. The simple way of looking at things, which is so much the mark of a noble nature, was regarded as a ridiculous quality and soon ceased to exist. Society had become divided into two ideologically hostile camps, and each side viewed the other with suspicion. As for ending this state of affairs, no guarantee could be given that would be trusted, no oath sworn that people would fear to break; everyone had come to the conclusion that it was hopeless to expect a permanent settlement and so, instead of being able to feel confident in others, they devoted their energies to providing against being injured themselves.

West remarks:

> There is much in this that may be applied to Orestês and his friends by a critic who, aloof as Thucydides, reads the play in his study. But Euripides was not writing for such persons. He was writing for a theater audience whose emotions he had enlisted on Orestês' side. What does the academic critic think that Orestês and Êlektra ought to have done? Taken their medicine like sportsmen, or like Socrates, hymning the supremacy of law, leaving Menelaos and Helen in possession of Agamemnon's house and throne?

The answer to some will be a resounding no, if for no other reason than that what may be proper and ethical and moral today need not always have been proper and ethical and moral. Times change and people change with the times. The Hippolyte and Phèdre of Racine are not the Hippolytos and Phaidra of Euripides. West writes of this misperception as follows:

In the last third of the play these paragons turn without a qualm to murder, hostage-taking, and arson in the hope of (a) taking revenge on Menelaos for failing to save them and (b) escaping with their lives. They would certainly have used bombs if they had had any. Now it is easy for us to say "Why, they are behaving like a modern terrorist group: this we can only condemn." But the ancient Athenian spectator will have applied different categories. Where we see crimes, he saw resourcefulness, a brilliant plan being carried out boldly and efficiently. It was self-evident to him that one seeks to preserve one's life and one's friends' lives and injure one's enemy. In Greek eyes the application of cunning and ruthlessness to such ends is admirable, whether in a Homeric hero or in a Resistance fighter, to all who sympathize with the cause. Our ancient spectator held no brief for Menelaos or Helen, and after seeing the affair from Orestês' and Êlektra's point of view all the way through, he was not going to be alienated by their use of an unscrupulous stratagem in order to come out on top. If Euripides had wanted him to be, his chorus would have shown the way. But the chorus remains supportive of Orestês and Êlektra: despite its horror at the murder of Klytaimnêstra, it approves of the murder of Helen.

II

If the behavior of Orestês, Êlektra, and Pyladês fails to reflect the temper of the time of the play's production in 408, there is still much in the play that does and almost certainly helps date it for us.

At the close of the fifth century democratic Athens was the scene of several oligarchic revolutions. In 411 it was the body of the Four Hundred that was set up to rule Athens. The *Oxford Classical Dictionary* defines Athenian oligarchy in comparison with a democracy. In a Greek democracy, particularly in Athens, political rights were extended to the totality of adult males in the "nonimmigrant population." As far as limitations in eligibility for the holding of office for these male citizens were concerned, there were, practically speaking, none, so slight were they. In an oligarchy, some of the free adult male citizen population were excluded from "even basic political rights," and even more of them might be excluded from office holding, thereby reducing "the amount of business which came the way of the full citizen body." In effect, then, democracy permitted political activity to the poor, whereas oligarchy not. Aristotle was inspired to say that "oligarchy is the rule of the rich and democracy is the rule of the poor."

West observes further of the oligarchy of the Four Hundred:

> With the Assembly restored to power, demagogues and hotheads like
> Cleophon once again came to the fore. There was a wave of recrimi-
> nations against all those compromised by the revolution. Hundreds
> were prosecuted and fined, deprived of civic rights, or put to death.
> As the witch-hunt continued, the unscrupulous took the opportunity
> to enrich themselves by blackmail or to settle private scores by mali-
> cious denunciation . . . Democracy was not seen at its best in those
> years.

That Euripides had every intention to record that albeit short-lived experience of oligarchy in 411 is testified to by the very way in which he altered
the myth of Orestês that he chose to deal with. In the traditional handling of
the myth, as in Aeschylus's *Oresteia,* or even Euripides' own *Êlektra,* Orestês
is immediately attacked by the vengeful Furies for his murder of his mother
Klytaimnêstra. He goes to Delphi for cleansing by Apollo but is pursued by
the Furies throughout Greece until finally he is directed by Apollo to Athens
where he is acquitted by Athêna at the court of the Areopagos.

In *Orestês* Euripides places the murder of Klytaimnêstra six days in the
past, and Orestês has not fled but is seen at the play's opening feverous and
hallucinating, stretched out on a bed in front of the palace tended by a dis-
traught Êlektra. Contrary to Aeschylus and other handlers of the traditional
myth, including Euripides in his *Êlektra,* the Argos of *Orestês* is not jubilant
at the end of the traditionally oppressive reign of Klytaimnêstra and Aigisthos;
rather, it rises violently against the two aristocratic children of the house of
Agamemnon, Orestês and Êlektra, with the intention of condemning them to
death for their crime and for the pollution they have brought on the city.

Euripides has created out of the stuff of the history he has just shortly
ago experienced the fable of his play. The Old Man in *Orestês* who just happens to be passing through town on his way from the country observes the
demos of Argos in Assembly, and we must assume that it was much like what
Euripides saw playing itself out at similar Assembly meetings on the Athenian Pynx in 411. The Old Man addresses Êlektra:

> But to get on with it—when every seat in the Assembly was filled, a
> herald rose up and asked: "Who will speak to the issue: is Orestês to
> be put to death for matricide?" Up sprang Talthybios, the same who
> helped sack Troy with your father. A toady of a man, never know what
> he thinks, talks out of both sides of his mouth at once, always bowing

to the first in power. He praises your father with high-flown phrases and then twists them round filthy criticism of your brother. And for what? Orestês, says he, set an example dangerous for parents. And all the while he smiles brightly at the friends of Aigisthos. But they're like that, heralds, all of them; jumping the fence, this side and that, whichever side holds the greater power. Next came Lord Diomêdês, advising not to kill you or your brother, but to satisfy religion by exile. His speech raised rounds of approval, but also disapproval. And then there arose a man whose mouth never rested. An arrogant, self-assured sort; a hireling if ever there was one. He spoke in favor of death by stoning for you and Orestês; but in truth he was nothing but a mouthpiece for Tyndareos. Another stood up then to argue the opposite. No great beauty, this man, but a man all the same, seldom seen in the town or marketplace, a small landholder, one of those we count on for the land's survival, shrewd, intelligent, a man eager to come to grips with the arguments. A man of discipline and free of corruption, whose life is above reproach. He argued for rewarding Orestês, son of Agamemnon, he said, wreathing his head with a garland, he said, for avenging his father's murder by killing that whore of a godless wife; that woman who was depriving us of all that, of taking up arms, of going off to war, if the men who stayed behind would undermine their houses and families by seducing the soldiers' wives. Those who were decent, at least, found him convincing, but no one spoke in support after that. Your brother then came forward, but his words, however eloquent, had no effect. The scoundrel won, the hireling, he got the most hands, the one who urged your and your brother's death. Poor Orestês had all he could do to persuade them not to kill you by stoning. And he only won that point by saying that the two of you would kill yourselves before the day's end.

If the demoralized populace of Greece was as badly off in 431 according to Thucydides, we have only to imagine the moral state of Athens after twenty-three years of warfare, a description which, according to M. L. West, does not include Orestês, Êlektra, and Pyladês. There are, of course, other critics who strongly disagree with this position regarding Euripides' central characters.

III
Without question, *Orestês* has elicited a multitude of contradictory responses from critics, and, as William Arrowsmith says, it "has long been an unpopular and neglected play, almost an unread one," and yet history testifies over-

whelmingly that it was the most famous and most performed play in classical antiquity. "Tragic in tone, melodramatic in incident and technique, by sudden wrenching turns savage, tender, grotesque, and even comic, combining sheer theatrical virtuosity with puzzling structural violence and a swamping bitterness of spirit," as Arrowsmith maintains, "like so many Euripidean plays, *Orestês* has had to pay the price for affronting the pat handbook theories of the well-constructed Greek play, and its very 'queerness' and bravura of bitterness have seemed to violate both the idea of tragedy and tragic dignity itself." Arrowsmith concludes:

> The *Orestês* can be accurately dated to the year 408 B.C.E., that is, just a year or so before Euripides, old, embittered, and disillusioned with Athens, withdrew in voluntary exile to Macedon, where he died a few years later. The political climate of the play itself graphically represents the state of affairs in Athens, and, presumptuous or not, I am tempted to see in the play Euripides' prophetic image of the final destruction of Athens and Hellas, or that Hellas to which a civilized man could still give his full commitment. It is a simple and a common symbolism: the great old house, cursed by a long history of fratricidal blood and war, brought down in destruction by its degenerate heirs. The final tableau is the direct prophecy of disaster, complete, awful, and inevitable, while Apollo intervenes only as an impossible wish, a futile hope, or a simple change of scene from a vision that cannot be brooked or seen for long because it is the direct vision of despair, the hopeless future.

Is it too much to suggest that in the early years of the twenty-first century the world has reached a place where in insanity and criminality it is in every way a parallel to that of Euripides' play, and that *Orestês* has every reason to be back in style and flourishing on our stages as a mirror to our own absurdity? Ovid, so long out of fashion because he didn't fit our previous image of ourselves, is back with a vengeance with his black humor and uncompromising pessimism. It may indeed be time once more for *Orestês*.

◆

BAKKHAI

I

In 408 Euripides, then in his early seventies, left Athens, most likely embittered and despondent over the course of the Peloponnesian War and the decline and degeneration of his beloved city, whose reduction to near chaos over the decades he had witnessed as well as warned against repeatedly in his work. His leaving was self-determined, voluntary exile, though possibly also encouraged by the invitation of King Archelaus of Macedon, a vast region in the north of Greece, a regent whose Hellenizing policy included extending patronage to various artists, sculptors, philosophers, poets, including Euripides. He lived for two more years, only to die there in 406. His son (or nephew) Euripides the Younger discovered among his effects three plays written during his residence in Macedon: *Bakkhai, Iphigeneia in Aulis,* and a third, *Alcmaion at Korinth,* now lost. Taking them back to Athens, the Younger Euripides produced them, most likely in 405, at the City Dionysia, winning for them the coveted first prize that more often than not had eluded the aged playwright during his lifetime.

II

Although most Athenian tragedies are based on myth, the source of *Bakkhai* is historical, however distant in the Bronze Age past, a time well before the year 1000. It concerns the introduction of the religious rites of Dionysos into mainland Greece, most likely from Asia Minor. David Kovacs points out that we know precious little about Dionysos in the classical period and earlier, but that we do know from the Linear B tablets that worship of Dionysos extends back at least to the Bronze Age palace civilization of Mykenê and Pylos that generated the tablets. As seen in *Bakkhai,* Kovacs continues,

> our earliest substantial witness, it was a religion of ecstasy, centered upon the experience of oneness with the god and with the *thiasos* (congregation or coven) of his worshippers. It seems to have provided, at stated times of the year, a release from conventional restraint, particularly for women, whose role in home and community was strictly circumscribed, allowing a brief period of truancy, not unlike Carnival, that paradoxically helped to maintain the usual order of things. Dionysos is credited with introducing viticulture and the liberating effect of wine. At Athens his two principal festivals, the City Dionysia in early spring and the Lenaea in late winter, become the venue for

tragedy and comedy. Some scholars have seen a link between the liberation from restraint offered by Dionysos and the assumption of other roles and personalities that makes drama what it is, and the earliest evidence we have of enactment by impersonation (drama) is the Dionysiac festivals of the sixth century. . . .

III

It is quite conventional when we think of Dionysos today to associate him primarily with wine, and with good reason. Wine is venerated in the play, and even the ancient prophet Teiresias praises the glory of the god's gift: "Human kind, young man," he says to the defiantly resistant Pentheus (who is at best sixteen or seventeen; he has down on his cheeks), "has two great powers."

> First, the goddess Dêmêter, or whatever you may call her, earth, perhaps, our source of solid food. And then this god, *this* god, this Dionysos, son of Semelê. He came later but he matched her gift when he invented for us the clear liquid juice of the grape. When we've drunk our fill, it brings an end to sorrow, brings sleep that drowns the day's cares and worries, the sole, the only remedy for our distress. Himself a god, he is poured in honor to the gods, to bring mankind their blessings. . . . Welcome this god to Thebes. Pour out wine in his honor. Wreathe your head with garlands and dance the Bakkhic dance.

Wine for Dionysos may be a major attribute, but to the classical Greek he was not exclusively, or even primarily, the god of wine, according to E. R. Dodds in his edition of the play. This is confirmed by the cult titles of Dionysos, such as the Power in the Tree, the Blossom Bringer, the Fruit Bringer, the Abundance of Life. According to Plutarch, as Dodds observes, the realm of Dionysos is the totality of nature: "—not only the liquid fire in the grape, but the sap thrusting in a young tree, the blood pounding in the veins of a young animal, all the mysterious and uncontrollable tides that ebb and flow in the life of nature."

IV

Wine, however, is not the only way for the follower of Dionysos to achieve personal oneness with the god, nor is it, as Dodds observes, the most important one. The Herdsman's description to Pentheus of the celebrating women in the clefts of Kithairon makes that very clear:

One of them seizes a wand and strikes a rock: an icy stream leaps out. Another plunges her wand into the earth: up springs Bakkhos in a flood of wine. Those eager for milk scratch the ground with their fingers: milk streams out. And pure honey spurts from the head of their wands!

It is only in the mind of the prurient and defensive young Pentheus that wine is misused in their rite. The Herdsman describes the women on the mountain:

> They were fast asleep, lying where exhaustion had dropped them; some leaning back against pine boughs, others resting their heads on pillows of oak leaves on the forest floor. Carelessly, perhaps, but modestly. Wine, yes, but not drunk, not as you say, sir, not driven to frenzy by shrieking flutes, not searching for sex on the mountain.

Dance, too, is a means to becoming *entheos*—one with the deity, as the Chorus of Asian Bakkhai sing at length of it in their entry song.

V

Criticism regarding the meaning of this greatest of Athenian tragedies is, perhaps, a futile endeavor. Read enough of the critics and you will, late or soon, find an interpretation that will suit you—at least for a time, for this play will change for you as often as you read it, and it demands repeated reading throughout a lifetime. As the reader changes, so changes the play. As one learns and experiences more, so the play is more profoundly experienced if not, indeed, better understood, for the play is securely founded on ambiguity, an ambiguity that is at the core of the character of Dionysos.

As the final section of the General Introduction in this volume discusses at length, Dionysos is a composite of opposites—hot-cold, light-dark, silence-sound, life-death, to name only a few. He is what any situation requires him to be. But above all else he is a force to be reckoned with, not to be subordinated, impossible to be ignored. He is the Id, but he is also the Superego, one and the same and at the same time utter opposites, eternally at odds with himself, both sides of the proverbial coin, just as he and Pentheus are blood relations, cousins, both of them Theban, and forever in conflict over the issue of *who rules here*. If Pentheus is the stonewalling tyrant, then Dionysos rises from inside him to tear down those walls, and the more resistance Pentheus offers, the more drastic is Dionysos's response. If Pentheus is Civilization, then Dionysos is the Discontent held prisoner within it. It is only when the two of them cease their internecine strife that a harmonious whole emerges and the energy once dissipated in struggle is turned to productivity, to the formation of an Ego that is stable, balanced, and creative, as indeed are the two ancient old men of Thebes—in this dream/nightmare of Pentheus—Kadmos and Teiresias, two who have it all together, who dance with Dionysos on the mountain and warn the hotheaded and inexperienced boy-king that there are things that are better taken on faith than fought against blindly, for death is a certainty waiting in the wings for his entrance.

$\diamond$

IPHIGENEIA IN AULIS

I

For the last quarter of the fifth century, the span of time from his earliest extant plays to his final one, *Iphigeneia in Aulis,* the time that also embraces the horrors of the Peloponnesian War (431–404), Euripides has most frequently used his art as a means not only of observing but of warning his beloved Athens regarding its tragic and lamentable decline not merely in fortune but ethically and morally as well—her humanity was compromised.

By the time of this his final play, two or three years before the end of that disastrous conflict, we may fairly well assume that Euripides realized the futility of his efforts as an artist to affect the history of his time and his people. In *Iphigeneia in Aulis* he appears not to be trying any longer to influence, but to be asking a question: Is war, any war, worth the price of a single life? That single life in the case of our play is Iphigeneia's. Will she or will she not be sacrificed to the Greek cause? That is the basis of the play's tension.

II

The crucial moment in the play is not Agamemnon's capitulation to the "need" for the sacrifice of his daughter Iphigeneia, but Iphigeneia's own change of mind regarding her sacrifice. She begins by cursing all who are instrumental in that decision, and within a very brief period of time she has accepted her fate, she will die, but she will die in "glory"; she bows, she says, to divine and mortal will, she will lead Greece to victory, she will save Greece and secure the safety of Greek womanhood from barbarian interference. Her speech ends:

I'm only mortal, who am I to oppose the goddess? That must never happen. My life belongs to Greece. Offer me up, then, kill me, and bring down Troy. That will be my monument. That will be my marriage, my children, and my glory for all time.

There is something terribly wrong here that goes far beyond the logical question regarding why this sudden, unexplained change of mind and heart occurs. So strange is it in fact that the speech works against itself, proving the exact opposite of what it intends. It is, furthermore, rife with jingoistic platitudes of patriotism that defend the deplorable mission (as Euripides sees it) of the Greek forces. She ends her speech with:

> Greeks were destined to rule, mother, not to serve, but to rule others, other countries, other people; to be ruled by others would be to make slaves of Greeks; and Greeks were born to be free.

A sentiment, no doubt, that warmed every Athenian heart in that Theater of Dionysos, for it was a sentiment dearly held, as well as one that helped usher them into the devastation of the Peloponnesian War.

III

Athens in the fifth century was a decidedly male society, one would better say a passionately male society, a syndrome best termed Male Ascendancy. But vitally connected to that concept is a term in Greek that is central in understanding the Greek character from at least as far back as the eighth century, and that word is *agon,* a term which the *Oxford Classical Dictionary* defines as denoting

> the informal and extempore competitive struggles and rivalries that permeated Greek life in the general fight for success and survival, especially philosophical, legal, and public debates; action between opposing sides in war. . . . A corollary of the agonistic drive was the prominence as a motive for action of *philotimia* (love of honor), which could turn into over-ambition and jealous rivalry, and, in its worst form, lead to *stasis* (strife) and political upheaval.

Needless to say, it is the "corollary of the agonistic drive" that most interests us here. *Agon,* to say the least, was a term primarily, if not exclusively, ascribed to the male. For instance, the place of woman was abysmally low in classical

Athens, a position rightly defined by the contemporary comparison: "women and slaves."

Given the circumstances, one wonders what Agamemnon would have done if the goddess Artemis had decreed that a male child of his should be slaughtered to bring the proper wind to sail to Troy. Perhaps what Kreon did in *Phoenician Women:* refused and immediately sent his son off to safety in distant regions. But Iphigeneia is female, and expendable, and let us not forget that the fifth-century night-shrouded hills outside Athens were more often than not alive with the cries of female babies exposed for no other reason than that they were female and cost a pretty dowry to marry off.

IV

In Agamemnon's self-justifying speech regarding Iphigeneia's sacrifice, he begins by describing the assembled Greek armies, the ships, the weapons, the armor, from all of Greece, "and," says he,

> they can't sail, can't sail to Ilion, can't pull down the famous towers of Troy, unless I offer you up as sacrifice, as the prophet Kalchas says the gods demand.

Is it too much to say that it sounds as if the boys have set their minds on a sweet treat and are being petulant about not getting it, for indeed that is precisely what they are doing, and when we try to figure out why, we arrive at the viable suspicion that they have had their male pride wounded. The wife of one of them, a Greek wife, one loathed and reviled by all for her whorish deed, has been abducted, indeed raped, by a wealthy Phrygian prince named Paris (who probably smelled better than they did) and hauled off to Troy as his prize. One suspects that it's not the value of the wife in question that riles them, but the fact that a possession, a *male* possession, has been purloined, a property, a "slave" who will bear him progeny to inherit his wealth—male children of course. But it doesn't end there. Agamemnon fears that unless he sacrifices his barely pubertal daughter the army will descend on Mykenê and kill him and every member of his family for denying them their military privilege, their *agon,* their way of demonstrating their male sense of honor, their manhood.

V

At the end of his speech Agamemnon avers that it isn't Menelaos to whom he is a slave, but to Greece, "the will of Greece." And why? Because "Greece must be free."

And if you and I can make it so, child, then we must. As Greeks we must not be subject to barbarians, but defend ourselves against the plunder and rape of Greek wives by brute force.

Vengeance for the "rape of Greek wives" is gratuitous; it is the word "barbarian" (twice used in this speech) that is the key here, a word used frequently in the play for the inhabitants of Troy, and one of the central words in Athenian tragedy, indeed in the vocabulary of the fifth-century Greek, a heritage extending at least as far back as Homer, and, we may assume, as far as the time prior to the Trojan War, possibly the twelfth century. To the Greek the term *barbarian* referred most generally to anyone who was not Greek but its most specific application was to the people of the East, namely Asia Minor.

The concept of barbarian may well be considered a major stumbling block in the history of ancient Greece. It refers to the *other*, the bête noire, the opposite of all that the Greek male considered himself, namely, the luxury, the refinement, the opulence so despised by the Greeks for its softness, its weakness, its—femininity. This is the Greek other, but that is not the root of the problem. What is at the core of that other, that other that is a projection of something more immediate and even more profoundly distrusted? The precise historical origin of the fear may never be known, but the core of the phobia is nothing else than Woman: the Feminine.

VI

At the end of the *Oresteia* that concludes on a glorious note of reconciliation and cooperation, the Furies, now at the service of the Athenian state, sing praises to that state, to Athens, they who once were vengeful furies, but who now are the Kindly Ones. Their last words in the play, however, are a warning:

> Give us reverence,
> your immigrant guests,
> and happy fortune is yours forever.

What in fact they are saying is: *We are women, the defenders of women, who agree now to defend men and women both in this mighty city of Athens; but mistreat the feminine, subject it to the indignity that you have in the past, and we will defend it as powerfully as ever we did in the past, we implacable forces born of Mother Night.* And that is precisely what happens repeatedly in Athenian tragedy of the fifth century: misused, repressed, dishonored, ignored, and rejected women fighting back at their male oppressors: Klytaimnêstra, Êlektra,

Antigonê, Dêianeira, Mêdeia, the Sphinx and Iokastê, Phaidra, Agavê. Cavander rightly calls the list "a formidable one for a culture in which the conventional idea of woman was as meek drudge, as childbearer who was not supposed to question her husband's tyranny, a kind of 'slave' with special rights. The theater in ancient Greece did indeed hold a mirror up to nature—to the Greeks' own nature, and in the mirror they saw what they could not otherwise see—their own hidden side." One wants to theorize that that confrontation explains the paucity of first prizes in Euripides' theatrical career.

That, then, is how the position of women reveals itself in Athenian tragedy. And in the history of fifth-century Athens we see it in the power achieved in the creation of the Delian League and in the consequences that led to the demeaning horrors of the Peloponnesian War and the ultimate collapse of Athens. Cavander writes:

> Since Greece had rejected (or "killed") her feminine, emotional, creative side, that which was despised appeared as something foreign, "outside." The contemporary Greek stereotype of the luxurious, "effeminate," slave oriental was in effect a projection of the unrecognized part of Greece itself. Historically, the neglected aspect took revenge in the lust for power and wealth that drove Athens, in particular, to increase her "empire" at the expense of other "Greek" values such as simplicity, autonomy, respect for the freedom of others; the revenge also maintained itself in the irrational and passionate feuding that accompanied the last quarter of the fifth century.

VII

What does it add up to? In the case of Iphigeneia in the body of extant Athenian tragedy, we have seen her as the young, simple, virginal girl who serves against her will as the final facilitator of the Trojan War. Without her sacrificial death there would be no war. In one play it has to do with a lack of wind, in another with too fierce a wind, and in still another, our play, with a wind blowing in the wrong direction for the Greek fleet at Aulis to set sail for Troy. In all but *Iphigeneia in Aulis* she dies against her will for reasons made clear in the foregoing. In our play she originally fights her death, but, for what reason we cannot know (unless she buys into her father's male defense of male action), she finally sees her way clear to offering up herself for the glory of Greece. That speech is, as we have seen, self-deceiving, it doubles back only to destroy its own tragic logic. Her sacrifice will not be to the glory of Greece, but to Greece's near-destruction and Troy's unqualified destruction. In the end it makes her as guilty of the devastation of the war as Helen herself, so roundly denounced in the play.

What can have been in Euripides' mind in putting such a blind and unreasoned speech in the mouth of this tragic and lovely young girl, one of the most memorable images of Athenian tragedy, a central though submerged theme even in those plays in which she does not appear? If the reasoning in the foregoing analysis is correct, and Euripides thought similarly regarding her death as symbolic of the death of the feminine aspect in the Greek male, then her absurd and unthinking capitulation in *Iphigeneia in Aulis* may be a sign that whatever warning power she may once have possessed is now run out, she has no longer the power of reason, no longer the radiance of the other youthful characters in Euripidean tragedy who also, and nobly, sacrifice themselves and in doing so save their cities. This final Iphigeneia of Athenian tragedy, two or three years from the fall of Athens, in effect leads Athens head-on into its doom. There is no way that the aged Euripides, who deserted in despair his beloved and fast-sinking Athens in 406 for Macedon, could not have known that the end was simply a matter of time—the same end that we see foreshadowed in the pitiable, cruel, because benighted, death of Iphigeneia. A death, furthermore, that betokened the death of what she once represented in the Greek male, the reasoned moderation and self-knowledge called for on the pediment of the temple of Apollo in Delphi and so little heeded in the course of the ancient history of the Greeks.

~◈~

RHESOS

I

Of the fact that Euripides wrote a play titled *Rhesos* there can be little doubt; that the extant play known as *Rhesos* is that play has been a matter of dispute since antiquity. Those who believe it to be genuine consider it an early effort, whereas those who reject it relegate it to an unknown writer of the fourth century. Which faction is correct is impossible to determine. One theory is that the genuine *Rhesos* by Euripides was lost, and when the extant play of the same name turned up in the fourth century, it was believed to be that lost play. Much the same division of attitude has persisted into our own time.

One aspect of the play that tends to identify it as genuine Euripides is the language. Cedric Whitman say of it "The language is certainly that of Euripides, as are some tricks of style and rhythm, and the lack of elevation and sparkle could be paralleled in other, lesser plays [of Euripides]." Richard Emil Braun writes that "As far as can be determined from the meager remnants of the corpus of Greek tragedy, the style, language, and metrical usages of the *Rhesos* most resemble Euripides' before 428. How much earlier the play may be, it is impossible to tell, but 445–441 is a good guess." The most recent commentary on the issue is by Edith Hall who writes:

> In the 1960s one respectable scholar published a spirited defense of the Euripidean authorship of *Rhesos*, arguing that its distinctive qualities are signs that it dated from early in [Euripides'] career. But most experts now agree that the ancient record somehow substituted the text we possess for Euripides' tragedy of the same name. There are several possible explanations for such a substitution: Euripides was widely imitated by other tragedians, and others bore his name, including his own youngest son, who was responsible for the posthumous production of *Iphigeneia in Aulis* and *Bakkhai*. The prevalent scholarly view holds therefore that *Rhesos* is the work of an unidentifiable playwright active in the fourth century B.C.E. (when there was a revival of interest in dramatizing themes from the *Iliad*), and as such it is a unique document, since all the other Greek tragedies date from the century before.

And *Rhesos* is indeed based in part on Homer, namely the bloody tale of Rhesos and Dolon from the tenth book of the *Iliad*. But there were at least two alternate treatments, one used by Pindar in a lost poem, and the so-called oracle version which, according to Kovacs, is the major source for the play.

II

Critical reception of *Rhesos* covers the entire spectrum of possibility. To begin with the worst, Kitto dismisses it out of hand in less than one sentence when he calls it "the miserable *Rhesos*." John Ferguson, not quite as dismissive, advises that *Rhesos* is a play "to see, to enjoy, and to forget." And Grube says of it: "The criticisms of those who would reject it mainly amount to saying that this is not the kind of play that Euripides could have written. . . ." Grube continues.

> That *Rhesos* is fundamentally different from any other extant tragedy is undeniable. It is a play of action, it is vigorous, direct, spectacular, there are many characters and many changes of situation. It is the

work of no mean playwright, but it has little or no tragic depth; it is a series of exciting events rather than a tragedy; the chorus are but one of the characters; the Athêna who appears in the middle of the play and actually directs the plot belongs to the epic rather than tragedy; characterization reaches no depth.

A recent translator of *Rhesos* (one who advocates the authorship of Euripides) describes it in these terms:

> A play about losers, Euripides' *Rhesos* has been treated itself as a loser of a play in our time. Some modern scholars, in fact, have advocated the loss of its attribution to Euripides, though his authorship is well-attested in antiquity. The grounds for this argument have been that the play is so anomalous and defective as tragedy as to render its creation by a great artist unthinkable. Even many of those who acknowledge its authenticity seek excuses for its "failings" by pointing out that it is a very early composition, if not the first play that Euripides ever wrote. It has been compared often to another early work of the playwright's, *Cyclops,* which is the only complete satyr play extant. This perception of *Rhesos* as an example of Euripides' artistic immaturity, marked by its affinities with the conventions of the funny, cruel satyr play, has had an isolating if not alienating effect on its standing among the rest of Euripides' tragedies. Yet, as Anne Pippin Burnett has argued, the play's odd singularity, defined by its hatred of war and debunking of heroism, its scorn for the small, mean, and ugly ways of men, and even its apparent distrust and ridicule of the conventions of traditional tragedy, makes a better case for than against the play's originality and authenticity. Though it will probably never escape its status as an egregious example of Euripidean tragedy, *Rhesos* deserves to be accepted on its own terms. It may be, as it were, the black goat of the flock, and it may, for better or worse, stand apart from the rest, but its strange bleating can also be music to our ears.

III

Edith Hall perhaps best summarizes a fair and equitable view of *Rhesos* for our time as, if not one of the towering literary texts of all time (it is certainly no *Oresteia* or *Oedipus at Kolonos*), then as a devilishly intriguing piece of theater, the very medium for which it was written (whether by Euripides or someone else), a crowd pleaser that almost without question must have pleased its audience no matter when it was written.

Rhesos certainly does not deserve the relegation to the margins of literary history that it has suffered. Perhaps more than any other play by Euripides, it needs to be read as a theatrical script for enactment by expert actors. It is not particularly great literature (although some passages, particularly in the choral odes, are not inconsiderable poetry). But it is likely to have been highly successful theater. The nocturnal, masculine, military atmosphere, with its passwords and watch fires, disguises, scouts and reconnaissance, will have enthralled the male spectators for whom it was designed, many of whom will have seen military action themselves.

She writes also of "flamboyant visual effects" offered by *Rhesos,* the waking of the sleeping Hêktor by the noisy entrance of the Chorus of Trojan Sentries, the arrival of Rhesos with "jangling bells on his shield," armor of gold, "twin spears" and "Thracian entourage." And then in the very middle of the play the unexpected arrival of Athêna (gods and goddesses in Euripides usually arrive at the end), to offer aid to the Greek spies Odysseus and Diomêdes in the Trojan camp; the same Athêna who then disguises herself (a first in tragedy) as Aphroditê so as to divert the attention of the sex-crazed Paris. This play, Hall asserts with very good reason, "which deftly telescopes within a single night of military subterfuge the story of the whole Trojan War, constitutes a fast-paced, action-packed, theatrical *Iliad* in miniature."

∾·

A Note on the Translation

Every translator feels obligated to explain his or her aim in making a translation, and that is a salutary endeavor, for at least it tells the innocent reader what to expect as well as what not to expect. As a translator for many years, I have always (perhaps even before deciding whether or not to buy a particular volume of translations) insinuated my fingers between the covers to peek briefly at the obligatory "note on the translation" that I know cannot help but be there. What am I looking for? Usually only one word; the word that must be the bête noire of the true translator: *accuracy*. What's accuracy to the translator—or the translator to accuracy—that he or she should lust for it? A flippant query perhaps, but perhaps not, for it is a question that boggles the mind of all but the pedant. And it is in the name of *accuracy* that many a translator's hour (lifetime?) has been wasted, not to mention the hours wasted on his or her product by the unsuspecting reader who sets out to enjoy a Dante or a Homer or a Goethe, only to plow his or her way through sheer will and in the end wonder what all the fuss has been about.

There is no question that there is a place for literal translation, for translation that is bound to the word. The most convenient example that comes to mind is the long-lasting and successful Loeb Classical Library that publishes the original text and the translation on facing pages. The aim of its volumes is to aid the reader with a little Greek (or Latin), or a lot of Greek (or Latin), but not quite enough to read the original by casting a glance at the translation when knowledge fails or falters. David Kovacs is completing a new six-volume Euripides in that series that admirably fulfills its function as support in reading the original. He says about his translation: "I have translated into prose, as literally as respect for English idiom allowed." And he's correct. He's also "accurate," but that's what the series' mission is to be, and for good reason. Yet what his translations are not (and I suspect he would agree) are performable versions for the stage, and for one reason: accuracy has destroyed the poetry.

But enough of this.

What is good translation? The answer to that question is different with each good translator who has ever wrestled with the problem. Listen to St, Jerome, the great fourth-century translator of the Bible into the Latin Vulgate, in speaking of Plautus and Terence and of their translations of Greek plays into Latin: "Do they stick at the literal words? Don't they try rather to preserve the beauty and style of the original? What men like you call accuracy in translation, learned men call pedantry. . . . I have always aimed at translating sense, not words." Fourteen hundred years later the translators of the King James Bible of 1611 expressed their thoughts on literal translation: "Is the kingdom of God become words and syllables? Why should we be in bondage to them?" And in the seventeenth century, John Dryden, the translator of many a classical text, from Plutarch to Virgil and Ovid, expressed his theory of translation at length, but most succinctly when he said: "The translator that would write with any force or spirit of an original must never dwell on the words of the author."

To bring it now to our own day and to the prolific translator of many classical and modern texts, William Arrowsmith: "There are times—far more frequent than most scholars suppose—when the worst possible treachery is the simple-minded faith in 'accuracy' and literal loyalty to the original." To read an Arrowsmith translation, say, of a classical Greek play, side by side with the original, is to see a fertile and poetic mind undaunted by the mere word of the original. He realized that he was translating a fifth-century BCE Greek play for a middle- to late-twentieth-century English-speaking audience and had one obligation: to make that ancient play work on the contemporary stage for an audience that had few if any ties to the play's original context or audience. His duty was to make it work and to make it work with style and the best poetic means at his disposal.

And finally the contemporary Roger Shattuck: "The translator must leave behind dictionary meanings and formal syntax. . . . Free translation is often not an indulgence but a duty." And to that one must add that dramatic texts require perhaps even greater freedom than nonverbal texts (and poetry in whatever form is a verbal text). On the stage, rhythm is every bit as important as what is being said; at times even more important. A stinging line has to sting not merely with what it says, but with how it says it, with its rhythm. One phrase, indeed one word, too many in a sentence destroys a moment that in the end can destroy an entire scene. Effect on the stage is everything, whether one is Aeschylus or Tennessee Williams. What to do with that rebellious word or phrase? Cut it if it adds nothing of importance. And if it is important and can't be cut, then write a new sentence that gets it all in, just be certain that it has grace and style and wit, or horror if that's what's needed, and serves the moment in the best and most theatrical way possible.

What, then, is the purpose of the translations in this book and its companion volumes? And the answer to that is simple. They are aimed at the theater, at performance, at as high a level of communication to a contemporary public as is possible. That was the aim of the plays' fifth-century author, and it must remain the aim of any translator, for a dramatic text performance is all. This doesn't mean that a text meant for the theater is not communicable to a reader. At the same time, however, any theatrical text is a challenge to a reader unacquainted with the exigencies of the stage. A novel, a short story, any piece of fiction, is a thing in and of itself; it communicates totally. And if it is great writing, it also sends the imagination on all sorts of flights of possibility. A dramatic text, on the other hand, is a part of a whole; it is not totally defined. It suggests, and in suggesting it invites the spectator/auditor to bring as much to the experience as is given, and the thing that is brought is imagination.

On the stage a scene between two characters is defined by the director who arranges the action, the stage movement, in such a way as to elicit as great a sense of tension or horror (whatever is called for) as possible. A scene in which two characters whisper to each other has one effect; but play the same text with a separation between the two characters (enforced or voluntary) so that they have to speak at full volume, or even shout, and you have another effect entirely—and possibly another kind of play as the result.

This, of course, is all the work of the director whose choices determine what the bare text will convey. For the reader that visualization is lacking and the imagination is called upon to provide it. No easy task for the neophyte to the theater. Reading a play is a test even of the most experienced theater person.

Nor will a supply of translator-generated stage directions do much good. The Greeks, of course, had no stage directions in their texts, and for the translator to add them is to freeze the play's meaning, as opposed to opening it up to all kinds of possible interpretation. The stage directions in the present texts are held to a minimum.

What these translations are not is philological. One might ask why? And the best response might be that there are many such translations around, and more currently in development. The Loeb Classical Library is actively pursuing a splendid contemporary renewal of its older texts with new ones, currently Sophocles and Euripides by Hugh Lloyd-Jones and David Kovacs respectively, as well as Aristophanes by Jeffrey Henderson. Aris and Phillips (Warminster) is gradually building up a splendid library of newly edited texts and highly annotated philological translations. Penguin Classics is in the midst of renewing its Euripides collection to replace the thirty-year-old Vellacott texts with new ones by John Davie. Oxford is underway with a Euripides series translated variously by James Morwood and Robin Waterfield. Each of these publications is translated, annotated, and provided with textual notes by classical scholars. It would be fair to say, then, that the philological translation scene of Greek tragedy and comedy is well covered.

But there are also other approaches being taken. One of the most distinguished is The Oxford Greek Tragedy in New Translations series. Begun in 1973 under the inspired general editorship of the late William Arrowsmith, it is only now coming to its too-long-delayed conclusion. Arrowsmith was a demanding classicist, but he knew intuitively that Greek drama was theater first and then poetry, even if for him those two factors existed on one and the same level. He invited major American poets (W. S. Merwin, C. K. Williams, and Anthony Hecht, to name a few) to work together with classical scholars (in Anne Carson he got both in one) in producing translations of astonishing theatrical brilliance—and, one must add, translations conceived in an astonishing degree of freedom for a major university press like Oxford.

The University of Pennsylvania Press has only recently published the latest complete Greek Tragedy and Comedy series under the editorship of David R. Slavitt and Palmer Bovie. It is a series that takes enormous risks and is bound to rub some academics quite the wrong way, and yet it is never less than exciting and provocative. Literal fidelity in the Penn series is frequently dismissed as pedantic, and frequent attempts are made (not always successfully) to adapt rather than merely translate; the intent being to bring the original into a modern frame of reference.

Perhaps the most famous translation of a classical text in the last decade is the *Oresteia* by Ted Hughes for production at Britain's Royal National Theatre. Here is a distinguished English-speaking poet attacking one of the monuments of world culture in a manner that is, to say the least, unique. It is, in fact, difficult to call what Hughes has done to the *Oresteia* a translation, and yet it is that all the same. But there is also in his work on that masterpiece of world theater almost as much of himself as there is of Aeschylus. He will begin a speech as an inspired translation and then, after a dozen lines or so, segue into a lengthy speech of his own. Apt, yes, given the context, insightful, but not Aeschylus. But should one complain? I think not. We're lucky to have his thoughts. Though it might have been more direct if the product had been labeled as an adaptation/translation, as was his *Alcestis* of Euripides.

Why, then, another attempt at the Greek tragedies? Perhaps because, though much good work has been done, there is still much to do and different things to try. The reader of the present texts will have to test those new attempts for him- or herself, but one factor of these new translations must be commented on, and that is the prominence of music, song, and dance in the plays. To understand the Greek theater properly is to give full weight to these utterly essential factors. The translations in the present volumes indicate very clearly where music, chant, song, and dance were called for in the original.

Whether a modern director chooses to use music as fully as did the classical Greeks is a personal choice. In any event, the change of mood dictated by chant, song, and music in the original must ideally be created in some way in any successful modern production. It can be accomplished with voice, with mode of delivery, with style of acting, but it must be with *something,* because there is a range of tones in these plays that must be dealt with other than realistically.

Again: What is the purpose (methodology, if you will) of the translations in the present volumes of the plays of Euripides? In a word, it is to heed the warnings and advice given to translators through the millennia by practitioners of the art from St. Jerome to Roger Shattuck, to allow the original texts to breathe freely rather than to be suffocated by demands that may be proper in the classics classroom but out of place in the study of the humanities and in performance on the stage.

One final comment must be added regarding the text of these volumes. Even in classical times, the plays of Aeschylus, Sophokles, and Euripides were subject to interpolation by producers, directors, and actors. In the case of an actor, for example, his aim was to amplify his role. In all but a very few instances such interpolations have been been excised on the basis of the most recent scholarship.

᠀

PHOENICIAN WOMEN

(ΦΟΙΝΙΣΣΑΙ)

CHARACTERS

IOKASTÊ *mother and wife of Oedipus*
POLYNEIKÊS *king of Thebes, son of Oedipus and Iokastê*
ETEOKLÊS *living in exile, son of Oedipus and Iokastê*
ANTIGONÊ *daughter of Oedipus and Iokastê*
KREON *brother of Iokastê*
MENOIKEUS *teenage son of Kreon*
TEIRESIAS *blind Theban prophet*
OEDIPUS *former king of Thebes*
CHORUS OF YOUNG PHOENICIAN WOMEN
FIRST YOUNG PHOENICIAN WOMAN *chorus leader*
TUTOR of *Antigonê*
THEBAN SOLDIER
SECOND THEBAN SOLDIER
THEBAN SLAVE *of Eteoklês*
ATTENDANTS, SERVANTS, SOLDIERS

PHOENICIAN WOMEN

Thebes.
In front of the royal palace on the Theban Akropolis.
An altar and statue of Apollo stand near the door.
Enter from the palace IOKASTÊ, aged, in dark robes, hair shorn.

IOKASTÊ: Great Sun, in the rush of flames of your swift-steeded chariot, what an evil ray you cast on Thebes, that day long ago, when Kadmos first entered this land from his home in seaswept Phoenicia! Here he married Harmonia, daughter of Kypris, and fathered Polydoros, father, they say, of Labdakos, who in his turn sired Laïos.

I am known here as the daughter of Menoikeus, and men call me Iokastê, for that's what my father named me. In time I married Laïos, and after long years, our marriage having proved childless, he went to Delphi to petition Apollo that he bless us with male heirs to carry on our house. "King of horse-rich Thebes," said Apollo, "do not defy the will of the gods by sowing male children, for if you do, you will die at the hands of your son and your house in future will be awash in a sea of blood." But Laïos in a moment of drunken abandon gave way to pleasure and planted in me a son. Then, realizing his error, he recollected the god's injunction and delivered the babe to his herdsmen for exposure in Hera's meadow by the crag of Kithairon, after first piercing its ankles with spikes of iron, from which he came to be known in Greece as Oedipus, meaning Swell Foot. But the child somehow came into the hands of the horse herders of King Polybos, who, instead of exposing it, took it back to the palace and lay him in the arms of their mistress, the queen. She took to her breast the pains of my labor, and persuaded Polybos to raise him as their own.

Years later, when the first signs of a reddish beard began to show, either because he had discovered for himself or heard through gossip, my son set off for Apollo's temple at Delphi to learn the true identity of his parents. It so happened that at the same time Laïos my husband also went off to Delphi to learn whether the son he had ordered exposed was truly dead. Traveling in the same direction, they reached a spot, the fork in the Phokis road, and Laïos's driver called out: "Stranger, clear the way for royalty!" But he paid no attention, my son, he continued on, he was proud; and in passing close, the horses' hooves wounded and bloodied the tendons of his feet. It followed— not to dwell on matters irrelevant to the disaster—that son killed father. He then took the chariot and gave it to Polybos, the father who had reared him.

Now, when the Sphinx began ravaging and preying on Thebes, and my husband being dead, my brother, Kreon, let it be known that anyone who solved the wise maiden's riddle would receive my hand in marriage. As it happened—who knows how—my son Oedipus discerned the meaning of the singer's song, took up the royal scepter, and, doing so, poor man, unwittingly married his mother, who herself was ignorant that it was her son she slept with.

I bore to my son two other sons, Eteoklês and mighty Polyneikês, and two daughters, Ismênê, named by her father, and the firstborn, whom I called Antigonê. But when he learned that our marriage bed was incestuous, Oedipus—who had endured all sufferings—performed on himself a dreadful bloody outrage in slaughtering his eyes, stabbing at them with the pins of golden brooches. When my two young sons' cheeks were shadowed with down, they locked their father away, out of sight, behind bolted doors, to hide from public view and censure the enormity of his shame— though it was no easy task to conceal. He's alive still, Oedipus, living in the palace. Driven near to madness by this treatment, he laid down a dreadful curse on his sons, that they should divide their inheritance, this house, with a whetted sword.

Fearful that the gods would fulfill the curse if they lived together, they determined that the younger of them, Polyneikês, would go into voluntary exile, and that Eteoklês should rule for one year, after which they would trade places on a yearly basis. But once Eteoklês had had a taste of kingship, he refused to relinquish the throne and himself banished Polyneikês from Thebes. He went to Argos then, Polyneikês, and married the daughter of King Adrastos, then mustered a mighty host of Argive warriors to march against Thebes, himself its commander. That army stands outside our seven gates at this moment, and Polyneikês demands his father's scepter and his rightful share of the land. In an attempt to forestall this strife between them, I persuaded one son to meet the other under a truce before resorting to force of arms. The messenger I sent said Polyneikês agreed to come.

Great Zeus, you who dwell in the glittering recesses of the sky, save us, bring my sons to an accord! The gods, if they are wise, ought not to allow misfortune to plague one man forever. *(Exit into palace.)*

(Enter onto the roof of the palace through a trapdoor the old TUTOR, followed by ANTIGONÊ who stops on the ladder only partially in view.)

(Music.)

TUTOR: Antigonê, fairest flower of your father's house, we're almost there. It was kind of her, your mother, to allow you to leave the safety of your chamber and come up here to view the Argive army—though I must say you begged her passionately enough. But stay right where you are for just a bit. I'll need to check for anyone in the road below. It wouldn't do to be seen up here. For me, a slave, it scarcely matters, but for you, a princess of the royal house, it's quite something else, and it would be all my fault. But I'll tell you all I know, all I saw and heard when I went to the Argive camp to deliver the truce to your brother and returned bringing his truce to our side. *(He surveys the area in front of the palace.)* No, I see nothing, no one around. Climb on up now, up those age-old cedar wood steps. From here you can survey the plains and the vast encampment of the enemy Argive army beside the waters and streams of Ismênos and Dirkê.

ANTIGONÊ: *(Sings.)*
Reach your hand,
reach your ancient hand
to my young hand,
and help me
rise to the roof.

TUTOR: *(Speaks.)* Here, take it, my dear. You've come at just the right time. The Argives are on the move, separating out one company from another.

ANTIGONÊ: *(Sings.)*
Oh lady Hekate,
daughter of Leto,
I see the whole field
flashing with bronze!

TUTOR: *(Speaks.)* Polyneikês hasn't come to trifle. Listen to the din and roar of his infantry and horsemen beyond number!

ANTIGONÊ: *(Sings.)*
    What of the walls,
    the stone walls built by
    Amphion with music?
    Are they secure?
    The bronze bolts at the gates
    tightly in place?

TUTOR: *(Speaks.)* No need to fear. The city inside the walls is safe.

ANTIGONÊ: *(Sings.)*
    Who is that man, there,
    with the white crest,
    leading his men?
    How he balances on his arm
    his bronze shield as if it were nothing!

TUTOR: *(Speaks.)* A Mykênaian by birth, they say, who lives by the waters of Lerna. Lord Hippomedon.

ANTIGONÊ: *(Sings.)*
    Ah! What a grand and fearsome sight!
    Like a giant born of the earth that you
    see in paintings! His face like a star,
    not like that of a mortal!

TUTOR: *(Speaks.)* Do you see that man crossing the river Dirkê?

ANTIGONÊ: *(Sings.)*
    Who is he?

TUTOR: *(Speaks.)* Tydeus, son of Oineus, who carries Aitolian Arês around in his heart.

ANTIGONÊ: *(Sings.)*
    Tell me, old friend,

is it he who married the sister
of Polyneikês' wife?
How strange his weapons.
Almost barbaric.

TUTOR: *(Speaks.)* All Aitolians, child, carry light shields and are very
accurate marksmen with their javelins.

ANTIGONÊ: *(Sings.)*
   Look! Over there! There!
   The monument of Zêthos!
   Who is that passing it?
   That youth with a head of long curls
   and a wild look in his eyes?
   A captain, surely,
   for he's followed by a crowd
   of men in full armor.

TUTOR: *(Speaks.)* Parthenopaios, son of Atalanta.

ANTIGONÊ: *(Sings.)*
   Then I pray that Artemis,
   mountain-ranging Artemis,
   destroy both him and his mother
   with her arrows,
   for he's come to sack my city!

TUTOR: *(Speaks.)* I pray for that, too, my child. But they come with
justice on their side, and I fear the gods will see that.

ANTIGONÊ: *(Sings.)*
   But where is that man, my brother,
   born with me of the same mother
   to a dreadful fate?
   Dear, dear old man,
   as I love you dearly,
   where is Polyneikês?

TUTOR: *(Speaks.)* Over there, beside Adrastos, by the tomb of Niobê's seven daughters. Do you see him?

ANTIGONÊ: *(Sings.)*
    I do, yes, but not clearly.
    What I see is a silhouette,
    the shape of his form, his chest.
    How I wish I were a cloud
    sped along on the wind,
    to go to my brother,
    my own dear brother,
    and take his sweet neck in my arms
    after so long, so long,
    poor unhappy exile of a brother!
    How glorious he looks
    in his golden armor, old man!
    Gleaming as the first rays of dawn!

TUTOR: *(Speaks.)* You'll be glad. He's coming, here, to this house, under a truce.

ANTIGONÊ: *(Sings.)*
    That one there, old man, who is he?
    In the chariot drawn by white horses?

TUTOR: *(Speaks.)* That's Amphiaraös, my lady, the seer. Those are animals for sacrifice with him, whose blood will stream across the thirsty earth.

ANTIGONÊ: *(Sings.)*
    Oh Goddess Moon,
    Selanaia,
    golden-circled light,
    bright-girdled daughter of Sun,
    how calmly he drives,
    gently goading now this horse, then that!
    But where is he, where is Kapaneus,
    that man who makes such dreadful threats
    against our city?

TUTOR: *(Speaks.)* Over there, working out the height of the walls from top to bottom, the easier to scale them.

ANTIGONÊ: *(Sings.)*
Hear me, Nemesis, hear me, come!
And deep-rolling thunders of Zeus,
and white-hot lightnings, come, oh come!
Nemesis who lays proud boasts to rest, come!
This is the man who boasts that by force
he will enslave the women of Thebes,
give them as captive prize to the women of Mykenê,
and to the Triple Fount of Lerna,
slaves to the waters of Poseidon's lover!
Never, lady Artemis, never,
never, golden-haired daughter of Zeus,
never let me suffer such slavery, never!

TUTOR: *(Speaks.)* It's time, my child, you return to the house and your quarters. You've seen what you wished to see. Because of confusion and panic in the city, a mass of women is descending on the royal palace. Women are a strange lot, they glory in finding fault, and give them the slightest prod in that direction they titivate a tale to absurdity. They take a strange delight in slandering each other.

(Exeunt TUTOR and ANTIGONÊ into the palace.)

(Enter the CHORUS OF YOUNG PHOENICIAN WOMEN exotically dressed.)

(Music continues. Song. Dance.)

YOUNG PHOENICIAN WOMEN: *(Sing.)*
Leaving the surging swell of the sea at Tyre,
leaving behind Phoenicia's seaswept island,
I have come,
I have come,
as a choicest offering to Loxias,
a temple slave for Apollo, shining Phoibos,
where under the snow-heavy peaks of Parnassos

he makes his home.
On shipboard I sailed the Ionian Sea,
while high in the sky a brisk West Wind
rode down the sky trail his breezy mounts,
below him Sicily's barren sea plains,
and high in the heavens he made lovely music.

My city's fairest offerings to Loxias,
I have come, I have come, to this Kadmeian land,
sent here, sent to the towers of Laïos,
kindred towers to the line of great Agênor.
Like gifts of gold, I now am Apollo's,
and yet the crystal waters await me,
Kastalia's ancient spring,
to moisten my hair in service to Apollo,
my maiden glory.

Oh rock-bound ridge of Parnassos,
whose twin peaks flame with the torches of dancers,
sacred, sacred to the revels of Dionysos,
oh wine-dripping vine that daily blossoms,
oh cave sacred to Apollo-slain Python,
and Lookout Point where the god took aim,
oh holy snow-clad mountain,
snow-blown summits,
how I wish,
how I wish I could dance for the immortals,
sacred to the god, free of fear,
dance in Delphi's earth-center hollow,
far, far from the terror of Thebes!

But Arês now stands before these walls,
Arês sets blazing bloodshed and war,
destruction, destruction for Thebes!
Stop him, oh stop!
Friends share the misfortune of friends,
and if these seven towers should fall,
Phoenicia will suffer no less than Thebes.
AIIII!

AIIII!
The blood in our veins is shared blood,
and children born are shared, shared,
descendents all of horned Io.
I also share in the pain.

A murky storm cloud of shields blazes,
giving shape to bloody encounter,
which soon Arês of Battles will witness,
as he brings to the sons of Oedipus
the evil blight of Spirits of Vengeance.
Oh Pelasgian Argos,
I tremble,
I tremble,
tremble at your power,
tremble at what the gods will send.
For this man who comes to win back his house,
comes with Justice,
with Justice he marches,
with gods on his side.

(Music out.)

POLYNEIKÊS: *(Enters alone, sword drawn.)* The gatekeepers eagerly
unbarred their gates to admit me, but once in the net I fear some
treachery will not let me out unbloodied. And so I turn my eyes every
which way on the lookout for trickery. At least this sword gives me
confidence. *(Wheeling quickly around.)* Ha! Who's there! Or do noises
shake me now? Even a bold man is wary in enemy territory. Still, I
trust my mother—and at the same time I don't. She arranged the
truce that brings me here—persuading me.
    Well, at least safety's not far off; there's the altar for sanctuary.
And the palace isn't deserted. I'll put up my sword and ask these
women who they are. *(He sheathes his sword. To the YOUNG
PHOENICIAN WOMEN.)* Ladies, tell me—I see by your dress you're
foreigners—where are you from? How did you happen to settle in
Greece?

FIRST YOUNG PHOENICIAN WOMAN: My country is Phoenicia, sir. And my people, the descendents of Agênor, sent me to Greece as choicest offerings in thanks for victory in war. The son of Oedipus, King Eteoklês, was about to send me to Apollo's holy oracle at Delphi when the Argive army marched against Thebes. But now it's your turn. Who are you, and why are you here in this city of seven-gated towers?

POLYNEIKÊS: My father is Oedipus, son of Laïos, and my mother, the daughter of Menoikeus, Iokastê. Thebans call me Polyneikês.

(Music. Song. Dance.)

FIRST YOUNG PHOENICIAN WOMAN: *(Chants.)*
    Oh kinsman of Agênor's sons,
    kin of my kings, who sent me!
    I kneel at your feet, my lord,
    in honor of my country's ways!
    You have returned, returned at last,
    to the land of your birth!

YOUNG PHOENICIAN WOMEN: *(Chant.)*
    IO! IO!
    Inside!
    In the house!
    Lady! My lady!
    Come!
    Come see!
    Throw the doors wide!
    Come out!
    Come out,
    mother of this man,
    mother who bore him!
    Listen!
    Why so long,
    so long?
    Come out and hold your
    son in your arms!

(Enter IOKASTÊ from the palace.)

IOKASTÊ: *(Sings.)*
    I heard your cry,
    your Phoenician cry,
    young women,
    but I am old,
    an ancient woman,
    and I drag my feet,
    my trembling steps,
    out to your shouting voices.

    Oh son, dear son,
    my baby,
    how long,
    how long the endless,
    countless days since
    I have seen you,
    your dear, sweet face!
    Come, hold me,
    the mother who bore you,
    your cheek on my cheek,
    your rich dark curls
    circling my neck!

    IOOO!
    IOOO!

    Oh child,
    I'd lost all hope for your return,
    never to hold you again,
    never your mother's arms around you!

(Releasing him, she steps back to observe him, then feebly dances around him, stroking him with her hands as she does so.)

    What can I say to you?
    How to relive, to recapture, how,
    by touch, by word, by dancing round you

with ancient, tottering feet,
this side and that,
here, there—
how to have again the joys of days long past?
(The dance ceases.)

Oh son, my son,
you left your father's house desolate,
exiled by your brother's outrage,
missed, much missed by friends,
missed, much missed by Thebes!
And so I weep,
weep and lament,
cut my white hair in mourning,
and my clothes, not white,
but these gloomy rags
of desolation and despair.

And he in the house,
the blind old man,
moans in longing for his sons unyoked,
free of the house, and seeks out the sword,
or the noose over the beam,
again, again,
cursing his sons with endless cries,
hiding himself in gloom.

As for you, my son,
I hear of a foreign marriage,
in a foreign house,
the joys of fathering foreign children,
an unspeakable pain,
a misery beyond forgetting to your mother,
and the house of Laïos long dead,
a marriage that brings an alien curse!

You denied me the right, the joy,
of lighting the torch,
the custom of a happy mother
at the wedding of her son.

The Ismênos was denied,
no water shared for the ritual bath.
And no shouts, no wedding songs,
heard in the streets of Thebes
at your bride's entry.

I curse them, these griefs,
whether the spawn of war,
or strife, or your father,
or the fate of this race run wild
in the house of Oedipus,
for the grief of these miseries
descends upon me!

FIRST YOUNG PHOENICIAN WOMAN: *(Speaks.)* The pains of
childbirth affect women deeply. All women love their children.

(Music out.)

POLYNEIKÊS: Mother, it was good judgment brought me to meet my
enemy; and yet at the same time how mad it was. All men love their
country, and whoever says differently loves playing with words, while
his heart lies elsewhere. I had such dread as I passed through the gates,
fearing my brother had planned evil against me, that I walked with
sword drawn and constantly on the lookout for danger. Only one
thing sustains me, our truce and your honesty. Without them I'd never
have entered the walls of my city. It was not without tears I walked its
streets, seeing after so long its altars and temples, the gymnasia, the
wrestling grounds, where I was trained, and the waters of Dirkê where
I bathed and swam with friends. And it is of these that I am deprived,
unjustly denied, and live in a foreign city where my eyes forever flow
with tears. And coming here I go from one grief to another, seeing you
with your head shorn, in black robes! What a misery! Mother, what is
more wretched than a family divided by hatred?

IOKASTÊ: Some god is bent on destroying the family of Oedipus, and this
is how he began. I gave birth to your father when it was unlawful,
your father then married me in a wicked marriage, and that's how you
were born. But why dwell on it? We endure what the gods send. Oh

how do I ask what I must ask, and doing so not grieve you! And yet what choice do I have?

POLYNEIKÊS: Ask anything, Mother. Leave nothing out. Our wishes are the same, yours and mine.

IOKASTÊ: What is it like to lose one's country? Is it dreadful?

POLYNEIKÊS: More dreadful than words can say.

IOKASTÊ: But what is it like? What is so difficult?

POLYNEIKÊS: Not to have the right to speak freely.

IOKASTÊ: But that's slavery, not to speak freely.

POLYNEIKÊS: You endure the arrogance and stupidities of power.

IOKASTÊ: How painful! Sharing the folly of fools!

POLYNEIKÊS: To gain advantage you play the slave.

IOKASTÊ: Exiles, so they say, feed on hope.

POLYNEIKÊS: Hope that seduces, but never delivers.

IOKASTÊ: And doesn't time teach the emptiness of hope?

POLYNEIKÊS: Hope that infatuates us with the impossible.

IOKASTÊ: How did you manage to live before marriage saved you?

POLYNEIKÊS: Sometimes the day provided, sometimes not.

IOKASTÊ: And your father's friends? They didn't help?

POLYNEIKÊS: Success is the only way! Misfortune goes begging.

IOKASTÊ: But surely your noble birth helped you?

POLYNEIKÊS: Wealth is all that matters. Rank doesn't feed you.

IOKASTÊ: Then a man's country *is* his dearest possession.

POLYNEIKÊS: There are no words to say it.

IOKASTÊ: How did you arrive in Argos? To what purpose?

POLYNEIKÊS: Apollo's prophecy. A prophecy to Adrastos.

IOKASTÊ: Prophecy? What prophecy? I don't understand?

POLYNEIKÊS: That his daughters would marry a boar and a lion.

IOKASTÊ: But what did you have to do with wild beasts?

POLYNEIKÊS: I don't know. He was summoning me to my fate.

IOKASTÊ: The god is wise. But how did you come to marry?

POLYNEIKÊS: It was night. I arrived at Adrastos's door.

IOKASTÊ: Searching for a bed, as any exile would?

POLYNEIKÊS: Yes. Then another arrived.

IOKASTÊ: Who was he? Poor man, as miserable as you?

POLYNEIKÊS: Tydeus, the son of Oineus.

IOKASTÊ: But how did Adrastos think you wild beasts?

POLYNEIKÊS: We fought over a bed.

IOKASTÊ: And so he understood the prophecy?

POLYNEIKÊS: Yes; he married us to his two daughters.

IOKASTÊ: And your marriage, was it a happy one?

POLYNEIKÊS: Happy, to this very moment. I have no complaint.

IOKASTÊ: How did you win the army you led to Thebes?

POLYNEIKÊS: Adrastos swore to his two sons-in-law that he would repatriate them to their rightful countries, but me first. Many chieftains of Argos and Mykenê have followed me here as a favor I'm sorely in need of, but which tears me apart, for I'm marching against my own city. I swear by all the gods that it wasn't I who willed to take up arms against my brother, it was he who willed it. But the end of this evil, Mother, lies with you: reconcile us, two brothers who share the same blood. And doing so, save from catastrophe me, yourself, and the whole city.

> It's a song sung often before, but I'll rehearse it nevertheless. It's said that prosperity and money are mankind's most valued possessions, and of all things under the sun there is nothing of greater influence. It's for this I've come with ten thousand spears. A man of nobility who is destitute is nothing.

FIRST YOUNG PHOENICIAN WOMAN: Here comes Eteoklês now, ready to parley. Iokastê, you're their mother, it's for you to reconcile your sons.

ETEOKLÊS: *(Enters with several ARMED ATTENDANTS.)* Mother, I'm here. This is a favor to you. What's your wish? I'm waiting. Will someone begin?

(He looks ferociously at POLYNEIKÊS who turns his back on him.)

IOKASTÊ: That's enough, Eteoklês! Haste is no answer to justice. Calm brings the greatest wisdom. And tame your ferocious gaze and enraged gasping for air. It's not a severed Gorgon's head you're looking at but your brother. And you, Polyneikês, turn and face your brother. Words will flow more easily if you look at him, and you'll both be better at listening. *(POLYNEIKÊS turns to face ETEOKLÊS.)* Now. I have advice for the two of you.

> When two friends meet, and each is angry with the other, they must hold fast to the reason for the meeting, and forget any wrong from the past. It's for you to speak first, Polyneikês my son. It's you

who have brought here the Argive army, claiming to have been wronged. I pray that some god reconcile your grievances.

POLYNEIKÊS: Truth of its own self tells a simple tale, and no just cause needs elaborate glossing; it speaks for itself. But the unjust cause, diseased at its core, needs every sophistic medicine it can find.
    In leaving home, I was guided by both of our interests, his as well as mine, regarding our father's inheritance. I also hoped to escape our father's curses uttered against us long ago. I left Thebes of my own free will, voluntary exile, yielding to this man the right to rule the land for a single year. He agreed, swearing an oath by all the gods, but he has proven himself false, has broken every pledge, and holds fast to the kingship as well as my share of the inheritance.
    If, now, I receive what is mine by right, I am prepared to dismiss the army to its own country, to administer my estate for one full year, and then to return it to this man for his just term. Only this will save me from sacking my city, from assaulting it with scaling ladders against its towers. But deny me justice and there is nothing less I can do. I call on the gods to witness that, for all my just action, I am most unjustly and impiously deprived of my country.
    These are the facts, then, Mother, simply stated and free of clever entanglements, but justly, in a way that speaks to both the humble and the clever.

FIRST YOUNG PHOENICIAN WOMAN: I may not have been raised a Greek, but what you say makes sense.

ETEOKLÊS: If men had one definition of justice and wisdom, there would be no such thing as disagreement. As it is, equal right and justice don't exist, except in name only, for each defines them differently. Words without substance. Here, then, Mother, is what I have to say, and I hold back nothing. I would, if I had the means, and if such things were possible, climb to the heavens where the constellations rise, and delve deep into the earth, if I could lay hands on absolute power. There is nothing greater than power, the greatest of all the gods! Resign it? Why? I have it. I want it. What man who respects his manhood would resign what is great for what is less than great? A coward.

What's more, Mother, I would feel shame if this man, who comes here with an army to sack the city, were to get what he wants. What a disgrace it would be for Thebes if fear of the Argive spear made me surrender my scepter to him. What right had he to come here to resolve an issue by force of arms, when speech can do everything that arms can do? So, if he chooses to live in this land on different terms, so be it. But I will not yield to his demands. I will never willingly surrender my kingship. Why, when I can rule, should I be this man's slave?

And so, let fire and sword advance, harness the horses and fill the plain with chariots! I will never surrender my kingship to him! In all things else, piety is the rule. But if injustice is to be done, let it be done in the pursuit of power!

FIRST YOUNG PHOENICIAN WOMAN: Men ought not to praise ignoble deeds. It's not a noble action, and hated by justice.

IOKASTÊ: Eteoklês, son—not everything about old age is misery. With age comes experience, and experience—it's not impossible—may speak with greater wisdom than youth. Why do you seek out the worst of divinities, my son? For that's what she is, Ambition, the worst. She knows no justice. How many prosperous houses, how many cities has she entered, and then deserted, desolate, in ruins! And yet this is the one who infatuates you. How much better, child, is Equality, she who binds friend to friend, city to city, ally to ally. Equality, men have found, is the basis of stability, of law; the other, the lesser, is always in opposition to the greater, and the source of all hostility. Who but Equality has given us numbers and the ability to distinguish between them? Who has established weights and measures for mankind? Night's dark eye shares equally its yearly round with Day's light. They both yield to necessity, and neither resents the other. If Night and Day can unite to serve men's needs, why can you not share equally with him? Where is justice in that?

And what's this obsession with tyranny, this injustice that you praise so extravagantly? What's so remarkable about it? Is it so grand to be the object of every eye? No! An empty gain! Or is it mountains of wealth in your house you long for? But what of the troubles that accompany it? Where's the advantage? More and more and more! It's only a word! To meet life's needs is sufficient for the man with sense.

Yes, now let me ask you a question—no, two, two in one—yes. Which would you prefer? To rule, or to save Thebes? Will it be to rule, I wonder? And when—or if—Argive spears conquer Thebes? What then? Captive Theban women dragged off by the hair, forced into slavery, raped by marauding Argive warriors? This wealth of yours, that you so lust for, will have come at a high cost to Thebes! But, then—you are an ambitious man. So much for that. Now to you, Polyneikês.

The favor Adrastos did you was sheer folly, and your coming to attack this city nothing less than madness! Let's assume you do sack Thebes—which heaven forbid!—how will you celebrate the death of your own city? What trophies will you set up along the Inachos? And how inscribe them? "Having torched his city, Polyneikês dedicates these arms in honor of the gods!"? Never let this be your fame in Greece, my son! And yet, what if he overcomes you, his forces superior to yours, conquers you? How will you return to Argos, leaving behind so many countless Argive corpses? Someone will say, some Argive: "Adrastos, what have you done? One misguided marriage, and Argos is ruined!" You're faced with two evils, my child: Fail at Thebes and you lose Argos as well.

Both of you, rein in this insanity! When two fools meet, the end is disaster!

FIRST YOUNG PHOENICIAN WOMAN: Gods, turn away disaster and reconcile again the sons of Oedipus!

ETEOKLÊS: The time for talking is past, Mother, and time wasted between now and the battle is wasted time! There will never be agreement between us except on my terms: I maintain power and I rule this kingdom. So spare me your tedious admonitions and let me be! *(To POLYNEIKÊS.)* And you—out of here, now!—or you're a dead man!

POLYNEIKÊS: And who'll do the honors, I wonder? What man is so invulnerable as to attack me and not pay for it with his life?

ETEOKLÊS: He's near, very near, not far. Do you see these hands? This sword?

POLYNEIKÊS: I do. But I also see a rich man clinging to life. A coward?

ETEOKLÊS: And you've brought all these men to fight a coward?

POLYNEIKÊS: Better a cautious captain than a careless.

ETEOKLÊS: Ah, the bold boaster with a truce to protect him.

POLYNEIKÊS: And you. I demand the scepter and my share of the land.

ETEOKLÊS: Demand denied. The house is mine. I'll keep it.

POLYNEIKÊS: More than your share!

ETEOKLÊS: Yes! Now get out of this country!

POLYNEIKÊS: Oh altars of my fathers' god—

ETEOKLÊS: —which you came to plunder!

POLYNEIKÊS: —hear me!

ETEOKLÊS: What god will listen to his city's invader?

POLYNEIKÊS: Temples of the white-horsed gods—

ETEOKLÊS: Gods who abhor you!

POLYNEIKÊS: —I am being driven from my land—

ETEOKLÊS: Yes, and you come to drive *me* out!

POLYNEIKÊS: —driven unjustly!

ETEOKLÊS: Call on the gods of Argos, not mine!

POLYNEIKÊS: Gods? You have no gods—

ETEOKLÊS: At least I'm no enemy to Thebes, as you are!

POLYNEIKÊS: —for you banish me without my share!

ETEOKLÊS: Yes, and I'll have your life to round out the bargain!

POLYNEIKÊS: Father, do you see my suffering?

ETEOKLÊS: And he hears as well what you're up to!

POLYNEIKÊS: And you, Mother?

ETEOKLÊS: How dare you! The word's obscene on your lips!

POLYNEIKÊS: Oh city! Oh Thebes!

ETEOKLÊS: Get off to Argos! Call on the waters of Lerna!

POLYNEIKÊS: I'm going! Don't worry! I thank you, Mother.

ETEOKLÊS: Get out of this land—now!

POLYNEIKÊS: I'm leaving. But first my father, let me see him.

ETEOKLÊS: Never!

POLYNEIKÊS: Then my sisters, at least.

ETEOKLÊS: Nor them.

POLYNEIKÊS: Oh sisters!

ETEOKLÊS: Why call on them, their worst enemy?

POLYNEIKÊS: Good-bye, Mother, I wish you much happiness.

IOKASTÊ: Yes, you see the happiness it's brought me!

POLYNEIKÊS: You've lost your son.

IOKASTÊ: My misery knows no limit.

POLYNEIKÊS: Because of a brother's outrage!

ETEOKLÊS: Am I not outraged in turn?

POLYNEIKÊS: Where will you be in battle?

ETEOKLÊS: Why ask me this?

POLYNEIKÊS: I'll be there to kill you.

ETEOKLÊS: I long for that, too.

IOKASTÊ: Oh my sons, what are you doing?

POLYNEIKÊS: You'll know soon enough.

IOKASTÊ: You must escape your father's curses!

ETEOKLÊS: Let the whole house be damned!

POLYNEIKÊS: My sword will never again be shy of blood! I call on the
land and the gods that gave me life to witness my pain, driven,
dishonored, insulted, from my home, like a slave and not the son of
my father Oedipus, the same as he, my brother!

  Oh city, whatever your fate, the blame is his, not mine. I came
to Thebes against my will, and against my will I wage this war.

  Phoibos, Lord of the Ways, farewell! And farewell, too, my
house, my home, the friends of my youth and the altars where we
offered honey to the gods! Will I speak to you ever again, I don't
know. But hope is still alive, and with the gods' help I know I will kill
this man and rule here in Thebes.

*(Exeunt POLYNEIKÊS, then IOKASTÊ into the palace. ETEOKLÊS
and his ATTENDANTS remain.)*

(Music. Song. Dance.)

YOUNG PHOENICIAN WOMEN: *(Sing.)*
  Kadmos,
  Phoenician Kadmos,
  came to this land,

came led to this land by an untamed calf,
no yoke on its neck,
and the calf,
in exhaustion,
as prophecy told,
rested in the fields,
the wheat-ripe fields,
where Kadmos was to build his house,
by Dirkê,
swift-flowing stream that moistens the plains
to luxuriant growth.
Here a mother bore a son,
son of Zeus,
Zeus,
divine,
earthborn mother,
Mother Semelê,
and about him,
soon, soon,
fresh green tendrils crept to the babe,
enfolding him in cool shady softness,
blessing on the blest,
on Bakkhic god,
god Dionysos,
god Bromios,
Dionysos,
god,
that Theban maidens and Theban women
danced,
danced,
a holy dance,
dance to Dionysos,
in honor,
shouting his ecstatic cry:
Evoë!

But the deadly dragon,
Arês' serpent,
Arês' dragon,

mortal to man,
kept watch with ever-circling eyes
on the streams that made the fields grow green,
Arês' springs and flowing waters,
eyes ever watchful.
And Kadmos came seeking lustral waters,
and Kadmos killed him,
Arês' serpent,
cast a rock with his beast-killing arms,
and smashed his head,
the man-killing dragon.
And Pallas Athêna,
motherless goddess,
commanded he sow in the fields' fertile furrows
the great serpent's teeth;
and from those fields rose men fully armed,
a marvel to see,
treading the earth.
But Slaughter,
cruel of heart and mind,
cut them down again to earth's level,
joined them again to earth's furrows,
bloodied earth that had given them birth,
revealed them to the sunlit earth.
And you, Epaphos,
on you I call, too,
ancient offspring of our ancestor Io!
IOOO! IOOO!
Come, oh come!
I call you with barbarian shout,
call you with barbarian prayer!
Come, oh come,
to this land,
this city,
to Thebes founded by your descendants,
and goddess Persephonê,
and dear Dêmêter,
ruler of all,
nurse of all,
Mother Earth!

Come, Epaphos,
with the torch-bearing goddesses!
Protect this land!
For the gods all things are possible.
(Music out.)

KREON: *(Enters from the side.)* I've looked for you everywhere, lord Eteok-lês. I made the rounds of the gates and guard posts to find you.

ETEOKLÊS: I'd hoped to see you, too, Kreon. Polyneikês' peace terms were unacceptable.

KREON: I've heard he has great plans for Thebes, thanks to his army and the marriage tie to Adrastos. But that's for the gods to deal with. Meanwhile I have something more pressing.

ETEOKLÊS: More pressing? What is it?

KREON: A prisoner. An Argive.

ETEOKLÊS: And his news?

KREON: They mean to cordon off Thebes with heavy artillery.

ETEOKLÊS: Then Thebes must meet them head-on in the field.

KREON: The field? Where in the field? Are you so naïve?

ETEOKLÊS: Out there, beyond the trenches.

KREON: But Thebes is weak, the enemy mighty.

ETEOKLÊS: Mighty, yes, in words!

KREON: The Argive force is famed throughout all Greece.

ETEOKLÊS: Is it? Well, they'll soon be Argive corpses!

KREON: I certainly hope so. But what an effort it will be.

ETEOKLÊS: I won't have my men cooped up inside these walls!

KREON: Victory is won by foresight and good counsel.

ETEOKLÊS: What are you saying? Take a different approach?

KREON: Consider *every* approach before you risk everything.

ETEOKLÊS: Well, then, a night attack? Surprise them by ambush?

KREON: By all means, if it gets you back safely.

ETEOKLÊS: Night is a great equalizer, and makes bold men bolder.

KREON: One misstep in the dark and it's over.

ETEOKLÊS: We'll attack while they're eating.

KREON: A fright tactic at best; what we need is victory.

ETEOKLÊS: The Dirkê's deep—too deep for retreat.

KREON: Better to be well on our guard.

ETEOKLÊS: All right, then, a cavalry attack?

KREON: They're barricaded, ringed round by chariots.

ETEOKLÊS: So what do I do? Surrender the city?

KREON: Surrender! No! Think it out! You're clever!

ETEOKLÊS: What plan is cleverer than mine?

KREON: Word has reached me that seven of the enemy captains—

ETEOKLÊS: Seven? And what will they do?

KREON: Each leads a company to assault our seven gates.

ETEOKLÊS: And we do what? I can't stand indecision!

KREON: Choose seven men to meet them.

ETEOKLÊS: In single combat, or in charge of a company?

KREON: In charge of a company. Choose your bravest.

ETEOKLÊS: Yes, to prevent them scaling the walls.

KREON: Generals along with yourself. No man can see everything.

ETEOKLÊS: Do I choose them for courage or intelligence?

KREON: For both. They feed off each other.

ETEOKLÊS: I agree. A commander at each of the seven gates, as you suggest. I'll see to it at once. To name each one would waste valuable time with the enemy camped at our walls. I'm going; this is no time to be idle. With luck I'll meet my brother face to face and kill him for coming to destroy my city. But if I fail, Kreon, it's for you to see to the marriage of my sister Antigonê to your son Haimon. You're also my mother's brother. What more need I say? See to her wellbeing in every way, for your sake and mine. As for my father, I have little respect for him. Only a fool puts out his own eyes. And if he has his way, he'll kill us with his curses. But there's one thing I've yet to do. I must learn if Teiresias has any advice. I'll send your son Menoikeus, your father's namesake, to fetch him. He'll gladly talk to you. To me he scarcely speaks. I once questioned his prophetic skills.

But you, Kreon, you and my city, on you I put this charge: If I succeed, if my cause triumphs, the body of Polyneikês must never be buried in this land of Thebes. And if it is, let him who buried him be put to death, even if one of the family. Bring my arms and armor! A contest of blood lies before us. We set out now with Justice that brings us victory. And to Caution, that most useful of deities, I pray to keep safe our city.

(Exeunt ETEOKLÊS with ATTENDANTS. KREON remains.)

(Music. Song. Dance.)

YOUNG PHOENICIAN WOMEN: *(Sing.)*
Arês,
god of suffering,
god of pain,
why,
why are you possessed by death,
why possessed by bloodshed,
ever in discord with the revels of Bakkhos?
Let loose your curls,
toss your hair,
let it flow to the joyous song of garlanded youth,
to the breath of melodious pipes
alive,
alive with the grace of dancing!
Why do you lead a joyless dance,
a dance of death where armies collide,
inspiring Argives to slaughter Thebans?
A dance of evil no music graces,
a grim rejoicing where no flute plays.
You whirl no thyrsos,
you wear no fawn skin,
but tall in your four-horsed chariot,
amid the ring of clattering bridles,
and thundering hooves along the Ismênos,
you inspire the sons of the Sown Men
to defend against Argives,
in bronze you deck them,
brazen shields and armor,
hostile,
and line them along great battlements of stone.
Strife is a terrible goddess,
Strife,
who contrived these woes for our kings.

God-hallowed glade teeming with wild things,
favorite haunt of goddess Artemis,
snow-clad Kithairon,
why when he was cast out to die,
abandoned,

left exposed on the hillside,
did you save him from death,
Iokastê's baby,
child adorned with golden pins,
Oedipus?
If only that winged monster from the mountains,
the Sphinx,
had never shrieked her dissonant songs in Thebes,
never brought pain,
never sorrow,
she,
sent by Hades to maim this land,
who with four-taloned feet
swooped down on our walls
to carry off the youthful sons of Kadmos,
high,
high into the pathless light
of the radiant empyrean.
But now another hate bursts forth,
another curse to plague the city
and the house of the sons of Oedipus.
What is not good can never be good,
nor unlawful sons be made lawful,
their mother's polluted brood,
their father's shame
who shared her bed of incest.

Oh Earth,
I heard in my Phoenician home,
heard once,
Earth,
that you gave birth,
long ago,
to the race of the red-crested,
beast-eating serpent,
whose teeth spawned men,
Sown Men,
the glory and the shame of Thebes.
And the gods came once,

long ago,
to the wedding of Harmonia,
sons of heaven,
and as Amphion played,
as his lyre strings sounded,
the walls of Thebes rose tall and proud
on the land between the two rivers,
where Dirkê and Ismênos
water the lush green plain.
And after that Io,
horned mother of our race,
bore kings to the line of Kadmos.
Blessed with countless and countless blessing,
this city stands crowned with the garlands of war.

(Enter TEIRESIAS led by his young DAUGHTER, one hand on her shoulder and a staff in the other. On his head is a golden chaplet. MENOIKEUS follows.)

(Music out.)

TEIRESIAS: Onward, dear child of a blind old man. Your eyes are to my sightless steps like stars that guide the seafaring sailor. Set my foot finally on level ground, and go before me so we don't stumble. Your father is a weak old man. And those lot tablets of divination you carry, guard them with your pure young hands. I prepared them at my holy seat of prophecy when I learned what the bird omens were. Ah, Menoikeus, my lad, Kreon's son, how much farther till we find your father? My legs are weary, my steps so many, our progress slow.

KREON: Courage, Teiresias! You're sailing into harbor with friends near. Take his arm, son. Like toddling children, old men need a helping hand.

(MENOIKEUS helps TEIRESIAS forward to face KREON.)

TEIRESIAS: Ah, yes, here we are, then. Why the so urgent summons, Kreon?

KREON: That can wait, old man. First catch your breath and recover your strength after your wearying climb.

TEIRESIAS: Yes, and right you are, weary's the word. I returned from Athens only yesterday. War there, too, against Eumolpos. I brought the Athenians a glorious victory. This golden chaplet I'm wearing— you see?—first fruit of the spoils of battle.

KREON: I take your victory chaplet as a good omen. As you know, a sea of troubles surrounds us, a great Argive wave ready to break. King Eteoklês, fully armed, is already on his way to meet the attack. He asks what we must do to save the city.

TEIRESIAS: If Eteoklês had asked me, I'd have shut my mouth and refused my oracle. But since it's you, I'll speak. This land has long been diseased, Kreon, ever since Laïos acted in disobedience to the gods and fathered wretched Oedipus, the son to be his mother's husband. The gory mutilation of his eyes was the gods' subtle device for teaching Greece a lesson. And the sons of Oedipus, hoping to cloak these things with the passage of time, let alone outwit the gods, fell into disastrous error. By denying him not only his rights, but the freedom to leave, they stung the miserable old man into a frenzied rage. Diseased, degraded by their treatment, he lashed out at them with terrible curses. What did I not do? What did I not say? And my reward? The hatred of the sons of Oedipus.

Death for them is near, Kreon, each at the other's hand. Corpse will fall on corpse, many, many, Argive and Theban limbs intertwining, and pitiful keening will resound throughout the land. And you, poor, wretched city, you will be destroyed with them if no one heeds my words. Best for Thebes is that no son of Oedipus live or rule in this land. They are possessed by a father's curse and will take Thebes down with them. But the force of evil here being stronger than the good, there remains one other way to deliverance. But to say what that is, even for me, is not safe, and bitter for those whose fate is to offer the city a sacrifice for its safety.

I'll go now. Farewell. One among many, I will suffer what comes. What else can I do? (As he turns to leave, KREON grabs him by the arm.)

KREON: Stop, old man!

TEIRESIAS: Take your hands off me!

KREON: Stay! Why are you running from me?

TEIRESIAS: It isn't I who run from you, but your fate.

KREON: How do we save the city and its people?

TEIRESIAS: You want to know now, but soon you won't.

KREON: But how could I not want to save my city?

TEIRESIAS: You really want to know? Is that what you want?

KREON: How could I want anything more?

TEIRESIAS: Very well, you'll hear the prophecy. But first, where is Menoikeus, who led me here?

KREON: Not far off. Quite near, in fact.

TEIRESIAS: Tell him to leave; to get as far from my prophecy as possible.

KREON: He's my son; he'll keep secret what he must.

TEIRESIAS: Then you'd have me speak in his presence?

KREON: He'll be pleased to hear what will save us.

TEIRESIAS: Here is my prophecy. To save your country, you must slaughter your son Menoikeus. I wouldn't have spoken, but you insisted.

KREON: What are you saying, old man? I don't understand!

TEIRESIAS: What is revealed, you must do.

KREON: How much evil you've said in so few words!

TEIRESIAS: Evil for you, for your city a lifeline.

KREON: I didn't hear! I wasn't listening! City be damned!

TEIRESIAS: This man is not the man he was; he changes course.

KREON: Go! I have no need of your prophecies!

TEIRESIAS: Has truth died because of your suffering?

KREON: On my knees I implore you, old man—

TEIRESIAS: Kneeling? Why? Accept your suffering! It can't be avoided!

KREON: Say nothing in the city! Do you hear me? Nothing!

TEIRESIAS: What you ask me is wrong. I can't keep silent.

KREON: What are you doing to me? Will you kill my son?

TEIRESIAS: That's for others. It's for me to speak.

KREON: How has this evil come upon me and my son?

TEIRESIAS: You're right to question and demand a reply. This boy must be
    sacrificed in the cave where the earthborn dragon, guardian of Dirkê's
    stream, first came to light. His blood will be a libation to Earth for the
    ancient crime of Kadmos, assuaging Arês' wrath, for Arês is avenging
    that serpent's death. Do this, and Arês will be your ally.
    If Earth receives fruit for fruit, and human blood for blood, she
    who once brought forth the golden-helmeted crop of Sown Men will
    favor you. One of their race must die: a child born of the dragon's jaw.
    You are the last of that race of Sown Men, a direct line on both your
    mother's and your father's side, as are your sons.
    Haimon is barred from sacrificial slaughter by virtue of his
    coming marriage; for though he has had no part of the marriage bed,
    he has a bride and by law is considered married. But this young colt,
    as yet unyoked by marriage, belongs to no one so much as Thebes, her
    sacrificial animal. By his death his city will be saved. His offering will

be a blight to Adrastos and the Argives in their homecoming, casting a dark doom of grief on their eyes for the death of so many. And his sacrifice will bring great glory to Thebes. It is for you to choose your fate. Save your son, or save your city. So much for my message. *(To his DAUGHTER.)* Lead me home, child. A man must be mad to practice prophecy. If he prophesies unwelcome prophecies, he is the enemy; and if out of pity he mitigates the truth, he is a liar who dishonors the gods. Apollo alone should prophesy: he alone fears no one.

(Exeunt TEIRESIAS and his DAUGHTER, his hand on her shoulder, leading him, as at their entrance.)

FIRST YOUNG PHOENICIAN WOMAN: Why so silent, Kreon, so quiet? I, too, am struck dumb with horror.

KREON: What's to be said? It's clear, at least, what I *must* say. Never will I sink so low, never, as to deliver up my son to Thebes to be slaughtered! All men love their children, and not one, not one, would give up his child to be killed. I want no praise for patriotism while my child is being slaughtered for his city! Myself, yes, I'm of an age, I'd offer my life for my city, I'm ready.

Hurry, son! Before the whole city learns, leave here, now, forget these wanton prophecies of seers! Out, out of the country! Now! He'll tell them, tell them all, the generals, the captains at the seven gates! Leave now, quickly, and your life is saved. Delay, and it's over, you die.

MENOIKEUS: Where do I go? What city? What friends?

KREON: Wherever you'll be farthest from Thebes.

MENOIKEUS: Tell me, I'll go.

KREON: Go past Delphi—

MENOIKEUS: Where to, Father?

KREON: Aitolia.

MENOIKEUS: Where then?

KREON: Head for Thesprotia.

MENOIKEUS: The temple at Dodona?

KREON: Yes—

MENOIKEUS: How will that protect me?

KREON: The god will guide you.

MENOIKEUS: What about money?

KREON: I'll send you money.

MENOIKEUS: Thank you, Father.

KREON: Be on your way now.

MENOIKEUS: First I'll see your sister Iokastê. She nursed me at her breast when my mother died. I'll say good-bye, and then be off to save my life.

(They embrace and MENOIKEUS starts for the palace.)

KREON: Hurry, son! There's no time to waste! *(Exit KREON to the side.)*

MENOIKEUS: *(About to enter, turns to the WOMEN.)* Women, how cleverly I dismissed my father's fears! Did you see? Using deceit to win my heart's desire! In trying to remove me from danger, he's depriving the city of its rightful fate, and making me look a coward. Cowardice in an old man may be forgiven, but to become a traitor to the country that bore me can never be pardoned. No! I'll save my city. I'll offer my life to my country. How could I endure the thought that men, free of oracles and the gods' constraints, stand fast by their shields in battle, fighting for their land, and never once shrink from the thought of death, while I, betraying my father, my brother, my city, desert my country, a coward! Wherever I live men would point me out for what indeed I'd be, contemptible. No, by Zeus who dwells among the stars, and bloody Arês, who established the Sown Men, risen from the earth, rulers of this land! I will go now and take my place on the towering battlement, sacrifice myself above the serpent's sacred lair, as the seer instructed, and save my city. *(Exit to the side.)*

(Music. Song. Dance.)

YOUNG PHOENICIAN WOMEN: *(Sing.)*
    You came, you came,
    winged brood of Earth
    and underworld Echidna,
    monster snake of hell,
    came to plunder the sons of Kadmos,
    bringer of ruin,
    bringer of tears,
    half woman, half beast,
    dreadful omen,
    on roving wings you came,
    with talons to feed on raw flesh!
    Once on a time,
    once,
    from Dirkê's banks,
    you snatched up young men
    with your sinister dirge,
    a Fury bringing murderous woes,
    a song of doom,
    a song of despair,
    a pall of death on all the land—
    and bloody the hand of the god who brought them!
    Mothers mourning,
    mourning young girls,
    laments poured from houses;
    cries of anguish,
    cries of agony,
    roared through the streets,
    rose and fell and rose again,
    a thunderous roar through all the city,
    when bloody talons
    snatched up another son of Kadmos!

In time wretched Oedipus came,
Oedipus sent by Pythian Apollo,
doomed Oedipus to the land of Thebes,
at first in joy he came,
then sorrow,
for he made a marriage,
an evil marriage,
marriage with his mother
that was no marriage,
in triumph he unraveled the riddle,
then brought pollution to the land he'd saved.
And now from bloody deed to bloody deed,
he brings his sons into bloody conflict,
casting them with his bloody curse
into bloody slaughter,
each of the other,
unhappy man.
I rejoice,
I rejoice for him who chose death,
death to save his city from ruin,
for though he leaves Kreon to mourn,
he brings glorious victory to Thebes
of the seven-gated towers.
I pray, I pray
I have sons like this, dear Pallas,
Pallas who brought on the dragon's death by stoning,
and turned Kadmos to the deed
that brought this grasping,
ruinous plague from the gods.

(Music out.)

THEBAN SOLDIER: *(Entering in a rush, pounds on the palace doors.)* Open
    up! Who's minding the gates? Open! Bring Iokastê! *(Silence.)* You! In
    there! Open! Hello in there! Why this delay? Open!

IOKASTÊ: *(Enters from the palace.)* Dear friend, what is it? Not news
    of Eteoklês' death, I hope. You were always beside him in battle,
    protecting him from enemy missiles. Is he dead? Eteoklês? Tell me.

THEBAN SOLDIER: Don't be frightened. No, he's alive. I assure you.

IOKASTÊ: The city walls, then? The seven gated towers? All safe?

THEBAN SOLDIER: The walls are secure. The city's safe.

IOKASTÊ: Were we ever in danger of defeat?

THEBAN SOLDIER: We were. It was close. But we proved the stronger.

IOKASTÊ: Please, one thing more? Polyneikês? Is he alive?

THEBAN SOLDIER: Both your sons are alive at this hour.

IOKASTÊ: Bless you! But tell me of the victory. How, when they had us blockaded, you forced the enemy from the gates. I so want to gladden blind old Oedipus with the news.

THEBAN SOLDIER: When Kreon's son, who gave his life to save the city, stood high on the battlement, and had plunged the deadly sword into his throat, your son ordered seven companies with seven commanders to the seven gates to ward off the Argive attack. He also organized cavalry and hoplite reserves to rush to any part of the walls where our defense needed strengthening. From high on the towers we then saw the Argive army with its white shields leave Temessos and, nearing our trenches, break into a run and encircle the entire citadel. Suddenly, from both sides, simultaneously, the roar of battle cries and braying trumpets rose to split the ears.

We fought at first with bows and javelins, and slings, distance weapons, and stones that we used to shower them. When we were winning, Tydeus and Polyneikês shouted: "Men of Argos, will you wait till you're torn to shreds by their missiles? Assault the gates in full force, hoplites, cavalry, charioteers, everyone!" Hearing the cry, at once they charged, every one of them. And many fell, heads laid open, and ours fell, too, tumbling, plunging from the high battlements, blood soaking the thirsty earth.

The Arkadian then, no Argive, Atalanta's son, hurled himself at one of the gates like a hurricane, calling for fire and axes to raze the city. But he was checked in his fury by Periklymenos, son of Poseidon, who hurled at his head a stone the size of a cart, a coping stone from the battlements, that shattered his fair-haired skull, bursting the sutures and bloodying his cheeks with their first bloom of youth. He'll return no more to his huntress mother of the fair bow. Seeing this gate well defended, Eteoklês rushed off to another, me beside him. I saw Tydeus then, massed round with companions, aiming their Aitolian spears at the topmost edge of the fortifications, forcing our men to abandon their posts on the battlements. But like a master of the hunt summoning his hounds, your son regrouped them and set them back once more on the towers. This danger contained, we sped off to other gates. But how to describe the raging Kapaneus? A long-necked scaling ladder in his grip, he boasted that not even the sacred fire of Zeus's thunderbolts could stop him razing the city from top to bottom. Rung after rung he climbed, his body coiled beneath his shield to protect against the shower of stones hurled down upon him. When just about to mount the battlement's height, Zeus struck out at him with a lightning bolt. The earth roared, striking terror into everyone. He fell from the ladder, his limbs torn from his body, his hair flown up to the sky, his blood splattering the earth, his arms and legs rolling like Ixion on his wheel, and his body fell, a flaming torch, to the ground.

When Adrastos saw that Zeus had taken sides with the enemy, he withdrew his men beyond the ditch. But no sooner our men saw this favorable omen from Zeus, out they rushed, chariots, cavalry, infantry, attacking the Argives at the very heart of their line. It was a chaos of ruin and destruction. Men leapt or were flung from chariots, wheels spun through the air, axel piled on axel, corpse on corpse. We've checked the towers' destruction for today. As for the future, that lies in the hands of the gods.

IOKASTÊ: The gods and fortune have done well by us. My sons are alive and the city has escaped unharmed. Poor Kreon, it seems, has reaped the bitter harvest of my marriage with Oedipus, having lost his son— a blessing for Thebes, but a personal pain for him. But tell me more. What are my two sons planning?

THEBAN SOLDIER: Don't ask what follows. So far the news is good.

IOKASTÊ: You rouse suspicions. How can I not ask?

THEBAN SOLDIER: What more do you want than your sons alive?

IOKASTÊ: To know if my future fortune is good. *(She restrains him.)*

THEBAN SOLDIER: Let go of me. Your son will need his subordinate.

IOKASTÊ: What evil are you hiding in the dark?

THEBAN SOLDIER: I refuse to deliver bad news after good.

IOKASTÊ: You will, unless you can vanish into thin air.

THEBAN SOLDIER: Ah, why couldn't you let me leave after the good news, and not force me to deliver the bad? Your two sons—I curse their shameful brashness!—mean to meet in single combat apart from their armies. To the assembled Argive and Kadmeian troops they both spoke words they should never have uttered.

Eteoklês was the first. From high on the battlements he called for silence in the ranks. "Commanders of the land of Greece, chieftains of Argos assembled here, and citizens of Thebes! What need have you to barter away your lives for me or for Polyneikês? To deliver you from that fate, I have determined to fight in single combat with my brother. If I kill him, I will rule alone in Thebes. If he defeats me, the throne, the land, the house are his. Argives: lay down your weapons and return to Argos with your lives, rather than leave your corpses to rot in our fields!"

Eteoklês having finished, Polyneikês rushed from the ranks to second his brother's speech, and Argives and Thebans both roared a shout of approval. In the no man's land between the two armies a truce was ratified and the commanders took oaths to abide by it.

These two young sons of ancient Oedipus then covered their bodies in bronze, decked out in arms and armor by their friends; Eteoklês by Theban nobles; his brother by princes of Argos. They stood resplendent in the sun, their faces ruddy, savagely ready to hurl the first spear. Friends came out from either side, offering encouragement, words like: "Polyneikês, it's in your hands now to raise a trophy to Zeus and bring glory to Argos." And to Eteoklês: "This is Thebes you're fighting for; win in glory and the throne is yours." Those were their words, urging them on to the fight.

The prophets then sacrificed sheep to interpret the fissures at the tips of the flame—a sign of moistness opposed to the fire—and the peak of the blaze that portends either victory or defeat. But if in any way, my lady, you have power to help, whether with wise words or magic charms, save your sons from this dreadful encounter. The danger is great.

IOKASTÊ: Antigonê! Daughter! Come out of the house! This is no ordinary day in our lives, by the gods' decree. At this moment your two brothers are racing toward death. We must stop them before they kill each other.

ANTIGONÊ: *(Enters from the palace.)* Mother, what new calamity have you to tell me?

IOKASTÊ: Your brothers' lives are rushing to an end.

ANTIGONÊ: What are you saying?

IOKASTÊ: They'll fight in single combat.

ANTIGONÊ: Don't say that! No—no—

IOKASTÊ: Yes, it's not pleasant. Come.

ANTIGONÊ: But where? You mean leave my quarters?

IOKASTÊ: To the battlefield.

ANTIGONÊ: I'd be ashamed in such a crowd.

IOKASTÊ: This is no time for modesty.

ANTIGONÊ: What will I do?

IOKASTÊ: Put an end to your brothers' quarrel.

ANTIGONÊ: How, Mother?

IOKASTÊ: By falling to our knees before them. *(To the THEBAN*
SOLDIER.) You! Lead the way to the battlefield! Let's not delay!
Hurry, daughter, hurry! If I reach my sons before the fight, I'm saved.
But if I find them dead, I'll die beside them.

(Exeunt IOKASTÊ, ANTIGONÊ, and the THEBAN SOLDIER.)

(Music. Song. Dance.)

YOUNG PHOENICIAN WOMEN: *(Sing.)*
AIIIII!
AIIIII!
My heart trembles,
trembles with fear,
fear and dread.
And pity,
pity pierces my flesh
for the mother of sorrows.
Which,
which of the sons,
which will first draw blood—
oh Zeus, oh Earth,
I weep for her pain!—
which will pierce his brother's shield,
his brother's neck,
his brother's life
with a bloody stroke?
TALAIN' EGO TALAINA!
Whose death will I weep for?
Whose corpse will I mourn?

FÉU DÁ!
FÉU DÁ!
Twin beasts,
blood-maddened minds,
spears brandished
to pierce the fallen foe,
slaying, slaying,
bloody end,

what led them,
the fools,
to choose single combat!
I will raise a foreign,
barbaric shriek,
to mourn the dead,
fit for the dead!
Their fate is near,
slaughter at hand!
The sword decides the future.
How evil the ill-fated slaughter
the Erinyës have brought!

FIRST YOUNG PHOENICIAN WOMAN: *(Speaks.)* Hush! No more
lamentation! Here is Kreon, his face heavy with gloom.

(Music out.)

KREON: *(Enters from the side.)* AIIII! AIIII! What shall I do? Weep and
moan for myself or my city, my city so clouded in sorrow that
Acheron is no darker? My son is no more, my son who gave his life for
his land, and won a noble name, but endless pain for me. I just now
took him from the dragon's cliff and brought his self-sacrificed corpse
back home in my arms, where my whole house wails in despair. I've
come here in search of my ancient sister Iokastê, I, an old man. She
must wash and lay out my dead son's body for burial. The living must
tend to the dead, giving honor to the god of the underworld.

FIRST YOUNG PHOENICIAN WOMAN: Your sister is gone, Kreon,
away from the house with Antigonê.

KREON: But where? Tell me? Some new catastrophe?

FIRST YOUNG PHOENICIAN WOMAN: Her sons are to fight in single
combat for the throne.

KREON: What are you saying? I didn't know. I was so concerned with my
own son's body.

FIRST YOUNG PHOENICIAN WOMAN: Your sister has been gone a long while. The deadly conflict must be over now, Oedipus's sons having settled their score.

(Enter the SECOND THEBAN SOLDIER.)

KREON: AIIII! I already see a sign! This man comes with no good news.

SECOND THEBAN SOLDIER: O TALAS EGO! How can I deliver such news? How do I express my misery?

KREON: Your words tell me the end has come.

SECOND THEBAN SOLDIER: O TALAS! I cry it again, for my news is a horror!

KREON: Tell it! Add to our full cup of misery!

SECOND THEBAN SOLDIER: Kreon—your sister Iokastê's sons are dead.

(Music. Chant.)

KREON: *(Chants.)*
    AIIII!
    AIIII!
    What grief,
    what suffering you bring,
    for me,
    for Thebes!
    House of Oedipus,
    do you hear?
    Two sons dead
    by the same
    disaster!

FIRST YOUNG PHOENICIAN WOMAN: *(Speaks.)* Yes, and would weep if it had a heart to feel.

KREON: *(Chants.)*
AIIII!
I cry for calamity!
AIIII!
I cry for disaster
in my misery!

SECOND THEBAN SOLDIER: *(Speaks.)* Do I dare tell you what is yet to come?

KREON: *(Speaks.)* What can there be more grievous than this?

SECOND THEBAN SOLDIER: *(Speaks.)* Your sister is dead along with her sons.

YOUNG PHOENICIAN WOMEN: *(Sing.)*
Howl,
cry,
raise,
raise the lament,
strike,
rain down blows,
strike,
blows on the head
with pale white hands!

KREON: *(Speaks.)* Poor, miserable Iokastê, to what an end that Sphinx's riddle has brought your marriage, your life! How did it happen, tell me, this slaughter the sons of Oedipus have made?

(Music out.)

SECOND THEBAN SOLDIER: You know of the city's success at the towers—the walls are not far off. When the young sons of ancient Oedipus had sheathed their bodies in bronze, they proceeded to the field between the two armies, eager to engage in single combat. Polyneikês spoke first; casting a glance toward Argos he prayed: "Lady Hera—for I am yours, since married to the daughter of Adrastos and living in his land—I pray you grant that I kill my

brother, that in victory I drench my fighting hand in his blood!"
Eteoklês prayed then, facing the temple of Pallas of the Golden Shield:
"Daughter of Zeus, grant that my victorious spear hurl from my hand
into my brother's chest!" When, like a flaring torch, the blare of the trumpet was set
ablaze, the signal for the start of bloody battle, they hurled themselves
upon each other like wild boars whetting savage tusks, their beards
white with foam. Lunging, each at the other, with spears, they
crouched for safety behind their shields, so that the iron would glance
off harmlessly. If one saw the gleam of the other's eyes above the rim,
he jabbed with his spear, hoping to be the first to strike. But their
spears were ineffectual; each kept his eyes safely behind his shield.

Eteoklês, sensing a stone in his path, kicked it aside with his
foot, and doing so exposed his leg. Polyneikês saw and at once
directed his aim at the target, so that his spear pierced his opponent's
shin guard, and the Argive army raised a mighty shout. All the while,
Eteoklês, seeing the arm that struck the blow exposed, let fly his shaft
at Polyneikês' chest, giving pleasure to his fellow Thebans—only to
have the point broken off. Deprived of his spear, Eteoklês backs up,
step by step, and, seizing a large stone, hurls it directly at Polyneikês,
breaking the pole of his spear in the middle. They are equal now, the
battle poised, neither of them with a spear.

Each of them now grasped for his sword and ramming their
shields together they made a thunderous clatter. Eteoklês then,
somehow, recalled a trick he'd learned in Thessaly. Disengaging
himself and pulling back his left foot while at the same time careful
to guard his belly, he thrusts forward his right leg and runs his sword
through Polyneikês' navel clear to the spine. Polyneikês, doubled over,
clutching his wound in agony, falls to the ground, blood gushing from
his body.

Eteoklês, thinking himself now victor and master of the field,
tosses aside his sword and proceeds to strip his brother of his armor,
so engaged in his task that he ignores his own safety. It was this that
proved his undoing. For Polyneikês, though gasping for breath, had
not let loose his weapon when he fell, and summoning what little
effort he had left, dashed his sword through Eteoklês' liver—
Polyneikês, the first to fall. They lie there now, side by side, bitter
earth between their teeth, dividing their sovereignty.

FIRST YOUNG PHOENICIAN WOMAN: Ancient Oedipus, how I mourn your misfortunes. Some god has now fulfilled your curse.

SECOND THEBAN SOLDIER: No, wait, there's more—more sorrows to tell. At the moment when her two sons had fallen and lay dying, their mother, with Antigonê, entered in breathless haste. Seeing them in the throes of mortal pain, she cried aloud her agony: "Oh my sons, though I came at once, my help has come too late!" Falling down beside them, she wept and mourned, lamenting that she had ever suckled them at her breast. "You, your mother's comfort in her age!" she cried. And at her side their sister wept: "Dear, dear brothers, who will now never see to my marriage!" Hearing his mother's voice, Eteoklês heaved a heavy sigh, then placed his dank, cold hand upon her, saying no word, the tears in his eyes telling her of his love. But his brother Polyneikês still had breath, and looking at his sister and ancient mother said: "Mother, I am dead. And yet it's you I pity, you and my sister here, and my dead brother—my brother who became my enemy, and yet was never less than the brother I loved. Bury me now, dear mother and sister, in the soil of my own land. And if the city rises in anger, appease them so that, having lost my share, at least I have this much. Now, Mother, close my eyes with your hand"—and here he himself placed her hand upon his eyes—"and so good-bye— the darkness is swift in coming—" Both then breathed out the last of their bitter lives.

And then a dreadful thing happened. Gripped by a fit of passion at the sight, their mother caught up a sword that lay by the corpses and ran it straight through her throat. She lies there now in their midst, embracing both her sons.

Both armies leapt to their feet, ours calling Eteoklês the winner, theirs claiming it was Polyneikês. Even the generals were arguing. The men rushed to seize their arms and armor. As chance would have it, we Thebans had sat down quite near to ours, the Argives some distance from theirs, and so we attacked them before they could arm. Not one of them stood their ground. The plain swarmed with hordes of fleeing men, and blood was thick on the field from those slain by our spears.

Once we had won, some of us set up a trophy offering to Zeus, while others stripped shields from the Argive dead and carried them inside the walls as war booty. Still others, along with Antigonê, are bringing the dead here for their people to mourn. Some of today's struggles have ended well for the city, others have brought bitter grief. *(Exit.)*

FIRST YOUNG PHOENICIAN WOMAN: No longer do we only hear of this house's misfortune, for now we see nearing the palace three bodies that death has joined, three lives that in death live in darkness.

(Enter ANTIGONÊ followed by SOLDIERS bearing on litters the bodies of ETEOKLÊS, POLYNEIKÊS, and IOKASTÊ.)

(Music. Song. Dance.)

ANTIGONÊ: *(Sings and dances.)*
No veil now covers the curls on my soft cheek,
no girlhood shame hides the blush,
the flush of my face,
as I come, in frenzy,
a bakkhant of the dead,
tearing loose the veil from my hair,
casting aside my saffron robe,
escorting the dead with endless groans.

AIIIII!
AIIIII!

Polyneikês,
how truly named you were!
Man of Strife!
Agony for Thebes!
And your strife,
your strife that was more than strife,
but killing upon killing,
slaughter upon slaughter—
that destroyed the house of Oedipus,
is now brought to fulfillment
in bitter bloodshed,
in bloodshed unspeakable!
House, oh house,

what song,
what groaning lament,
what musical wail of tears,
tears,
shall I call on to mourn you,
as I bring these three slain kindred bodies,
mother and sons,
to delight the vengeful Fury,
deadly Erinys?
Long ago,
long, long,
she destroyed the house of Oedipus,
that day he unriddled her riddling song,
the raucous singer's song,
hard to grasp,
the riddling Sphinx,
and killed her,
killed.

IO MOI MOI!

Oh Father,
Father I love,
what man,
what man of Greece,
what man of barbarian soil,
what noble prince of the distant past,
has suffered so,
suffered so many evils of human bloodshed
for all to see?
Poor woman that I am,
what bird hidden high in pine tree or oak
will come mourning a mother's loss and
sing a lament in tune with my misery,
I who will live a long life of loneliness,
a life, a life of eternal tears?
(She tears hair from her head.)

On which shall I cast first

the offering of hair torn from my head?
On these milkless breasts of the
mother who nursed me,
or on the gaping wounds
of my poor brothers' bodies?

(She places it on all three corpses.)

OTOTOTOI!

Father Oedipus!
Ancient blind Oedipus!
Come out!
Come out of your house!
Show the misery that fate has dealt you!
A long life dragged out in agony!
You who once, long ago,
brought murky darkness down on your eyes!
Do you hear,
do you hear in the courtyard,
wandering aimlessly,
or lying alone in the misery of your bed?

(Enter OEDIPUS from the palace, alone, supported by a staff.)

OEDIPUS: *(Sings.)*
Daughter,
Antigonê,
I heard your tears,
your pitiful tears,
calling for me, and
came, this staff
leading on my
blind steps.
Why have you
called me to the
light
from the dark
of my chamber?

Me, a bedridden,
ancient specter,
a gray phantom of
air and mists,
a soul from the
grave,
a hovering dream.

ANTIGONÊ: *(Sings.)*
Father,
the news you must know is disastrous.
Your sons are dead.
And Iokastê as well,
your support in all things,
dear Father!

OEDIPUS: *(Sings.)*
AIIIII!
AIIIII!
The pain,
the pain I must cry aloud!
The misery!
Three lives are no more!
What was their fate?
Tell me, child!

ANTIGONÊ: *(Sings.)*
I say this, Father,
not to reproach or mock you,
but with pain and sorrow.
Father,
the Spirit of Vengeance let loose by your curse,
burdened with sword and fire and brutal conflict,
has fallen on your sons—
my dear, dear Father!

OEDIPUS: *(Sings.)*
AIIII!
AIIII!

ANTIGONÊ: *(Sings.)*
    Why this lament?

OEDIPUS: *(Sings.)*
    My sons—

ANTIGONÊ: *(Sings.)*
    Your suffering is great, I know.
    But what if you still had sight,
    still saw the sun in its course,
    what then would be your pain
    if you saw these wretched corpses?

OEDIPUS: *(Sings.)*
    My sons' death I know,
    I understand.
    But what of my wife, child?
    What fate destroyed her?

ANTIGONÊ: *(Sings.)*
    Her cries and tears were heard and seen
    by all as she offered her breast to her children,
    a suppliant offering a suppliant breast.
    There,
    in that meadow covered with lotus,
    where they fought with spear shafts,
    lions in a den,
    she found her sons at the Êlektran gate,
    their wounds' gore cold,
    Arês' libation which Hades accepts.
    Seizing a sword of hammered
    bronze from the bodies,
    she dipped it into her own flesh,
    dyeing it,
    and sank down in grief
    on the bodies of her sons.
    These many sorrows, Father,
    are heaped on our house today by the god
    who brought them to fulfillment.

(Music out.)

KREON: Enough of mourning. The time has come to turn our thoughts
to burial. Listen to me, Oedipus. When your son Eteoklês gave to
Haimon the dowry and the hand of your daughter Antigonê in
marriage, he gave to me the right to rule this kingdom. I have no
choice, therefore, but to turn you out of this land. Teiresias told me
quite clearly that Thebes would never flourish so long as you live here.
And so you must go. I say this with no arrogance, nor as your enemy.
It is Thebes I must think of, and to protect it against the Avenging
Spirits that attend you.

OEDIPUS: Oh Destiny! You made me from the start a thing of misery!
Even before I saw the light of day from my mother's womb, even
unborn, it was prophesied to Laïos by Apollo that I should be my
father's murderer. O TALAS EGO! No sooner was I born, than the
father who made me saw in me his enemy, and tried to kill me—for it
was to be his fate to die at my hands. He sent me then, still reaching
for the breast, to make a wretched meal for wild beasts! But I was
spared! Rescued! AIIIII! How I wish Kithairon had fallen to the dismal
depths of Tartaros for not ending my life! Miserable wretch that I am,
I then killed my father, and came to my poor mother's bed, and made
with her children, sons, sons who were also brothers, that I have now
destroyed, putting upon them curses I had from my father! Fortune's
fool I may be, but not so foolish as to think I tore out my eyes and
killed my sons without the contriving of some god.

What to do with the ancient wretch now? Who will come to
guide his shuffling, blind footsteps? The dead woman here? Yes—
yes, if she were alive. Or my fine yoke of sons? But they are far from
me now. Or am I so young I can still fend for myself? How do I do
this? Where?

Why do you destroy me so utterly, Kreon? Exile me from
this land and I am dead. And yet, I refuse to clasp your knees in
supplication, and prove myself to be base. I was a king! I will never
betray the nobility of my blood!

KREON: It was well said that you would not clasp my knees; for I, in my
turn, cannot allow you to live in this city. As for the bodies of these
dead, one is to be taken into the palace; the other, the corpse of

Polyneikês, who brought with him an army to destroy his native country, cast him out unburied beyond our borders. A proclamation will be read to Thebes that anyone caught garlanding or burying this body will have as his reward: death. Enough of mourning, Antigonê, for these three corpses. Into the palace now.

ANTIGONÊ: Dear Father, what miserable creatures we are, surrounded on every side by evil. I pity you more than I pity the dead. Your life has not been one of light and shade, but of darkness from the first. But you, Kreon, this land's new ruler, I ask you, why this outrage to my father, why banish him from his country? And why lay down laws for a miserable corpse?

KREON: This was Eteoklês' counsel, not mine.

ANTIGONÊ: A foolish decision that only a fool would follow.

KREON: An order is an order.

ANTIGONÊ: Not if that order is evil and spoken in malice.

KREON: It's unjust, you say, to throw his body to the dogs?

ANTIGONÊ: The penalty you impose on him is unlawful.

KREON: He came as an enemy to destroy his own city.

ANTIGONÊ: Yes, and he paid with his life for it.

KREON: So let him pay with his burial as well.

ANTIGONÊ: What was his crime? He came for his rightful share.

KREON: I'll say it again: this man will not be buried!

ANTIGONÊ: And I say: let the city forbid it, I *will* bury him.

KREON: Then you bury yourself as well, alongside him.

ANTIGONÊ: How splendid for two friends to lie side by side.

KREON: Seize this woman and take her into the palace!

ANTIGONÊ: *(Falling to her knees, she holds POLYNEIKÊS' corpse.)* No, I will never let loose of this body!

KREON: The gods have decreed otherwise, young woman.

ANTIGONÊ: They've also decreed that the dead are not to be outraged.

KREON: Dust and libations will never touch this body!

ANTIGONÊ: I beg you, Kreon, in the name of his mother Iokastê here—

KREON: Don't waste your time. My mind will not be changed.

ANTIGONÊ: At least let me wash his body.

KREON: This, too, the city forbids.

ANTIGONÊ: Then let me bind his wounds.

KREON: This corpse will be shown no honor!

ANTIGONÊ: At least, dear brother, I can hold and kiss you. *(She does so before she can be stopped.)*

KREON: You mustn't! These tears will pollute your marriage!

ANTIGONÊ: Marry your son? You're insane! Not while I live!

KREON: You have no choice! How will you escape it?

ANTIGONÊ: That night I'll have a dagger in my bed.

KREON: How dare she insult us! The audacity!

ANTIGONÊ: Let this sword's iron be witness to my oath!

KREON: Why so desperate to be free of this marriage?

ANTIGONÊ: I'll share in my wretched father's banishment.

KREON: Yes, there's nobility in you—but foolishness, too.

ANTIGONÊ: And share his death!

KREON: Go! You'll never kill my son! Get out! *(Exeunt KREON and his SOLDIERS into the palace.)*

OEDIPUS: Daughter, how can I thank you for your love, but—

ANTIGONÊ: How could I marry with you alone in exile?

OEDIPUS: —stay here, be happy; I can endure my own troubles.

ANTIGONÊ: But, Father, you're blind. Who will guide you, my dear?

OEDIPUS: Wherever fate has me fall, there I will lie.

ANTIGONÊ: Where is that Oedipus who solved the famous riddle?

OEDIPUS: He is no more. A single day raised and destroyed him.

ANTIGONÊ: Then why shouldn't I also share your pain?

OEDIPUS: A daughter and her blind father in exile?

ANTIGONÊ: No shame, my dear, but noble—if she's wise.

OEDIPUS: Then lead me to your mother so I may touch her.

ANTIGONÊ: There! Touch the face of the dear old woman.

OEDIPUS: Dear mother, dear wife—how wretched your suffering—

ANTIGONÊ: A world of grief is joined in this pitiable form.

OEDIPUS: Where are the bodies of Eteoklês and Polyneikês?

ANTIGONÊ: Very near you; stretched out beside each other.

OEDIPUS: Place my unseeing hands on their poor faces.

ANTIGONÊ: There! Lay your hands on your dead sons.

OEDIPUS: Dear fallen sons, miserable as your miserable father.

ANTIGONÊ: Dear Polyneikês! Dearest name to me!

OEDIPUS: Apollo's prophecy even now reaches fulfillment.

ANTIGONÊ: What prophecy? Is there more misery to come?

OEDIPUS: That after long wandering I will die in Athens.

ANTIGONÊ: Where? What Attic fortress will receive you?

OEDIPUS: Sacred Kolonos, home of the god of horses. But come. It's time.
See to your blind old father, since you are so eager to share his pain.

ANTIGONÊ: To exile, then; to miserable exile!

(Music. Song. Dance.)

ANTIGONÊ: *(Sings.)*
Stretch out your hand, Father!
Your dear hand!
And I will escort,
will escort you,
like a fair breeze
a ship.

OEDIPUS: *(Chants.)*
There.
On my way.
Journey's beginning.

With you,
misery's child,
to guide me.

ANTIGONÊ: *(Sings.)*
And that I am,
I am,
saddest of all
the girls of Thebes.

OEDIPUS: *(Chants.)*
Where shall I put my
ancient foot?
Come, child,
be my staff!

ANTIGONÊ: *(Sings.)*
This way,
this,
put your foot here,
here,
your ancient foot, Father!
Plant your foot here!
You have as little strength
as a dream,
my dear!

OEDIPUS: *(Chants.)*
IOOO!
IOOO!
Pity this old man!
Pity! Pity!
Wretched old man
in miserable exile!
IOOO!
IOOO!
What things I have
suffered,
have suffered!

ANTIGONÊ: *(Sings.)*
    Suffered?
    Why speak of suffering?
    Justice is blind to
    men of evil!
    Justice does not punish
    man's foolish deeds!

OEDIPUS: *(Chants.)*
    I am the man
    who soared to the
    pinnacle of wisdom,
    the man who unriddled
    the beast woman's
    treacherous riddle!

ANTIGONÊ: *(Sings.)*
    Why hark back
    to the days of the
    Sphinx?
    Let's hear no more talk
    of past successes.
    These miseries you
    suffer
    were in store
    from the start,
    waiting, waiting:
    to wander in
    exile
    down endless
    roads,
    and one day to fall, Father,
    and die—
    wherever.

(Exeunt ANTIGONÊ and OEDIPUS, she leading, his hand on her shoulder.)

*

ORESTÊS

(ΟΡΕΣΤΗΣ)

CHARACTERS

ÊLEKTRA *sister of Orestês*
HELEN *wife of Menelaos*
HERMIONÊ *daughter of Helen and Menelaos*
FIRST NOBLE ARGIVE WOMAN *leader of the Chorus*
CHORUS OF NOBLE ARGIVE WOMEN
ORESTÊS *son of Agamemnon*
MENELAOS *brother of Agamemnon, husband of Helen*
TYNDAREOS *king of Sparta, maternal grandfather of Orestês and Êlektra*
PYLADÊS *friend of Orestês*
OLD MAN *servant of Agamemnon, a peasant*
PHRYGIAN SLAVE
MALE ARGIVE CITIZENS
ARMORED HOPLITES
APOLLO
ATTENDANTS
SLAVES

ORESTÊS

Mykenê in Argos.
In front of Agamemnon's palace.
Six days after the murder of Klytaimnêstra.
ORESTÊS lies asleep on a pallet.
ÊLEKTRA sits on the ground beside him.

ÊLEKTRA: There is nothing, nothing so terrible, no terror, no suffering
sent by the gods, nothing, but humankind is liable to endure it.
Consider Tantalos, that man who was the happiest of men (and I don't
mean to mock his fate), Tantalos, born, they say, of Zeus, the son of
Zeus, who now hovers in midair terrified by a huge rock looming over
him. This is his penalty, or so the story goes, for one day sitting at
table with the gods, as if an equal in their midst, he was gripped by
that most vile of all diseases, insolence, and his tongue got the better
of him.

Tantalos had a son, Pelops, and Pelops was the father of Atreus,
for whom the goddess Strife spun out a fate that he would engage in
warfare with his brother, Thyestês. Ah, but why must I linger on these
obscenities of my house?

Well—Atreus slaughtered Thyestês' children and served them
up to their father in a terrible feast. I pass in silence over what
happened next, and move on to the sons of Atreus by Krêtan Aëropê:
Agamemnon, glorious Agamemnon—if glorious he was—and
Menelaos. Of them, Menelaos married Helen whom the gods abhor,
while Agamemnon, lord of men, married Klytaimnêstra, an alliance
that was the gossip of all Greece. By her Agamemnon had three
daughters, Chrysothemis, Iphigeneia, and I, Êlektra—and a son, one
son, Orestês, all from one mother, a mother so detestable that she
wound her husband in an endless mesh of folds and killed him. For
what motive, you ask? I'll leave that vague, leave it for the world to
guess at. It isn't a proper subject for a young virgin.

And then there's Apollo. How does one speak of a god's
injustice? And yet, he persuaded Orestês to murder his mother, the
woman who bore him, an act not highly valued in men's eyes; still, he
did as the god told. And I helped him, helped in a way not unseemly
for a woman—I helped kill her. Since then poor Orestês has taken to

his bed, ill, ravaged by a savage sickness, whirled into fits of madness by his mother's blood—notice how I say "mother's blood" instead of naming the names of the Dread Goddesses who pursue him with their terror.

It's six days now since fire cleansed our mother's bloodstained body, and in that time he has taken neither food nor washed his body. When he's sane, when he's relieved for a time of his affliction, he hides himself in the folds of his cloak and sobs, or else he leaps from his bed like a colt bolting free of the yoke, charging wildly about.

In the meantime, the city of Argos has passed a degree denying anyone the right to shelter or warm us at their fires, even to speak to us, for we are matricides. Today is the day the Argives will vote in assembly whether we're to live or die, and if death is our fate, if it is to be by stoning. And yet we have some hope of escaping death. Menelaos has only now arrived from Troy after long wandering, his ship resting at anchor in Nauplia's harbor.

As for her, the spiller of so much blood, Helen, he sent her ahead in darkness to our palace. A politic move, for those fathers whose sons lie dead beneath Troy's walls, seeing her in daylight, might stone her. She's here now, there, inside the house, wailing, weeping her sister's death, and the house's ruin.

But she's not without consolation. She has here her daughter Hermionê to comfort her. Menelaos, you see, on his way to Troy brought her from Sparta and entrusted her to my mother for safekeeping. Helen rejoices in her Hermionê who helps her forget her troubles.

As for me, I keep watch, hoping every moment to catch sight of him, of Menelaos, without whom all hope is lost, so feeble is our strength. A house battered by fortune is a sorry thing.

(Enter HELEN, alone, from the palace carrying libation jugs and a small clipping from her hair.)

HELEN: Êlektra, my dear, how are you? Poor thing, still unwed after all these years. And your brother, how is he? No, my dear, I have no fear of pollution in speaking with you; to my mind the guilt belongs to Apollo. Yet I do mourn the fate of my sister—poor Klytaimnêstra. I never saw her again after that god-sent madness drove me to Troy. But I feel her loss, I do, and I mourn for her.

ÊLEKTRA: Why waste words to spell out for you, Helen, what you can see for yourself: I sit here by his corpse, an eternal vigil—for that's what he is, a corpse, his breath is so shallow. Don't misunderstand, I don't mean to ridicule his troubles. But here you are, you, you and your husband, smug with your flush of success, and we, we in the depths of our misery.

HELEN: How long has he been lying there?

ÊLEKTRA: Since the day he shed his mother's blood.

HELEN: The poor man! And the way she died, too!

ÊLEKTRA: Yes, it was all too much for him.

HELEN: Êlektra, my dear, would you do something for me?

ÊLEKTRA: Yes, well, that depends; there's my brother—

HELEN: Would you go for me to my sister's grave—

ÊLEKTRA: My mother's, you mean? Why?

HELEN: To take this lock of my hair and these libations.

ÊLEKTRA: She's your sister and you can't go yourself?

HELEN: I'm ashamed to show my face to the Argives.

ÊLEKTRA: A bit late, isn't it? Where was your shame before?

HELEN: Your words are more truthful than kind.

ÊLEKTRA: What is it exactly shames you?

HELEN: The fathers of the dead left behind at Troy.

ÊLEKTRA: And well you should be. Your name is well known in Argos.

HELEN: Do it for me, please; save me this fear.

ÊLEKTRA: No. I couldn't face my mother's tomb.

HELEN: But think of the disgrace to send a servant.

ÊLEKTRA: Your daughter, then. Hermionê. Send her.

HELEN: An unmarried girl isn't seen in public.

ÊLEKTRA: Think of it as payment. My mother raised her.

HELEN: Yes, that's true. I'll send her. Hermionê! Hermionê dear, come out please! *(Enter HERMIONÊ from the palace.)* I want you to take these, dear, these libations and this cutting of my hair, and go to Klytaimnêstra's tomb. When you're there, I want you to pour out the honeyed milk and wine, and then, standing on the mound, say: "Your loving sister Helen, too frightened of the Argives to come herself, sends you these libations." Ask her then to look with favor on me, on you, on my husband, and on this miserable pair destroyed by a god. Assure her I will do all in my power to honor my sister in all ways proper to the dead.

    Very well, my dear, take these offerings, and hurry, do you hear? And when you've finished, come back promptly.

(Exit HERMIONÊ with the libations and hair cutting as HELEN returns to the palace.)

ÊLEKTRA: Nature! What a curse to humankind! Did you see her? Did you? So carefully trimming her locks not to mar her beauty? The same old Helen. I pray the gods may hate you, may pour out their loathing on you for destroying me, my brother, and all of Greece!

(THE CHORUS OF NOBLE ARGIVE WOMEN is seen approaching and entering.)

(Music. Song. Dance.)

ÊLEKTRA: Oh, no! My friends! Here they come again. These women
who sing with me in my lamentations. They're sure to wake him and
start him raving and me weeping. Dear, dear women, step softly,
softly, so lightly it can't be heard. You mean well, I know, but seeing
his frenzy will destroy me.

NOBLE ARGIVE WOMEN: *(Sing.)*
Hush,
tread lightly,
lightly,
make no sound.

ÊLEKTRA: *(Sings.)*
No,
away from
the bed,
away!

NOBLE ARGIVE WOMEN: *(Sing.)*
Yes,
we obey.

ÊLEKTRA: *(Sings.)*
Speak, speak softly
as the gentle panpipe.

NOBLE ARGIVE WOMEN: *(Sing.)*
There,
my song as
gentle as indoors.

ÊLEKTRA: *(Sings.)*
Yes, that's right!
Now tiptoe closer,
closer to me,
but quietly,
softly!
Tell me
why you've come.

He's sleeping now,
asleep,
at peace.

NOBLE ARGIVE WOMEN: *(Sing.)*
How is he?
Tell me, dear.
Tell me what's happened.

ÊLEKTRA: *(Sings.)*
He breathes,
breathes, but his
breath is
shallow.

NOBLE ARGIVE WOMEN: *(Sing.)*
Poor boy!
Keep him safe, you gods!

ÊLEKTRA: *(Sings.)*
Don't wake him,
please!
Brush sleep
from his eyes
and you will
have killed him.

NOBLE ARGIVE WOMEN: *(Sing.)*
Such terrible suffering
for a god's command!

ÊLEKTRA: *(Sings.)*
The pain,
ah,
the pain!
The terrible wrong
the god cried out!
Injustice
screamed from

Apollo's tripod!
A mother's murder
to answer a father's!

NOBLE ARGIVE WOMEN: *(Sing.)*
   Do you see?
   There!
   He's moving!
   The covers!

ÊLEKTRA: *(Sings.)*
   Stirring,
   yes,
   your cries have
   disturbed him!
   Shhh!

NOBLE ARGIVE WOMEN: *(Sing.)*
   No, look there,
   he's sleeping,
   sleeping.

ÊLEKTRA: *(Sings.)*
   Leave us!
   Leave the house!
   Get back!
   Oh, please go!
   Quiet!
   Shhh!

NOBLE ARGIVE WOMEN: *(Sing.)*
   He's resting now,
   he'll sleep,
   he'll sleep.

ÊLEKTRA: *(Sings.)*
   Let him,
   let him.

(Chants.)

Oh queen, great mistress of night, majesty!
You who bring sleep to mortals in pain!
Come to us, rise from your cosmic abyss,
soar and descend on Agamemnon's palace,
where all is ruined,
where all is lost!

(ÊLEKTRA turns to the WOMEN who again approach the bed; sings.)

Shhh!
Be still!
So much clatter!
You'll wake him,
wake him!
Away from the bed!
Let him
sleep!
Be kind!

NOBLE ARGIVE WOMEN: *(Sing.)*
Where will it end?
How? Where?

ÊLEKTRA: *(Sings.)*
Death,
death.
There's nothing else.
He refuses to eat.

NOBLE ARGIVE WOMEN: *(Sing.)*
Then death will come.

ÊLEKTRA: *(Sings.)*
And I must
die with him.
Apollo's victims,
he and I,

sacrifice
of an evil oracle,
sacrifice of an
oracle
of blood,
to kill a mother
for a father
killed.

NOBLE ARGIVE WOMEN: *(Sing.)*
It was just!

ÊLEKTRA: *(Sings.)*
But evil!
Mother,
mother
who gave me life,
you killed
and were killed,
you destroyed us all,
father,
children,
me,
your son,
blood of your blood,
destroyed,
destroyed,
as good as dead,
and you,
you are
with the
dead,
and my
life,
my days,
my nights
are weeping,
wailing hot
tears,

no husband,
no children,
a life
lost in
sorrow.

(Music out.)

FIRST NOBLE ARGIVE WOMAN: Êlektra, look! See if he's died, your brother. You're nearest to him. He looks so lifeless, has he stopped breathing?

(ÊLEKTRA inspects ORESTÊS who suddenly wakens.)

ORESTÊS: Sweet Sleep! Sleep, lovely enchantress who comes when needed! Nurse against illness! How welcome you were! Goddess of forgetting to whom the sick man prays—*(Looking about him in surprise.)* What's this? Where have I been? Where am I? I can't—can't remember—can't recall—all gone—

ÊLEKTRA: Dear boy, you we're asleep. I was so glad for you. May I touch you, dear? To prop you up?

ORESTÊS: Yes, take hold, take hold, help me—thank you. Wipe it away, won't you, the crust on my mouth and eyes—

ÊLEKTRA: I will, dear boy, gladly—there. This is no hardship for a sister's hands.

ORESTÊS: Hold me, hold me up—yes, and my hair, so filthy, brush it from my eyes. I can barely see.

ÊLEKTRA: Poor, dear head! And these curls so matted! You haven't washed the whole time lying here—what a savage you look!

ORESTÊS: Help me lie down again. When the madness passes the body goes limp. No strength anymore.

ÊLEKTRA: There. A bed's a good thing for the sick. The greatest pain is needing it in the first place.

ORESTÊS: No, set me up again. Turn me round. There's just no pleasing the sick.

ÊLEKTRA: Shall I put your feet on the ground? So you can walk? It's been a long time since you did. A change might be welcome.

ORESTÊS: Yes, at least I'll look well. Better that than nothing.

ÊLEKTRA: *(Helping him to sit up.)* All right, now, Orestês, there's something I have to tell you; so listen to me while the Furies leave your mind in peace.

ORESTÊS: Good news, I hope. I've had enough of the other.

ÊLEKTRA: Menelaos has come—Uncle Menelaos, here in Argos. He's moored his ship at Nauplia.

ORESTÊS: Menelaos? Here? In Argos? Light at last in our troubles! The man who owes our father for so much!

ÊLEKTRA: Here, yes, in Argos! And here's the proof. He's brought Helen with him from the walls of Troy.

ORESTÊS: I'd envy him more if he'd survived alone. He's brought disaster with him with that wife.

ÊLEKTRA: What a fine brood of daughters Tyndareos fathered! Helen and our mother! Hated at home, disgraced in the eyes of Greece.

ORESTÊS: Yes, and you be different from them, you hear? Not just words to be mouthed, but in the heart. *(Rises and begins displaying signs of madness.)*

ÊLEKTRA: Orestês! Your eyes! How wild they are! How quickly it comes; just now you were sane.

ORESTÊS: Mother, no, don't! Don't set them on me! I see them, see them, bloody-eyed girls, snakes, coming, coming! Noooo!

ÊLEKTRA: Shhh! Quiet! Dear boy! Be quiet! Back to bed now, you hear? Better to lie down. Nothing you see is really there, dear.

ORESTÊS: Apollo! Apollo! Save me! They're coming! Leaping, charging! I *see* them! Bitch-hound faces with gorgon eyes! Dread Goddesses! Priestesses of the Dead! *(ÊLEKTRA attempts to lead him to the bed; he struggles.)* Let go! You're one of them! Furies! Grabbing me, grabbing! Wrestling, dragging me down to hell! Let go your grip!

ÊLEKTRA: I won't! I won't let go! My arms around you! I won't—let go— I—*(ORESTÊS violently breaks free of her grip around his waist.)* Where is there help now, where? Alone I can do nothing, nothing, the gods are against us. *(She covers her head in the folds of her robe and weeps.)*

ORESTÊS: The bow, bring me the bow, the horn-tipped bow, Apollo's gift! *(He receives the imaginary bow from an imaginary attendant.)* Defend yourself, he said, when they come, when the goddesses come to terrorize you with raging fits! *(He sets an arrow to the invisible bow.)* There's soon to be a goddess shot by a mortal if you don't listen and leave me, leave my sight, now, now! *(He shoots the arrow.)* See? Do you see? How it eats up the distance! Flying, flying, feathers flashing! At you! At you! Á! Á! Fly, why don't you, fly! Graze the heavens with your wings! Tell Apollo—tell Apollo it's his oracles are to blame! *(Coming to himself.)* ÉA! ÉA!
what   what is this
why am I   breathing
hard   gasping
why am I here   out of bed
I remember   yes   storm
great storm,
      past now, past,
calm waters,
          calm—

(He sees ÊLEKTRA, head hidden in her robe, sobbing.) Sister? Why are you weeping? Why are you hiding your head? I'm so ashamed.

What right have I to involve you in my pain? And you a young
woman. Don't be grieved because of me. I did it, I, killed Mother,
spilled her blood. You agreed, I know, but I did it—did it at Apollo's
command—he's to blame, it's him I blame for this unholy deed,
though all he gave was words, mere words, not actions—Apollo.
I know now what Father would say, Father, if I saw him face to
face, Father, if I asked him should I do such a deed as kill my mother,
he would take my face in his hands and beg me, implore me, not to
drive my sword through her neck, the mother who bore me. Will it
bring me back to life, he would ask? Will it fail to bring the plague
down on you, he would ask, as it does now?

Dear, my dear, dear Êlektra, let me see, let me see your face.
There, don't cry, don't, no matter how terrible it may be. When you
see me in despair, you must relieve me of my torment, comfort me in
my pain, my madness; and I must do the same for you when I see you
weeping, be at your side, advising, comforting; and I will be. This is
what those who love each other should do.

I want you to go in now, into the palace, poor, dear, suffering
soul, and I want you to sleep, and eat, and wash. Where would I be
without you if you left me now, if you took ill sitting here, tending
me? You're all I have; everyone else is gone, abandoned me.

ÊLEKTRA: No, no I can't, not leave you. This is my place, here beside you.
If you die, I die; if you live, I live: it's all the same. I'm a woman.
What could I do? How would I survive without Father, without
brother, without friends? But if you think it best, I'll go. But you must
lie down, too, lie down again, now. *(She helps him onto his bed which
first she straightens.)* There. And if the confusion, if the terror comes
again, you mustn't let it get to you, hold it off, and never leave your
bed, you hear? So. I mean, even when an illness is only in the mind,
still it tears at us and leaves us helpless. *(Exit into palace.)*

(ORESTÊS returns to his bed.)

(Music. Song. Dance.)

NOBLE ARGIVE WOMEN: *(Sing.)*
    AIIII!
    AIIII!

Wild-running goddesses,
winged on the wind,
frenzy-bringing,
weeping, wailing goddesses of the deep,
who rejoice in lament,
dark-hued Eumenides,
who drum the taut air in search of blood justice,
blood punishment for blood,
free him, we pray you,
free him, the son of warlord Agamemnon,
free him of madness that sets his mind raging!

Poor man,
poor wretched man,
who acted out a terrible deed,
a deed that wrestled you down and destroyed you,
a shout from the holy tripod of prophecy,
tormenting the halls of holy Delphi,
holy of holies,
earth's navel!

Great Zeus!
Listen!
Where is mercy?
Mercy for this boy?
Son, what is this agony,
this demon haunting your house,
misery on misery that drives you mad,
vengeance,
vengeance for your mother's blood?
I pity you!
I grieve, I grieve!
Great happiness for man is brief.
It never lasts.
God upsets it like a sail mast cracked,
and over it turns in a hostile sea,
washed over by waves,
bottom-side up.

What other house could we better honor
than this born of Zeus and Tantalos?

(Enter MENELAOS and his retinue.)

(Music out.)

FIRST NOBLE ARGIVE WOMAN: And here is the king himself, lord
Menelaos. Welcome, great King, who launched a thousand ships
against Asia! With heaven's help you accomplished all you prayed for
and glory and success are yours!

MENELAOS: House of my fathers, I greet you with joy and sadness!
With joy for my return from Troy; with sadness to see this house so
set round by evil. Agamemnon's fate I learned as I approached Cape
Malea. Glaukos, son of Nêreus and god of sailors, a prophet whose
word is infallible, rose up before me out of the waves and said:
"Menelaos, your brother is dead; his wife has given him his last
ablution." I wept at this, wept hard, as did my sailors. And then when
we came ashore at Nauplia, and I sent Helen on ahead to the palace,
fully expecting soon to embrace my brother's boy Orestês and his
mother, thinking them both well, I heard the news. An old salt told
me of the dreadful murder of Tyndarcos's daughter.
      But tell me now, young women, where I can find him, Orestês,
who steeled himself to this horror. When I saw him last on my way
to Troy he was a babe in his mother's arms. I would never know
him now.

ORESTÊS: *(Rises from his bed and comes forward.)* I'm here, Menelaos,
the Orestês you're asking for, and only too willing to testify to my
crimes. But first I kneel a suppliant at your feet, though I have no
suppliant's branches. Save me, I beg of you, from this disaster! You've
come at the right moment.

MENELAOS: Good god, what is this?

ORESTÊS: A living corpse!

MENELAOS: Your hair! Look at it! An animal!

ORESTÊS: It's my crimes torment me.

MENELAOS: Your eyes—how wasted.

ORESTÊS: At least I have my name left.

MENELAOS: No, I can't, I can't look!

ORESTÊS: It's Orestês who killed his mother.

MENELAOS: Spare me the grizzly details.

ORESTÊS: And Fortune spare *me*?

MENELAOS: Your sickness—what is it?

ORESTÊS: Conscience. I see my horrors.

MENELAOS: No riddles. Speak sense.

ORESTÊS: Anguish, then. Yes, anguish will do.

MENELAOS: A hard mistress; but there are cures.

ORESTÊS: And madness, my mother's blood.

MENELAOS: Which began—?

ORESTÊS: The day I raised her grave mound.

MENELAOS: Where? At home? By the pyre?

ORESTÊS: The pyre. I was collecting her bones.

MENELAOS: Who was with you?

ORESTÊS: Pyladês, who helped me kill her.

MENELAOS: What form do these visions take?

ORESTÊS: Three women—they look like Night.

MENELAOS: I know. I don't dare name them.

ORESTÊS: That's wise. They're awesome.

MENELAOS: And they drive you mad for the murder?

ORESTÊS: God, the torture! They hound me!

MENELAOS: What do you expect?

ORESTÊS: But I have a way out.

MENELAOS: Death? Don't be stupid.

ORESTÊS: Apollo ordered the murder.

MENELAOS: A foolish move for a god.

ORESTÊS: What are we but their slaves?

MENELAOS: What relief does he offer?

ORESTÊS: He's in no hurry. Gods are like that.

MENELAOS: How long has she been dead?

ORESTÊS: Six days. The pyre's still warm.

MENELAOS: How quickly they work.

ORESTÊS: I avenged my father; I was true to him!

MENELAOS: What good has that done you?

ORESTÊS: Nothing. Nothing at all. Now or ever.

MENELAOS: And the city?

ORESTÊS: They shun me. They won't even speak to me.

MENELAOS: Have your hands been purged of her blood?

ORESTÊS: No. They shut their doors in my face.

MENELAOS: Who? Name me a name.

ORESTÊS: Oiax. My father's enemy at Troy.

MENELAOS: Punishing you for Palamêdes' death.

ORESTÊS: I had nothing to do with it!

MENELAOS: Who else? Aigisthos's men?

ORESTÊS: Yes. They've got the city on their side.

MENELAOS: I presume you have your father's throne?

ORESTÊS: When they won't even let me live?

MENELAOS: What are they planning? Be specific.

ORESTÊS: A vote. They're voting today. Against me.

MENELAOS: And you haven't escaped?

ORESTÊS: I'm surrounded. Armed troops every way I turn.

MENELAOS: Whose? Enemies'? Argive forces?

ORESTÊS: The people, out for my death. What else can I say?

MENELAOS: Poor boy, you're out of rope.

ORESTÊS: And that's why I need you, Menelaos. You're my only way out
    of this. Here you are, home again, the image of success; but you must
    share it, uncle, share it with your loved ones in their desperation.

Don't horde it, don't, your good fortune, the benefits, the power, all for yourself. Share it, and share some of our miseries, as is only right. And doing so, you will repay the debt you owe to my father for his great favors to you. What are friends worth who disappear in adversity?

FIRST NOBLE ARGIVE WOMAN: Menelaos, look, Tyndareos of Sparta, dragging along on his ancient legs, hair shorn and dressed in black for his daughter.

ORESTÊS: Dear gods, I can't, I can't see him, Menelaos! Of all men, I want to see him least of any. For what I've done, for what I've done to him! He raised me as a child, loved me, carried me on his arm. "Agamemnon's boy," he called me, and Lêda, too, his wife, loved me as much as their own sons! And—and what kind of love have I returned them? A sad showing. Where can I find darkness to cover my face? Where is a cloud thick enough to hide me?

TYNDAREOS: *(Enters with ATTENDANTS.)* Where is he, where, where is my daughter's husband? Where is Menelaos? Pouring libations at Klytaimnêstra's grave, I heard it, heard that he was back, beached at Nauplia with his wife, after all these years. And safe, too, they said, safe in his skin. So take me to him, take me, show the way. I want to stand beside him and take his hand in mine again at last.

MENELAOS: Welcome, old sir, that shared his wife with Zeus!

TYNDAREOS: Ah, welcome to you, too, Menelaos! *(He catches sight of ORESTÊS.)* But what's this? What's this? The serpent that killed his mother, here, in front of the house, eyes poisoned, darting sick lightning flashes! Evil! Evil! Menelaos, surely you aren't talking to this creature? How I loathe him!

MENELAOS: And if I am? A brother's son. A brother I loved.

TYNDAREOS: Agamemnon's son? And he's turned out *this?*

MENELAOS: Yes, and down on his luck, and still to be honored.

TYNDAREOS: Your years among barbarians have made you one, too.

MENELAOS: The Greek way, I believe, is to honor one's kin.

TYNDAREOS: It's also Greek not to rise above the law.

MENELAOS: Soberly seen, compulsion makes one a slave.

TYNDAREOS: This may be your view; it isn't mine.

MENELAOS: Yes, because anger and age lead to no wisdom.

TYNDAREOS: Wisdom? What has wisdom to do with him? If right and wrong are as clear as day to everyone, then no one ever acted as stupidly as this man. He ignored what is right, ignored what is justice, and so upset the very practice of Greek law. When Agamemnon died, struck on the head by my own daughter—a deed of such horror I can never condone it—he should have charged her, this one, charged his mother, formally, haled her into court, made her pay the penalty for murder and bloodshed, pay with expulsion from the house and exile, and in doing so, religious propriety would have been met, as met it should have been.

Had he done so, he would have been praised for the sanity of his behavior, and for honoring both law and the gods, and he would be known as righteous, and not as a fool in the lap of disaster. As it is, his fate is no better than hers. Yes, he was right in condemning her act, but his act in killing her was more evil still.

Think, Menelaos, just think! Here is a man whose wife murders him, and then that man's son murders his mother to avenge the father, and then that son in turn is murdered by his wife, and *his* son— well, and on it goes! Is there an end? I ask you! Our forefathers knew well how to handle these matters. They banished them, banished murderers from public view, disallowed them to meet or speak with anyone, until—and here it comes!—until they had purged their hands of their victims' blood by exile, rather than by demanding another death. In this way they avoided the vicious cycle of murder and revenge that knows no end. As for me, I despise unfaithful wives, and my own daughter first of all, Klytaimnêstra, who killed her husband, and Helen, Helen, too, your wife, and also my daughter, I will never approve, never, never speak to her again. And you, Menelaos, for you I have little respect. You went to Troy for the sake of a vile woman, to win her back, to bring back your whore.

I can do without my daughters, but the law I cannot do without, and I will fight to the end to defend that law and end this bloody, brutal lust that turns men into beasts, corrupts our cities, and pollutes the very earth we walk on. *(Turning on ORESTÊS.)* As for you, *boy*, you ingrate, you inhuman wretch! What shred of humanity did you feel when your mother begged for her life, bared her breast, the nipple that suckled you, pleading? I may not have seen that dreadful sight, and yet my ancient eyes run with tears at the thought.

But I know this, and I know it without question: heaven, the gods, all creation loathes you for your murder. It is the gods who drive you into your insane frenzy, the gods who hold you responsible and make you pay for what you did to her. Witnesses? What need have I for witnesses? I see all I need to see, and I know what I know.

Be warned, Menelaos. Act on impulse, choose to defend this man, and you defy the will of the gods. Let happen what must happen. Let them stone him to death, the city as one. In dying my daughter had what she deserved; but she never deserved death at the hands of her child; a murder beyond all bounds. My life has been fortunate in all things, except for my daughters. In them fortune failed me.

FIRST NOBLE ARGIVE WOMAN: A man fortunate in his children is a happy man. To have failed in that is to know disaster.

ORESTÊS: Oh, sir—I love and respect you, your age, the gray of your hair; and knowing I am bound to distress you, I fight back my words rather than offend your honor. I tremble at your age, dear old man. And yet I must—I must speak. What was I to do? I was faced with two choices, two duties, each of them compelling, but each in conflict. On the one hand stood my father, on the other, my mother, your daughter. It was my father planted the seed of me, and your daughter whose field nurtured and gave me birth. As for your daughter—that woman I can't bring myself to call mother—she whored herself in disgrace with another man. I realize in saying this I blacken myself as well as her, but I have no choice.

I killed him, Aigisthos, her lover, her secret husband lurking in the house, and then slaughtered her, my—mother—both of them—an evil act, and yet for one purpose only: to avenge my father. I hated my mother, yes, and my hatred was justified. She betrayed him, betrayed her husband, away from home, at arms, commander of the combined forces of Greece, and she polluted his bed with an unholy alliance. And knowing she was guilty, did she punish herself? No. Rather to avoid punishment by her husband, she punished him, killed him, killed my father! By all the gods—or should I shrink from mentioning gods, for it's they who sit in judgment over murder—but what if I had said nothing, in silence condoned my mother's action, what would *he* have done to me, *he,* my father's ghost, my murdered father's ghost? Hounded me, driven me insane with the Furies bound with a father's hatred! Or is it only my mother is avenged by gods and he with no gods at all, and his hurt the greater?

And what's this? Forgotten Apollo? Delphi's god that sits at earth's navel? Apollo we obey blindly? Apollo whose command was to kill her, to kill my mother? Should he not be accused, the immoral god? Should he not be put to death for his crime? Kill him! Kill the guilty one! The sin's not mine, it's his! What was I to do? Is the god not worth his word to clear me of pollution? Where do I turn, to whom, when the god who ordered me to murder will not save me?

You, sir, it was *you* who destroyed me, *you,* when you fathered an evil daughter. Thanks to her, to her brazen audacity, I've lost my father and killed my mother for it! No, no one must say what I did was wrong, but only that I who did it ended in misery.

FIRST NOBLE ARGIVE WOMAN: Women by nature are an impediment to man, and with them they bring bitterness.

TYNDAREOS: Insolent, outrageous, spiteful *boy!* How dare you answer as you have? Every word you say incites me to greater anger, fires me to seek out your death! I came here to pay homage at my daughter's tomb, but your death will garnish that event and bring me even greater joy.

I'm going now to meet the Argives in assembly, to convince them—and they need little convincing—to bring down on your and your sister's heads all the fury of this enraged city, and see you pay the penalty of death by stoning! Yes, and she deserves death even more than you. All your childhood she stuffed your ears with hatred and more hatred. Message upon message to inflame your anger against your mother. Babbling of her nightly dreams of Agamemnon's ghost and the things he told her. Tattling her tales of your mother's adultery, that I pray appalled the gods below with its evil stench as much as it disgusted us here on earth! All of it, all, fuel to kindle the fire in you, and the fire of hatred that raged in this house!

As for you, Menelaos, I say this, and test me to see if I mean it: if you put any value on our relationship, you will in no way impede the gods' design for the death of this man. He will be delivered to a death by stoning at the city's hands. And if you interfere, never again set foot on Spartan soil. Be warned, and choose your friends wisely. To do otherwise will draw a line between you and men of piety.

Slaves, take me away from this house.

(Exeunt TYNDAREOS and ATTENDANTS.)

ORESTÊS: Yes. Good. Go your way. Let me say to Menelaos what I have to say without the nuisance of your old age interrupting. Why are you pacing like that, Menelaos, so lost in thought? What's troubling you?

MENELAOS: No, quiet, I'm thinking. I have a decision to make and don't know which way to turn.

ORESTÊS: Don't rush, then. Haste makes no good decisions. Listen first to what I have to say, and then decide.

MENELAOS: Yes, right, go ahead. There are times for speech and times for silence. This is a time to speak.

ORESTÊS: You'll forgive me if I speak at length, but length, at times, can be more persuasive. Let me say, first, Menelaos, that it's not anything of yours I'm asking for. What I'm asking is that you give back what my father gave to you, what you owe to him, the favor you owe my father. And, no, it's not money, I assure you, but my most precious possession: my life. I'm guilty of a crime, Menelaos, and I don't deny it.

My father once mustered an army to lay siege to Troy, and in doing so he did a wrong. But it was done for you, and a very generous wrong it was, too. He did it to undo Helen's wrong in deserting you. He was a good brother to you, Agamemnon, side by side in battle, shield to shield, fighting to win back your wife. It's now for you, Menelaos, to undo my wrong. I ask you, then, to return my father's favor. Just as he gave you back Helen, so you can give me back my life. Nor will it take ten years, but one day, one day only, by taking a stand for me and saving my life.

As for that event at Aulis, my father's slaughter on your account of my sister Iphigeneia, I give you that in all good faith, no need to turn your hand on Hermionê. I give you her life. All things considered, it's for you to have the upper hand, and for me to concede. And so I ask you to return my father's favor, to offer to him my life, and in doing so save the house of Agamemnon, for if I die, the house dies with me.

Not possible, you'll say. But isn't that the point? When else but in times of crisis do we help each other? Who needs help when the gods grant success? When heaven helps, we have friends enough. We all know, all of Greece knows, how you love your wife, and I don't mean that as flattery to disarm you, but in her name, Menelaos, in Helen's name, I beg you—*(Turns away; to himself.)* How can I do this? How can I have sunk so low? But I have no choice. *(He falls at MENELAOS's feet.)* Our whole house, uncle, our whole family, depends on this. You share my father's blood in your veins, then imagine now that his spirit listens to me in the world below, that he hovers over you and that you hear him through me, through my voice. *(He rises.)* Well—I've made my claims. You've seen me beg for my life, for survival, no man should be ashamed of that.

FIRST NOBLE ARGIVE WOMAN: I may be only a woman, but I beg of you to help them. It's in your power.

MENELAOS: I think you know, Orestês, the respect I have for you. After all, you're family, and what else should one do for family but help them bear their burden of troubles, assuming, of course, the gods provide the means.

Yes, well, if only I could, which is to say, had the means. But, you see, I've come not all that well prepared. After all my long wanderings, what have I left but a few remaining fighting men and weapons, and add to that, we're worn to the bone, myself included. So a pitched battle isn't exactly the way to win ancient Argos. Words, on the other hand, gentle words, are worth a try; persuasion is no weak weapon; tact, diplomacy—worth, as I say, a try. I mean, you don't win big with little means. It's stupid even to think so. For when the people grow angry and fall into a rage, it's like trying to extinguish a fire out of control. Whereas if a man holds back a bit, giving way a little here, a little there, waiting for just the right moment, who knows, it might blow itself out. And if it does, well, then, you get everything you wanted from them in the first place.

Sailing and politics are keen bedfellows. Stretch your sail too taut and the ship dips and keels; but trim your sails, allow a bit of slack, and she rights herself again. The gods hate nothing so much as overdoing it; and the same can be said for the people. And so, my task is to save you not by force of arms, as you might imagine—we'd be trounced in the bat of an eye—but by clever cunning. No, force is not the answer. My single spear won't turn the tables on your troubles.

(Exeunt MENELAOS and his retinue.)

ORESTÊS: Traitor! Good for waging war when it's for a woman, but a washout when it's the cause of your own kin! That's right! Turn tail and run! It's like you, you bastard! Forgotten Agamemnon, have you? His claims? His friendship? Your brother? Then this is the end of his house—the last of Agamemnon's house, my house. You're abandoned, father, deserted by your friends when your luck deserted you. And I'm betrayed, too, by my last refuge, the only man left to save me from death by the Argives.

But look, here's Pyladês! Running fast as he can. My dearest friend! Come all the way from Phokis. How sweet a sight it is to see him! No sailor ever welcomed a calm more dearly than I my truest friend in adversity! Pyladês!

PYLADÊS: *(Enters running.)* I'm here, Orestês, and winded, too, for my run through town. I hurried because I heard the city was meeting in assembly—I saw it myself—to condemn you and your sister to death—today, in fact. Dear friend, dear Orestês, my cousin and loving comrade, for you're all of these to me—tell me what's happened, tell me everything.

ORESTÊS: I can be brief, Pyladês. I'm a dead man.

PYLADÊS: Then so am I. I love you. Lovers share.

ORESTÊS: Menelaos has betrayed me and my sister.

PYLADÊS: When the wife's a whore, the husband's a bastard.

ORESTÊS: He might as well not have come where I'm concerned.

PYLADÊS: Then the rumor's true? He's returned?

ORESTÊS: At last—and rushed to prove himself a traitor.

PYLADÊS: And Helen with him? Helen on board?

ORESTÊS: No, the other way round, she brought *him.*

PYLADÊS: And where is this woman who all but wiped out Greece?

ORESTÊS: There, in my house, if I can call it mine?

PYLADÊS: What did you say to your uncle?

ORESTÊS: Not stand by to see me and my sister killed.

PYLADÊS: How did he answer that, I'd like to know?

ORESTÊS: What you'd expect from a false friend, to be cautious.

PYLADÊS: And his excuse? Tell me that, I'll know all.

ORESTÊS: That father of noble daughters came along.

PYLADÊS: Tyndareos you mean? In a rage over your mother?

ORESTÊS: Right. And Menelaos took *his* side against Father's.

PYLADÊS: Refusing help, I dare say.

ORESTÊS: Oh, he's a spearsman, all right, around the ladies.

PYLADÊS: It can't be worse. Death is certain, then?

ORESTÊS: They cast their votes today. The charge is murder.

PYLADÊS: I hate to ask, but what will the vote decide?

ORESTÊS: Life or death. Few words, but heavy with meaning.

PYLADÊS: Then why not escape, you and your sister, now?

ORESTÊS: You haven't seen them? Guards at every road?

PYLADÊS: Yes, I saw armed men blocking the streets.

ORESTÊS: Our house is under siege like a towered city.

PYLADÊS: It's your turn now to ask me. I, too, am ruined.

ORESTÊS: Disaster on disaster. What happened? Tell me?

PYLADÊS: Strophios, in anger, banished me. My own father.

ORESTÊS: In a public or private matter? What was the charge?

PYLADÊS: Taking part in your mother's murder. He calls me outcast.

ORESTÊS: So, then—my pollution is yours, too.

PYLADÊS: I'm no Menelaos. I can take it.

ORESTÊS: But the Argives, won't they want to kill you, too?

PYLADÊS: They have no right over me. I'm a Phokian.

ORESTÊS: Vicious leaders can make a mob do anything.

PYLADÊS: Yes, and with good leaders it's a different story.

ORESTÊS: All right, then, it's time we plan together.

PYLADÊS: What needs doing?

ORESTÊS: Suppose I went to the assembly and said—

PYLADÊS: —that you acted justly—

ORESTÊS: —as my father's avenger?

PYLADÊS: Careful, they just might arrest you.

ORESTÊS: What do I do, then? Die here? Cowering in silence?

PYLADÊS: No, that's a coward's way.

ORESTÊS: What, then?

PYLADÊS: Can you survive by staying here?

ORESTÊS: Not a chance.

PYLADÊS: But if you go you may be saved?

ORESTÊS: With luck.

PYLADÊS: That's better than staying here.

ORESTÊS: I'll go, then?

PYLADÊS: And if you die, at least you'll die nobly.

ORESTÊS: Yes, and avoid cowardice.

PYLADÊS: More than by staying.

ORESTÊS: And I've justice on my side.

PYLADÊS: As long as it seems so to them.

ORESTÊS: They may take pity on me—

PYLADÊS: Yes, your noble birth could sway them.

ORESTÊS: —angered at my father's death.

PYLADÊS: What matters is how they see it.

ORESTÊS: I'll go, then. I must. At least I'll die a man.

PYLADÊS: Good for you.

ORESTÊS: Do we tell my sister?

PYLADÊS: Definitely not!

ORESTÊS: Yes, what a scene that would be—tears.

PYLADÊS: And a bad omen.

ORESTÊS: Better to say nothing.

PYLADÊS: You'll save time.

ORESTÊS: There's only one thing stopping me.

PYLADÊS: What's that?

ORESTÊS: That the goddesses might drive me mad.

PYLADÊS: Don't worry, I'll be with you.

ORESTÊS: It's not pleasant, touching a sick man.

PYLADÊS: Not for me, as long as it's you.

ORESTÊS: But my insanity could strike you, too.

PYLADÊS: You're not to worry about that.

ORESTÊS: Then you wouldn't hesitate?

PYLADÊS: We're friends, Orestês—why would I hesitate?

ORESTÊS: All right, then. Lead me. Steer me on my path—

PYLADÊS: It's love leading you, my friend. Let me help you. *(He helps ORESTÊS to his feet.)*

ORESTÊS: —to my father's grave—

PYLADÊS: Why there?

ORESTÊS: To pray for his help in my deliverance.

PYLADÊS: Yes, and I think he just might listen.

ORESTÊS: As for Mother's grave, don't let me set eyes on it.

PYLADÊS: I know—she was your enemy. But let's hurry now. We mustn't arrive late, after they've condemned you. Your illness has made you weak, so lean against me, I'll support you. We'll then make our way through town, crowd or no crowd, and let them jeer if they dare. I do this proudly and with no shame. How do I prove my love better than when you most need help?

ORESTÊS: "Get friends as well as kin," the proverb says. And could it be more true? The love of a man whose heart is bound to yours is worth ten thousand relatives.

(Exeunt PYLADÊS supporting ORESTÊS.)

(Music. Song. Dance.)

NOBLE ARGIVE WOMEN: *(Sing.)*
 Where are they now,
 where the prosperity,
 where,
 where the prowess that with pride

once reigned across Greece
and beside the banks of Trojan Simoïs?
Gone, all gone now,
gone again,
deserting the house of Atreus,
a house once happy.
Gone, all gone its
greatness,
gone its glory.
It began so long,
so long ago,
in the ancient violence,
Tantalid violence:
a golden lamb,
slaughter of children,
princes slaughtered,
sons served up in a gruesome feast,
and the curse of blood,
spreading, spreading,
down ages of time,
murder for murder,
till now it sweeps up
the living descendents of Atreus's line.
There is no good,
none, none,
in piercing a mother's flesh with steel,
steel born of fire,
in raising high the offending sword,
black with her gore,
brandishing it to the great eye of heaven.
Impious madness of the doer,
delusion of a maddened mind!
Pierced with the fear of death,
Tyndareos's daughter screamed in her terror:

FIRST NOBLE ARGIVE WOMAN: *(Sings.)*
    "Son,
    my child,
    this is evil you do!

In avenging your father
you will rot in infamy!"

NOBLE ARGIVE WOMEN: *(Sing.)*
 Does earth know greater sickness,
 greater grief,
 than a son staining his hand
 with a mother's blood?
 He who did this deed,
 who raised the knife,
 is hunted,
 goaded now by ravening Furies,
 son of Agamemnon,
 made mad for the murder,
 red eyes rolling,
 flashing,
 darting,
 that saw the mother,
 her breast bared from her golden robes,
 pleading, pleading,
 and brought down the knife
 on the mother's neck,
 stabbing, stabbing,
 for his father's fate.

 (Music out.)

ÊLEKTRA: *(Enters from the house.)* Where is Orestês? Where has he gone,
 tell me. Another attack of the goddesses?

FIRST NOBLE ARGIVE WOMAN: No, not that. He's gone to the
 meeting of Argives.

ÊLEKTRA: But why? Who persuaded him?

FIRST NOBLE ARGIVE WOMAN: Pyladês. But look, here's an old man
 surely with news. He'll tell you.

OLD MAN: *(Enters from the town, excited.)* Lady Êlektra, daughter of great Agamemnon, I bring you bad news.

ÊLEKTRA: Then we're lost. Your words are clear enough.

OLD MAN: The Argives have voted. You and your brother will die today.

ÊLEKTRA: OIMOIIIIII! Finally it's come, what I most feared, what I most lamented! But tell me about the trial. What Argive arguments condemned us to death? And will it be death by stoning or by the sword?

OLD MAN: As it happens, ma'am, I was coming into town from the fields, hoping to learn the latest of you and Orestês. I always loved your father, and his house was good to me, peasant that I am, providing my daily bread. And when it comes to loyalty to friends, I'm as true as any man. But, as I said, coming into town, I saw a crowd climbing the hill and taking seats where, as they say, old Danaös called the first public assembly in Argos, that time Aigyptos took him to trial. Seeing this, and all that crowd of people, I went up to one of them and asked: "What's all this?" I said. "What's happening? All this bustle! Have we been invaded?" "Look there," he replied and pointed, "don't you see him?" And I looked, and there saw Orestês. "On his way," he said, "to stand trial for his life." And I saw a sight then I never hope to see again, never wanted to see in the first place. I saw there Orestês and Pyladês, coming along together, Orestês done in, limp and dejected, diseased, held up in his friend's embrace, helping him along, tending his illness like a brother, Pyladês, every bit as downcast as his friend.

But to get on with it—when every seat in the Assembly was filled, a herald rose up and asked: "Who will speak to the issue: is Orestês to be put to death for matricide?" Up sprang Talthybios, the same who helped sack Troy with your father. A toady of a man, never know what he thinks, talks out of both sides of his mouth at once, always bowing to the first in power. He praises your father with high-flown phrases, and then twists them round filthy criticism of your brother. And for what?

Orestês, says he, set an example dangerous for parents. And all the while he smiles brightly at the friends of Aigisthos. But they're like that, heralds, all of them; jumping the fence, this side and that, whichever side holds the greatest power.

Next came Lord Diomêdês, advising not to kill you or your brother, but to satisfy religion by exile. His speech raised rounds of approval, but also disapproval. And then there arose a man whose mouth never rested. An arrogant, self-assured sort; a hireling if ever there was one. He spoke in favor of death by stoning for you and Orestês; but in truth he was nothing but a mouthpiece for Tyndareos.

Another stood up then to argue the opposite. No great beauty, this man, but a man all the same, seldom seen in the town or marketplace, a small landholder, one of those we count on for the land's survival, shrewd, intelligent, a man eager to come to grips with the arguments. A man of discipline and free of corruption, whose life is above reproach. He argued for rewarding Orestês, son of Agamemnon, he said, wreathing his head with a garland, he said, for avenging his father's murder by killing that whore of a godless wife; that woman who was depriving us of all that, of taking up arms, of going off to war, if the men who stayed behind would undermine their houses and families by seducing the soldiers' wives. Those who were decent, at least, found him convincing, but no one spoke in support after that.

Your brother then came forward, but his words, however eloquent, had no effect. The scoundrel won, the hireling, he got the most hands, the one who urged your and your brother's death. Poor Orestês had all he could do to persuade them not to kill you by stoning. And he only won that point by saying that the two of you would kill yourselves before the day's end. Pyladês, with tears flowing, is bringing him now, followed by friends and supporters, weeping and moaning, a bitter sight that will move you deeply.

So it's time for you to prepare. A sword, a noose, to help you from life. Your noble birth served you no good; and Apollo and his Pythian tripod have been your ruin. *(Exit.)*

(Music. Song. Dance.)

NOBLE ARGIVE WOMEN: *(Sing.)*
Pelasgia!
My country!
Come mourn with me!
I begin,

I begin the lamentation!
My face bloodied by tearing white nails,
beating my head,
beating, beating,
beating for Persephonê,
fair child goddess of the world below!
I cry to this land,
this Cyclopian land,
to mourn with me,
mourn,
the pains of this house!
Shear your hair, maidens,
and cry for pity,
pity for those about to die,
heirs of the men who fought for Hellas!

Gone is the house,
gone, gone,
gone the long line of Pelops's children,
ancient house,
house once happy,
house once envied for its blessings,
gone now, gone,
doomed by the gods,
by the gods' envy,
doomed by the blood vote of the people's hatred.
IOOO!
IOOO!
Generations of suffering,
toiling mankind,
fleeting race,
behold how fate cuts short your hopes
with the stroke of death.
Years pass,
centuries flow,
and only sorrow remains for man,
sorrow and impermanence,
and nothing is known,
life is unfathomable.

ÊLEKTRA: *(Sings.)*
> Let me rise to the rock,
> soar to the rock,
> suspended in space between earth and sky,
> torn from Olympos by raging winds,
> great rock hung midair on golden chains.
> Take me there,
> take me,
> to Father Tantalos, ancient Tantalos,
> father of my fathers, founder of my house,
> to howl out the horrors my house has seen.

> First, the winged race of Pelops's chariot,
> shearing the sea near the surge of Geraistos,
> and Myrtilos tossed to his death
> in the white waves.

> That death brought the curse that brought
> grief to my house,
> grief and blood,
> grief and torment.

> And then the lamb with fleece of gold,
> golden ram from Hermês' flocks,
> fatal prodigy portending terror,
> brought bloody ruin and death to Atreus,
> horse-rich Atreus,
> a feud in the blood that turned the sun
> on a backward course,
> and Zeus in anger gave new tracks to the Pleiades.

> And that death brought deaths,
> death on death,
> Thyestês' horror,
> Thyestês' feast,
> the faithless bed of Krêtan Aëropê,
> deceitful Aëropê,
> and now to home,

to Father and me,
the blood-borne fate,
the house's law.

FIRST NOBLE ARGIVE WOMAN: *(Speaks.)* Êlektra, look, Orestês, a
man now condemned to death; and Pyladês with him, truest of
friends, loyal as a brother, carefully guiding his stumbling steps—a
trace horse leading the infirm.

(Enter ORESTÊS supported by PYLADÊS.)

(Music out.)

ÊLEKTRA: Dear Orestês! Oh dear gods! How can I bear to see you there
with death and your grave so near! Seeing you for the last time!
I can't—I can't bear it!

ORESTÊS: Enough of this! No more of your womanish tears! Accept what
is! There's no other choice, hard as it may be!

ÊLEKTRA: Not cry? How? Look around you, at this light, this radiant,
gleaming air that we'll never see again—never to see the sun!

ORESTÊS: Enough, I said! The Argives have killed me once, don't you kill
me, too! Enough!

ÊLEKTRA: But you're too young to die. So young and so unfortunate. You
should *live*, and yet you *can't*!

ORESTÊS: Stop this, please, listen to me, don't unman me as well, or I'll
soon be weeping with you.

ÊLEKTRA: You're telling me not to cry—but how do I do that?
We're going to die, Orestês. Life is precious; to lose it is a matter
for tears to anyone.

ORESTÊS: There's no delaying. It's now, it's today, the appointed day, and
our only choice is between a noose and a sword.

ÊLEKTRA: Dear brother, I want *you* to kill me. No Argive must insult the honor of Agamemnon's house.

ORESTÊS: My hands still run with my mother's blood, I won't have yours there, too. You must kill yourself whatever way you choose.

ÊLEKTRA: If I must, I must. I choose the sword, and I won't be far behind you. But now I want to hold you.

ORESTÊS: Enjoy the empty pleasure, then, if there *is* pleasure for those staring death in the face.

ÊLEKTRA: Dearest Orestês, there's nothing I hold dearer than you. Our souls are one.

ORESTÊS: See what you've made me do now? Tears after all. But now let me hold you. What shame can be left for a man in my place?

(They embrace, then part.)

ÊLEKTRA: How I wish one sword could kill us both, and then to share the same coffin.

ORESTÊS: There could be nothing sweeter. But who's there to bury us now? No family, no kin, no one.

ÊLEKTRA: And Menelaos? Did he say nothing? Nothing to save you? The same, the base Menelaos, who betrayed my father?

ORESTÊS: He never once showed his face. No, his eyes were elsewhere, glued to the throne, so why save his brother's children when they'd only frustrate his design? But come now, we must do the heroic thing, we must prove ourselves true children of Agamemnon, by dying a noble death. I'll prove my nobility to these Argives by plunging a sword through my heart. And your brave death must mirror mine.

Pyladês, I want you to preside over our death. And when we are dead, clothe us and lay out our bodies in a single tomb beside our father's grave. Farewell! I'm off to do what must be done. *(He turns to enter the palace.)*

PYLADÊS: No! Stop, Orestês! Wait! How could you think I'd even *want* to live with you dead?

ORESTÊS: But what has my death to do with you?

PYLADÊS: How can you ask that? Life isn't possible without my friend.

ORESTÊS: But you haven't killed your mother, as I did mine.

PYLADÊS: No, but I helped you. My suffering should be the same.

ORESTÊS: No, Pyladês, it's for you to live, not die with me. Go back to your father. You have a city, a people, I have none. You have a father's house to inherit, and the refuge of great wealth. As for your marriage with my unfortunate sister, the marriage I gave you to honor the ties of our friendship, that of course can never be; but you'll find another wife to bear you children. Those bonds that once bound us are broken now. And so, dear friend, friend I held so close to my heart, farewell— for you still can, and we cannot: faring well is what the dead are denied. *(He turns again as if to leave.)*

PYLADÊS: How little you understand my thinking, Orestês. May the fruitful earth never receive my blood, nor the bright, clear sky my soul, if ever I treacherously betray you, abandoning you to save myself! I was your partner in murder, and I affirm that proudly! I also plotted the deed, all of it, everything you're now being punished for. So I have every right to die with you and with her.

I agreed to the marriage once, and that, to me, makes her my wife. How could I ever return to Delphi, that grand city of the Phokians, and justify myself? I who stood by you in friendship before trouble came, but once it came denied your friendship? How? No. Not possible. Your fate and mine can never be divided. All right, now. Since we're dying together, let's plan how Menelaos will suffer with us.

ORESTÊS: Pyladês, dearest friend, if only I could see this I could die happy.

PYLADÊS: Trust me. Just don't rush to the sword.

ORESTÊS: Anything to get revenge on an enemy.

PYLADÊS: And keep your voice down; I have little faith in women.

ORESTÊS: These women you can trust. They're friends.

PYLADÊS: Let's kill Helen and get Menelaos where it hurts.

ORESTÊS: But how? I'm ready, if we can make it work.

PYLADÊS: We'll butcher her, cut her throat. She's hiding in there.

ORESTÊS: Yes—putting her seal on all my property.

PYLADÊS: Not for much longer. Her new husband is Hades.

ORESTÊS: But how can we do that? She has foreign slaves.

PYLADÊS: Slaves? Do you think I'm afraid of Phrygians?

ORESTÊS: Men who hold mirrors for her, bring her perfumes.

PYLADÊS: You mean she's come lugging the comforts of Troy?

ORESTÊS: Greece, you know, was never large enough for her.

PYLADÊS: Slaves are no match for men born free.

ORESTÊS: Bring this off and I'll happily die twice over.

PYLADÊS: So would I, as long as I'd avenged you.

ORESTÊS: Lay it out. Tell me your plans.

PYLADÊS: We'll enter the house as if ready to kill ourselves.

ORESTÊS: And then what? What comes next?

PYLADÊS: We make a scene, we weep, we tell her our troubles.

ORESTÊS: Making her burst into tears, while laughing inside.

PYLADÊS: Just as we'll be doing.

ORESTÊS: What then?

PYLADÊS: We'll have swords hidden in our clothes.

ORESTÊS: First we'll have to get rid of her slaves. How?

PYLADÊS: We'll lock them up in various parts of the palace.

ORESTÊS: And those who won't keep quiet we'll kill.

PYLADÊS: After that, the deed follows its own course.

ORESTÊS: Killing Helen. Yes. I take your meaning.

PYLADÊS: I thought you would. Now, here's the beauty of the plan. If we were putting to the sword a virtuous woman, it would be murder, pure and simple, bringing no glory on us. As it is, we'll be executing justice, making her pay for the emptying out of Greece, for the fathers and sons who died in her name, the husbands whose deaths made young wives widows. Cries of joy will rise up, altars will burn with thank offerings, and blessings and rewards will shower down upon us for having slaughtered the man-killing bitch!

No longer will you be known as The Mother Killer. That will be past, and from then on men will call you The Slayer of Helen Who Slew Many Men. It isn't right, not right, that Menelaos should thrive while you, your father, your sister should die, and then your mother— well, I'll say no more on that subject. For him to take over your house, when it was Agamemnon's spear that won back his wife, is unthinkable! I would invite Death to take me if I failed to run that woman through with my sword! And even if we fail in killing Helen, at least we can set fire to the palace before we die. But one thing is certain, either we die a noble death, or nobly succeed in our mission.

FIRST NOBLE ARGIVE WOMAN: Tyndareos's daughter deserves the loathing of women. She's disgraced her sex.

ORESTÊS: What can be more precious than a loyal friend? Neither wealth nor kingly power, nor all the people of Argos can take his place! It was you and no one else, dear friend, who devised the murder of Aigisthos. It was you who stood by me then in time of danger and shared that danger with me; and now again you deliver my enemies into my hands for vengeance, and again refuse to desert me.

    Forgive me, Pyladês, if by praising you too much I embarrass you. I'll say no more. I know my death awaits me, but before I die I want to do harm, great harm, to my enemies, to those who betrayed me, and make a misery of their lives who made a misery of mine. I am, after all, the son of Agamemnon, who ruled all Greece, not by virtue of royal succession, not as a tyrant, but because he deserved it— and yet, he did acquire a certain godlike might. I will never shame him by dying the death of a slave. No. My life ends that of a free man. I *will* be avenged on Menelaos! If we achieve only that one good thing, fortune will have blessed us. And yet, if somehow we manage to kill without being killed, all the better, a great good fortune from somewhere—that's my prayer. It's a sweet thought, a hope, to cheer the heart—and costs nothing.

ÊLEKTRA: I have it, Orestês! The answer! A way out for all of us!

ORESTÊS: Divine providence? Yes. Where do we find it? But I know you for a serious mind, Êlektra.

ÊLEKTRA: All right, then, listen. You, too, Pyladês.

ORESTÊS: Go on. Why delay good news?

ÊLEKTRA: You remember Helen's daughter—? But of course you do.

ORESTÊS: Hermionê, yes, Mother raised her.

ÊLEKTRA: She's off to Klytaimnêstra's tomb.

ORESTÊS: To do? What are you thinking? What hope is there?

ÊLEKTRA: To pour libations in her mother's name.

ORESTÊS: And what has this to do with our survival?

ÊLEKTRA: You must take her hostage on her return.

ORESTÊS: How does that effect the three of us?

ÊLEKTRA: All right. Once Helen is dead, if Menelaos tries to harm any of us—no matter which, we're all in this together—you must threaten to kill Hermionê. Draw your sword and hold it at her throat. Then, if after seeing Helen's body in a pool of blood, he decides to save his daughter's life, and offers to spare your own, release the girl to her father. But if fury and pride get the better of him and he tries to kill you, then you slit the girl's throat. I suspect if he comes on strong in the beginning, he'll soften as things progress. He's a coward by nature, he won't fight. This is my plan for our survival. So—I've said what I had to say.

ORESTÊS: Your mind is the mind of a man, Êlektra, your body the paragon of womanhood. Such a woman deserves life, not death. What a loss you'll suffer, Pyladês. Or if both of you survive, what a blessing she'll bring to your bed!

PYLADÊS: It's what I most hope for: to lead my bride to Phokis and the singing of wedding songs.

ORESTÊS: As for your plan, it can't be improved upon, but first we must catch that whelp of an unholy father. But when will Hermionê arrive?

ÊLEKTRA: She can't be much longer; the time's just right.

ORESTÊS: Good! Êlektra, stay outside here for when she returns. And no one enters before the murder's complete. If anyone comes, alert us by pounding on the door or crying out to us. As for us, Pyladês, we go in and take up arms for the final ordeal.

      Oh father dwelling in the halls of impenetrable Night, Orestês your son calls you to come to his aid!

ÊLEKTRA: Come, Father, come, if you hear us in the caverns of earth; we call for you, your children, being killed in your cause!

PYLADÊS: Agamemnon, my father's great kinsman, hear my prayer, too: save your children!

ORESTÊS: I killed my mother!

ÊLEKTRA: I laid my hand on the sword!

PYLADÊS: I made him bold, urging him on!

ORESTÊS: I did it for you, Father!

ÊLEKTRA: I didn't betray you!

PYLADÊS: Hear their reproaches, and save your children!

ORESTÊS: I pour you a libation of my tears!

ÊLEKTRA: And I of my lamentations!

PYLADÊS: Enough! The time to act is now. If prayers are heard inside the earth, he hears you. Great Zeus our ancestor, and holy Justice, grant success to this man, this woman, and to me—three kinsmen who face a single trial, a single judgment.

(Exeunt ORESTÊS and PYLADÊS into the palace. The door remains open.)

(Music. Song. Dance.)

ÊLEKTRA: *(Sings.)*
Women,
women of Mykenê,
dear friends,
noble women of
Argos—

NOBLE ARGIVE WOMEN: *(Sing.)*
What is it, my lady?
What orders have you for us?

For that is your title still
in our Argive city.

ÊLEKTRA: *(Speaks.)* —come, some of you, take up positions here on the
carriage road, you others over there, at the path. We must guard the
house.

NOBLE ARGIVE WOMEN: *(Sing.)*
    Why, dear friend?
    Why do you give us this task?

ÊLEKTRA: *(Sings.)*
    I'm frightened,
    frightened
    someone might come,
    catch my brother
    at the kill,
    and make our troubles
    even worse.

    (The women divide into two groups, each at the direction of a LEADER.)

LEADER A: *(Speaks.)* Hurry now! Come! Take your positions! I'll guard the
eastward road.

LEADER B: *(Speaks.)* And I the westward.

ÊLEKTRA: *(Sings.)*
    Turn your eyes
    in every direction.

NOBLE ARGIVE WOMEN A AND B: *(Sing.)*
    This side and that,
    and back again,
    following your command
    with our careful gaze.

ÊLEKTRA: *(Sings.)*
    Never stop searching,
    turn right and left.

NOBLE ARGIVE WOMEN A: *(Sing.)*
>   There's someone in the path!
>   Careful!
>   Who can he be,
>   this peasant coming to your palace?

ÊLEKTRA: *(Speaks.)* This is the end, then, friends! It is finished! He'll tell the enemy of the young lions inside, ready to leap on their prey!

NOBLE ARGIVE WOMEN A: *(Sing.)*
>   No.
>   No one.
>   The road is empty.
>   There's no one in sight.

ÊLEKTRA: *(Sings.)*
>   You there!
>   The other side!
>   Is it secure?
>   Give a good report
>   that all is clear!

LEADER B: *(Speaks.)* Nothing! No one! Keep careful watch over there! All's safe here!

LEADER A: *(Speaks.)* The same this side! Not a soul to be seen!

ÊLEKTRA: *(Sings.)*
>   Wait, I'll go to the
>   door and listen.

(She puts her ear to the door.)

NOBLE ARGIVE WOMEN A AND B: *(Sing.)*
>   You in there!
>   Why so slow?
>   Why this quiet?
>   Slash her!
>   Slash the victim!
>   Let her blood flow!

(Pause, as all listen.)

ÊLEKTRA: *(Speaks.)* They don't hear! What's wrong? O TALAIN'EGO KAKON! Has her beauty blunted their swords?

NOBLE ARGIVE WOMEN A AND B: *(Sing.)*
Some Argive soldier
soon will run to her rescue!

ÊLEKTRA: *(Speaks.)* Keep a sharp lookout! This is no time for idleness! You! Circle round over there! And you! Over there!

(They change positions.)

NOBLE ARGIVE WOMEN A AND B: *(Sing.)*
I move along the path,
searching in all directions!

(In changing position, they merge again into one group and halt at the sound of HELEN's cries from inside.)

VOICE OF HELEN: *(Speaks.)* IOOOOO! Pelasgian Argos! Murder! Treachery!

ÊLEKTRA: *(Speaks.)* Did you hear? Ha? Now their hands are bloodied! Helen's voice!

NOBLE ARGIVE WOMEN: *(Sing.)*
Zeus,
Great Zeus,
lend power to these
young lions' arms!

VOICE OF HELEN: *(Speaks.)* IOOOOO! Menelaos! Help me! Help! They're killing me!

NOBLE ARGIVE WOMEN: *(Sing.)*
Strike!
Strike her!

Again!

Again!

Slay the destroyer with your double-edged swords!

Slay the traitor to husband and country!

Slay her who slew Greeks in uncounted numbers,
by the river's edge,
by the merciless sword,
where weapons of iron made tears fall on tears,
tears on tears by Skamander's banks!

FIRST NOBLE ARGIVE WOMAN: *(Speaks.)* Silence! Silence! There's someone coming! I hear it! Footsteps! The path by the palace!

(Music out.)

ÊLEKTRA: *(Seeing the approach from off.)* Women, oh dear, dear women, it's Hermionê, to be sure! And just in time, too, in the middle of the slaughter! We must keep our voices down, no shouting now. Look at her there—walking straight into our net. And what a catch she is, if catch her I can! Compose yourselves, look natural, your face must betray nothing of what's happened in there. I'll choose a sullen disposition to meet her with, labored with grief, as if I know nothing of these goings-on. *(Enter HERMIONÊ.)* Ah, Hermionê dear, have you just come from Klytaimnêstra's grave? Decking it with floral wreathes and pouring libations to the dead?

HERMIONÊ: I have, and I won her good graces. But on the way back I was frightened when at a distance I heard shouting in the palace.

ÊLEKTRA: Yes, well, things have happened that call for tears.

HERMIONÊ: Not more trouble, Êlektra! Tell me what's happened.

ÊLEKTRA: Orestês and I have been sentenced to death by the Argives.

HERMIONÊ: No, it can't be! Not my own cousins!

ÊLEKTRA: There's no other way. The yoke of Necessity is on us.

HERMIONÊ: Then this was the cry I heard inside the palace?

ÊLEKTRA: He fell at Helen's knees, crying out.

HERMIONÊ: Who? I don't understand. Who at her knees?

ÊLEKTRA: Poor Orestês. Pleading to spare our lives.

HERMIONÊ: I see. No wonder the palace rang with cries.

ÊLEKTRA: What better reason can there be? But come, dear, come into the house and help your cousins plead for their lives. Fall down at your so prosperous mother's feet and beg her not to let Menelaos stand by and watch us be killed. Remember how my mother raised you. Show pity on us, help us in our troubles. Join us in our struggle; only you can save us. Come, I'll lead you in.

HERMIONÊ: I will, I will! I'll hurry! If I have any power in this matter, you're saved.

(ÊLEKTRA leads HERMIONÊ to the door, through which she enters the palace. ÊLEKTRA then remains at the door, looking in.)

ÊLEKTRA: *(Calling inside.)* Friends, comrades, here is your prey! Seize her!

VOICE OF HERMIONÊ: *(From within.)* OI'GO! What men are these?

VOICE OF ORESTÊS: *(From within.)* Silence! You're here to save our lives, not yours!

ÊLEKTRA: Seize her! Hold her! Put your swords to her throat and keep them there! Menelaos must see that he has *men* to deal with now, not cowardly Phrygians! Show him what a coward deserves! *(ÊLEKTRA enters the palace, closing the doors behind her.)*

(Music. Song. Dance.)

NOBLE ARGIVE WOMEN: *(Sing.)*
IO! IO!

Friends!
Come!
Your feet!
Come!
Stamp your feet!
Raise them high!
Raise, raise a shout,
a noise before the palace,
a mighty noise that the Argives know nothing,
nothing of the bloody deed done here,
here in the palace,
here,
and come,
in fright,
armed,
in fright,
to help her in her deserved distress!
See it,
I must see it before they come,
the bloodied corpse,
the murdered corpse,
the Helen corpse,
spread,
spread out before me in the house,
or hear it told me by one of her slaves,
for some of the tale I know,
some not.
But one thing I know,
justice,
divine justice,
has come,
come to Helen,
vengeance on Helen,
Helen who made all Greece shed tears,
tears on tears,
and all for him,
that accursed,
that accursed man of Ida,
who led all Hellas to Troy,
Paris!

(Amid cries of AIIIII! AIIIII! there are noises of hasty scrambling about on the roof of the palace; then there appears a PHRYGIAN SLAVE out of his wits with terror and clambering to climb down the façade to ground level.)

FIRST NOBLE ARGIVE WOMAN: *(Speaks.)* Shh! Hush! One of her Phrygian slaves! He'll tell us what has happened inside from the looks of him.

PHRYGIAN SLAVE: *(Sings.)*
    I have run,
    I have fled,
    I have escaped death
    from an Argive sword,
    sped away in barbarian slippers,
    over cedar-wood timbers and Doric porticoes,
    away, away,
    running scared in barbarian flight!
    Oh Earth!
    Great Earth!

    AIIII!
    AIIII!

    Run!
    Run where?
    Oh tell me, ladies, foreign ladies!
    Into the brightly shining sky?
    Or down to the sea
    that bull-headed Ocean
    embraces as he circles Earth?

FIRST NOBLE ARGIVE WOMAN: *(Speaks.)* Tell us, Trojan, Helen's slave, what is it?

PHRYGIAN SLAVE: *(Sings.)*
    Ilion, Ilion!

    OMOI MOIIII!

Oh rich and fruited soil of holy Ida's mount,
oh blessèd city, holy Troy,
Phrygia's glorious citadel!

AIIII!

How I lament your fall,
lament with loud barbarian cry,
in Asian grief, raise my dirge, my moan,
for your destruction, you,
victim of the bird-born vision of beauty,
swan-white whelp of Lêda,
Helen ruinous, ruinous Helen,
Erinys, Avenging Fury
Helen!

AIIII!

Helen high on the walls of Troy,
Apollo's polished battlements!

OTOTOTOI!

The dirges, the dirges!
Unhappy Troy,
unhappy land of Dardanos!
Unhappy plains where Ganymede rode,
bedmate of Zeus!

FIRST NOBLE ARGIVE WOMAN: *(Speaks.)* Tell us what happened in
there; tell us clearly.

PHRYGIAN SLAVE: *(Sings.)*
    AILINON!
    AILINON!
    So begins the lament of barbarians,

    AIIII!
    AIIII!

for the blood of kings spilled by murderous swords.
But I will tell you, tell you all, ladies,
ladies, will tell you all that happened.
Into the palace two lions came,
two matched lions, two Greek lions,
twin lions in every way.

One was the son of a general father,
Agamemnon,
commander,
the other the son of Strophios,
full of guile,
like Odysseus in that,
silent in deception,
but loyal,
loyal to friends, and bold,
bold,
bold with the best in battle,
skilled in ways of warfare,
and a man-killing serpent.
Curse him for his cold-blood schemes!

Inside,
they fell at the throne of Pariswife Helen,
one here, one there,
eyes wet, faces smeared, blotted with tears,
arms around her knees then,
Helen's knees,
grasping, clutching, suppliants' hands.

Leaping, bounding, they came at a run,
her slaves, Phrygian slaves,
whispering among themselves,
telling of terror,
foul play a-brewing,
some uncertain,
others suspecting,
mother murderer near,
entrapping Tydrareos's daughter in his crafty net.

FIRST NOBLE ARGIVE WOMAN: *(Speaks.)* And where were you? Already on the run?

PHRYGIAN SLAVE: *(Sings.)*
  In Phrygian fashion I fanned a breeze,
  a breeze past Helen's locks,
  Helen's lovely hair,
  with a round of plumes,
  while in her fingers, her white fingers,
  she twirled the strands of the distaff,
  the linen strands that fell to the floor,
  thread to sew gifts from Trojan spoils
  for sister Klytaimnêstra,
  Klytaimnêstra, sister,
  purple-dyed garments,
  gifts from luxurious spoils of Troy.

  Orestês then spoke,
  addressing the woman,
  the woman of Sparta:

  "Daughter of Zeus, rise from your couch,
  come, come to the hearth,
  the ancient hearth of forefather Pelops,
  to hear my words."

  He led her then,
  led her,
  and she followed,
  followed,
  not knowing what would be.

  Meanwhile his Phokian accomplice,
  evil man, evil,
  had other business in mind.

  "Clear out, you Phrygian scum,
  out of here, out!"

He locked us up here and there,
in the house, the stables, the porches,
every which where but near our mistress.

FIRST NOBLE ARGIVE WOMAN: *(Speaks.)* What then?
What happened next?

PHRYGIAN SLAVE: *(Sings.)*
Oh Mother,
great Mother,
mighty, mighty
Mother of Ida!

AIIII!
AIIII!

The horrors I've seen,
the sufferings, pains,
murderous, lawless,
here,
here in the palace,
the royal palace!

Out of the dark of their robes,
their purple-dyed robes,
from hiding,
two swords are drawn,
two swords brandished,
eyes flying every direction
to see they were alone!

Like wild boars, boars of the mountains,
they took their stand before the woman,
saying:

"It's your time now,
your time to die!
Your death?
Blame it on your

coward of a husband,
on him who deserted his
brother's children to
death here in Argos!"
And she cried,
she cried,
she cried out:

"OMOI MOIIIII!"

Her pale arm clasped to her chest,
she beat her breast, her head,
blow on piteous blow,
and runs,
runs this way,
that way,
on flashing golden-sandaled feet,
in flight,
in flight.

But Orestês,
his Argive boot planted stoutly,
with missilelike fingers has her by the hair,
her neck yanked back,
back to his left shoulder,
meaning to plunge
the dark sword in her throat.

FIRST NOBLE ARGIVE WOMAN: *(Speaks.)* And what did you Phrygians
do to help her?

PHRYGIAN SLAVE: *(Sings.)*
Hammering, pounding,
on doors, on jambs, on frames,
our shouts resounding,
echoing through the halls,
we leveled with crowbars and levers
the posts and frames of massive, mighty doors,
and ran from every direction to aid her,

one of us toting stones,
another a bow,
and another still, his sword drawn.

And then there was Pyladês,
Pyladês, Hêktor-like, invincible,
Hêktor the Phrygian,
or like Aias, great Aias in his triple helm,
the Aias I saw,
saw at Priam's gates.

Steel then met steel in a resounding clash,
but not for long,
for we proved, we Phrygians,
how greatly inferior in war might,
in Arês' war game, we were born
compared with the warriors of Greece.
One of us fled,
another lay dead,
a third was wounded,
and a fourth fell to his knees, begging for life.
For safety we fled to the shadows.

Hermionê then, poor Hermionê,
enters as her wretched mother,
the mother who bore her,
is being killed,
sinking to the floor in death.

Like Bakkhai then,
freed of their thyrsoi,
eager to snatch a whelp of the mountains,
they rush to seize the prey in their grasp,
then turn to finish the slaughter of Helen.

But where is she now?
Where to be seen in all the palace?
Oh Zeus and Earth!
Daylight and Deep Night!

Vanished from sight!
By drugs or magic or deceiving gods?
How?

What happened then, I cannot say.
Stealing from the house,
I ran, ran, for safety, for escape!

And Menelaos, what of him,
who sweated and toiled to win back a wife
brought from Troy?

In vain, in vain he struggled for Helen.

FIRST NOBLE ARGIVE WOMAN: *(Speaks.)* One thing follows another!
Is there no end? Look! Orestês, armed, rushing in haste from the
palace!

(Enter ORESTÊS abruptly from the palace, sword in hand.)

(Music out.)

ORESTÊS: Where is the one who fled my sword?

PHRYGIAN: I kneel, my head to the ground, in barbarian fashion.

ORESTÊS: This isn't Troy! It's Argos!

PHRYGIAN: The wise man prefers life, wherever he is.

ORESTÊS: Did you shout to bring help for Menelaos?

PHRYGIAN: No, lord, no, for you; it's you deserve it.

ORESTÊS: What are you saying? Helen perished justly?

PHRYGIAN: Justly, yes, even with three throats to cut!

ORESTÊS: You're lying, coward! I don't believe a word of it!

PHRYGIAN: No? Not for ruining Greece? Not for ruining Troy?

ORESTÊS: Swear you're honest, not flattering me, or I'll kill you!

PHRYGIAN: I swear by my life! Would I swear falsely by that?

ORESTÊS: *(Moving his sword nearer to the PHRYGIAN's throat.)* Were all
the Phrygians as terrified of steel as you?

PHRYGIAN: Take it away! Up close its gleam is deadly!

ORESTÊS: Afraid of turning to stone, as at sight of a Gorgon?

PHRYGIAN: Gorgons I don't know, but of turning to a corpse.

ORESTÊS: Afraid of death? A slave? Death the liberator?

PHRYGIAN: Even a slave lives for the light of the sun.

ORESTÊS: Well said! Saved by your wits. Go inside now.

PHRYGIAN: You won't kill me, then?

ORESTÊS: You've been spared.

PHRYGIAN: Praise god for that!

ORESTÊS: But I'm about to change my mind.

PHRYGIAN: The worse for me.

ORESTÊS: What a fool! Why would I stoop to bloody your neck?
By birth, you're not a woman, and your cowardice denies your
manhood. What are you? No, I came from the palace to put an end to
your racket. Rouse Argives with a cry and they're quick to respond.
But let him return, Menelaos, back within sword range, let him come
to show off his long blond curls!

(Exeunt the PHRYGIAN to the side, and ORESTÊS into the palace.)

(Music. Song. Dance.)

NOBLE ARGIVE WOMEN: *(Sing.)*
    IOOOO!
    IOOOO!
    Disaster strikes the house!
    Disaster, sisters, conflict,
    another struggle,
    to rend the house,
    the line of Atreus!
    What do we do?
    What?
    What now?
    Do we tell them?
    The city?
    Or do we stay silent?
    Silence,
    yes,
    silence is best.
    Look!
    Look there!
    Oh look!
    The roof!
    The roof!
    Smoke billowing!
    A warning message!
    They're lighting torches,
    torches to fire the palace,
    to bring down in flames
    the great house of Tantalos,
    never tiring in their struggle,
    no end to the slaughter!
    The end is in god's hands,
    always,
    always as he would have it;
    but how great, how great
    is the power of the Avengers,

Spirits of Vengeance!
The house has fallen,
fallen,
been thrust into a sea of blood
by that fall of Myrtilos
from his chariot.

FIRST NOBLE ARGIVE WOMAN: *(Speaks.)* But I see Menelaos
approaching in haste. He's heard of what's happened. *(Calling inside.)*
You in there! Descendants of Atreus! Bolt the doors! Now! It can't
be too soon! A man riding high on prosperity is a mighty foe for
someone down on his luck, as you are, Orestês!

(Music out.)

MENELAOS: *(Enters with armed SLAVES and ARGIVES.)* I've heard it all!
It's brought me here! The violence, the appalling crimes of those twin
lions! Am I to call them men? Inside there! Open the doors! *(To his
SLAVES.)* You, put your shoulders to use, push in the gates! At least
I'll save my daughter from those bloody murderers!

*(As the SLAVES approach the doors, ORESTÊS and PYLADÊS appear
on the roof with HERMIONÊ between them, ORESTÊS' sword at her
throat, while ÊLEKTRA carries lighted torches.)*

ORESTÊS: You! Hands off those doors! That means you, Menelaos, you
with your towering arrogance! Or I'll rip a stone from this ancient
cornice and smash your head! Don't worry the doors. They're bolted.
You won't be coming in to rescue anyone.

MENELAOS: ÉA! Torches on the roof, men, under siege, a sword at my
daughter's throat!

ORESTÊS: Which would you rather? Ask questions or listen to me?

MENELAOS: Neither; but it looks as if I'll be listening.

ORESTÊS: For what it's worth, I intend to kill your daughter.

MENELAOS: Give me my wife's body so I can bury it.

ORESTÊS: Ask the gods for that. But I *will* kill your daughter.

MENELAOS: Will the mother murderer add more blood to his hands?

ORESTÊS: The father avenger whom you abandoned to death.

MENELAOS: Wasn't it enough spilling your mother's blood?

ORESTÊS: I'll never tire of killing whorish women.

MENELAOS: And you, Pyladês? Are you a part of this murder?

ORESTÊS: His silence is your answer. I do the talking.

MENELAOS: And you'll regret it, unless you have wings to escape on.

ORESTÊS: Escape? No. We're setting fire to the palace.

MENELAOS: Your father's house? Your family's? How can you do this?

ORESTÊS: To keep it from you. Then I'll slaughter her over the flames.

MENELAOS: Kill her, then. But I'll make you pay.

ORESTÊS: Be quiet! Accept your misery as justified.

MENELAOS: That sword! Take it away from my daughter's throat!

ORESTÊS: Ah, then you lied.

MENELAOS: Will you really kill her?

ORESTÊS: The truth at last.

MENELAOS: OIMOI! What do you want of me?

ORESTÊS: Go to the Argives—persuade them.

MENELAOS: Persuade them to do what?

ORESTÊS: Not to kill us.

MENELAOS: Or you'll kill my child?

ORESTÊS: That's how it is.

MENELAOS: And you say you deserve to live?

ORESTÊS: Yes, and to rule.

MENELAOS: Rule? Where? What?

ORESTÊS: Here, in my father's country.

MENELAOS: *(Sarcastically.)* What a splendid sight! You—at the sacred basins!

ORESTÊS: Yes, and why not?

MENELAOS: Sacrificing victims before battle!

ORESTÊS: You, I suppose, are better suited?

MENELAOS: My hands are pure.

ORESTÊS: And your heart?

MENELAOS: Who'd speak to you?

ORESTÊS: Anyone who loves his father.

MENELAOS: And the one who respects his mother?

ORESTÊS: Is a lucky man.

MENELAOS: Which leaves you out.

ORESTÊS: Yes—I have no love for whores.

MENELAOS: Oh Helen, poor Helen—

ORESTÊS: And me? What about poor me?

MENELAOS: —I brought you back from Troy only for slaughter!

ORESTÊS: If only it were so!

MENELAOS: After all my toil and labor!

ORESTÊS: None of which was for me.

MENELAOS: I've suffered terribly.

ORESTÊS: Because you refused to help us.

MENELAOS: You have me pinned.

ORESTÊS: You pinned yourself, you swine. Come, Êlektra! It's time to torch the house! And Pyladês, of all friends the most loyal, you fire the battlements!

MENELAOS: Land of Danaös! Founders and men of horse-loving Argos! Come, come quickly, come now with weapons! Arm yourselves! Run to us here to help! Come to the rescue! Here is a man, hands still wet with his mother's blood, forcing violence on your city, violence to save his life, the mother-killer!

(Enter from the city a rush of armed ARGIVES CITIZENS, among them HOPLITES in armor, who join with MENELAOS's men to storm the palace.)

(APOLLO appears on a platform above the roof. His first words halt in their tracks the men below.)

APOLLO: Enough, Menelaos! Lay aside your whetted anger! It is Apollo, son of Lêto, who addresses you. And you, Orestês, you with your sword poised at this girl's throat, do likewise and hear the message I bring. As for Helen, who, in your rage against Menelaos, you were keen on killing, but could not, I rescued her, snatching her from under your sword, at Zeus my father's orders. As a daughter of Zeus, it is hers to have life immortal. She will sit enthroned in the vast folds of heaven beside her brothers Castor and Polydeukês, a guiding star for seamen. So much, then, for Helen.

You, Orestês, will cross this country's frontiers for the plains of Parrhasia, where you will live the circuit of one year, a land to be named in honor of your exile. From there you will proceed to the city of Athêna and be tried for matricide by the three Eumenides. There, on the Hill of Arês, gods will sit in judgment, casting the sacred verdict for your acquittal.

Then, Orestês, you will marry the woman against whose throat your sword now rests: Hermionê. Achilleus's son, Neoptolemos, intends she will be his, but that will never be. Neoptolemos will come to Delphi seeking from me reparation for his father's death, but he will fall to a Delphian sword. Êlektra. Give her in marriage to Pyladês to whom you've promised her. The life awaiting him will be a happy one.

You, Menelaos, allow Orestês to rule in Argos. As for yourself, rule in Sparta, enjoying it as a dowry from your wife—the wife who has been your source of endless torment. But that's now at an end. Marry again. Another wife for your house. *(Motions to HELEN who joins him on the platform.)* Helen's beauty brought Greek and Trojan together for one reason: War—so that many would die, many men, and relieve the earth glutted of mortals. She was a tool, Helen, an instrument, merely, in the hands of gods. As for Argos, I will reconcile it to Orestês, setting all things right. It was, after all, I who compelled him to murder his mother.

ORESTÊS: Great Apollo! Great god of truth, not falsehood! And yet when I heard your voice, I trembled with fear that it was not yours, but the voice of some Avenging Spirit. But all has turned out well, and I obey. With this motion—I release Hermionê from slaughter and accept her in marriage with her father's permission.

MENELAOS: Helen, daughter of Zeus, farewell! I envy you your home among the gods. I count you blest indeed. Orestês, I offer to you herewith my daughter in marriage, as Apollo commands. As both of us are from noble houses, I wish you all success and blessing, and not least myself who give her to you.

APOLLO: Go your ways, then, each of you, as I have assigned, and end your quarrels.

MENELAOS: We can only obey.

ORESTÊS: I agree, and so mend our differences, Menelaos, and accept your oracles, lord Apollo.

(Music.)

(Exeunt through the roof of the palace ORESTÊS, HERMIONÊ, PYLADÊS and ÊLEKTRA, emerging below as pairs through the palace doors.)

APOLLO: Go, each of you, each on his way! Honor Peace, the loveliest of goddesses! I now lead Helen to the Halls of Zeus, high among the flaming stars, where she will sit enthroned, a goddess forever, beside Hera and Hêbê, the wife of Heraklês, honored with her brothers, the sons of Zeus, with unending libations, a star to guide sailors to safety on the surging sea.

(APOLLO and HELEN disappear.)

(Exeunt all diversely.)

*

BAKKHAI

(BAKXI)

CHARACTERS

DIONYSOS

PENTHEUS *King of Thebes, grandson of Kadmos*

KADMOS *an old man, founder of Thebes, former king*

TEIRESIAS *an old, blind prophet*

AGAVÊ *daughter of Kadmos, mother of Pentheus*

CHORUS OF ASIAN BAKKHAI *female followers of Dionysos*

FIRST BAKKHÊ *chorus leader*

MALE SLAVE

BAND OF THEBAN MAENADS

GUARD

HERDSMAN

SOLDIERS

GUARDS

ATTENDANTS

BAKKHAI

Thebes.
Morning.
Before the Royal Palace.
Enter DIONYSOS.

DIONYSOS: I am here. I. Dionysos. Fire-born son of Zeus. Here in Thebes. I, once born of Semelê, daughter of Kadmos, in a blinding burst of lightning. I, a god who have hidden my godhead and assumed for now human form, disguised as my own priest. I stand here at the source of the River Dirkê and the waters of Ismênos, and I behold, here, by the palace, the tomb of my mother, thunderstruck, and the ruins of her house, smoking still with the flame of Zeus's fire; eternal testament to Hera's savage jealousy.

Praise to Kadmos for creating this precinct sacrosanct to his daughter's honor. I, in turn, have covered it over with the fresh grape-heavy green of the vine. I have left behind the treasure-rich fields of Lydia and Phrygia, crossed over the sun-drenched plains of Persia, and through the walled cities of Baktria, across the inhospitable country of Mêdia, of blessèd Arabia, and all of Asia that hugs the salt sea with high-towered cities filled with Hellenes and Barbarians together.

Once I had set my dances and established my rites in Asia, I came to this Hellene land to reveal myself to its people as what I am: a god. Thebes was the first of the cities of Hellas to shriek in ecstasy, whose women I clothed in fawn skin, and whose hands I armed with my green fennel wand, in battle a spear wreathed with ivy. And all because my mother's sisters—even *they*—denied that I, Dionysos, was son of Zeus, saying that Semelê was bedded by a mortal man, and then passed off her shame onto Zeus—a clever trick devised by Kadmos, and *that*, with slanderous tongues, they say, is why Zeus slew her: because she lied! And so from their homes I drove them, raging in their frenzy, stung with madness, to wander the mountain forests. I forced on their backs the garb of my sacred rites, frightening all the women of Thebes to run from their houses in rabid fury. And there, with the daughters of Kadmos, they sit, all as one, beneath green firs, on roofless rocks. This city must learn, like it or not, that it lacks the

wisdom of initiation into *my* Bakkhic rites. Once accomplished,
I must then, in honor of my mother Semelê, be revealed as the god I
am. Son of Zeus.

King Kadmos now has passed both throne and honors onto
Pentheus, his daughter's son, her young son, who revolts against the
gods by opposing *me*, excluding *me* from his libations, and never in
his prayers turns thought to *me*. Therefore to him, and to all of
Thebes, I will make known my godhead. And when I have won my
blessèd victory, I shall proceed to other lands, revealing myself a god.
But if these Thebans rage, take up arms against my Bakkhai, force
them from the mountain back to Thebes, then shall I lead them on
against the foe. It is for this that I have taken on this human guise and
enter the scene—a mortal.

Women! Come! Women who left behind Tmolos, Lydia and
other barbarian lands to follow and worship me! Come! Take up our
native Phrygian drum, my drum and Rhea's! Make the earth tremble
with the sound! Make them roar at the gates of Thebes! At the gates of
Pentheus's palace! Make his house shake at its foundations! Let the city
of Kadmos see and hear you in the fearsome glory of your mightiness!

I'm going now to the chasms of holy Kithairon where my
women, my Bakkhai, my worshipers, wait for me. I will join their
whirling dances! *(Exit.)*

(Enter the CHORUS OF ASIAN BAKKHAI.)

(Music. Song. Dance.)

ASIAN BAKKHAI: *(Sing.)*
Down,
down,
down from Asia's plains,
down,
down from Tmolos,
sacred Tmolos,
holy mountain,
I fly,
I soar,
in Bromios's name,
in honor of the Roaring God,

sweet labor that is no labor,
joyous weariness,
to praise,
to exalt,
to sing to the honor of Bakkhos,
Bakkhos,
holy Bakkhos!

Who is in the road,
who,
who is in the streets,
in the house,
who?
Make way!
Make way!
And let no irreverence be spoken,
no evil,
but speak with mouths of holy silence,
and I will sing his praises,
holy,
holy praises,
sing the ancient song,
the honored hymn,
to Dionysos!
Oh blest, blest,
blest is he whose heart soars,
soars high with god's love,
who knows in his heart god's secret mysteries!

Blest is he
who lives his life
in purity in god's sweet service;
whose spirit cries out in oneness with god,
who dances,
dances with holy joy,
holy,
to Bakkhos's glory,
who joins in dance on the holy mountain,
Bakkhos's sacred band,

pounding,
pounding,
pounding with naked feet,
naked,
naked feet the holy mountain;
who knows oneness with god,
oneness in holy purification!

Blest who honors the rites
of Great Mother Kybêlê,
who brandishes on high,
who shakes,
shakes the ivy-wound wand,
Dionysos's wand,
who sings,
sings,
sings the praises of god,
who crowns his head with ivy,
crowns his head in holy service
of Dionysos!

Rise up!
Rise up, Bakkhai!
Bakkhai, rise up!
Bring home,
bring him,
the god,
the Roaring God,
son god of god,
Dionysos!
Bring him,
bring him down,
down from the mountains,
down from the hills of Phrygia,
bring back the god,
bring him back to Hellas,
Bromios,
down to the wide streets,

the spacious squares fit for dancing.
Bring him,
Bromios,
Dionysos,
Roaring God!
Bring him,
Dionysos,
born of Semelê in a blast of lightning,
ripped from her womb by Zeus's thunderbolt,
a fiery birth,
and she died,
died,
her own light snuffed with the blinding flame.

All at once,
Zeus,
son of Kronos,
with god's deft hand,
opens wide his thigh,
a second womb,
and placing there the Roaring God,
closes his flesh with golden clasps,
concealing his son from Hera's rage,
the anger of Zeus's wife who never saw him,
the Roaring God.

And Zeus,
when the Fates had made him perfect in time,
Dionysos,
gave birth,
bore his newborn son,
the bull-horned god,
Dionysos,
and with garlands,
wreaths of snakes,
crowned his head with snakes,
snakes that all his holy Maenads,
all god-frenzied Bakkhants wear wound in their hair.

Oh Thebes,
Thebes,
you who raised Semelê,
crown your heads,
crown your heads with ivy,
abound,
abound with evergreen,
bright-berried bryony,
consecrate,
make yourselves holy,
holy to the god,
make yourselves holy with sprouts of oak and fir,
be Bakkhants,
wind yourselves in dappled fawn skin
and ropes of twisted wool,
raise up the wild wand,
god's violent wand,
holy it is,
holy, holy,
and all the land will dance,
dance to the god,
dance,
for whoever leads the worshiping bands to the mountain,
to the hills,
where women wait,
whoever leads them is Bromios,
is Dionysos,
bands of women freed from their looms,
to the mountain,
dance ecstatic on the mountain in the frenzy,
the madness,
of Dionysos.

And you,
you sacred caves of Krete,
you secret chambers of the Kurêtës
where Zeus first saw the light of the sun,
where triple-crested Korybantës
raised high their feet in dance,

dance,
and stretched tight the skin of the beast on the drum,
the drum they made for me,
and catching the tense rhythm of Bakkhic joy,
melted it,
gentled it,
sweetened it with the soft cry,
the soft-crying voice of Phrygian flutes
and gave,
gave it to her,
to Mother Rhea,
a rhythm to the shout,
the ecstatic revel shout of Bakkhants,
and satyrs took it then,
the drum,
raving satyrs,
dancing satyrs,
whose orgies now,
sacred to Dionysos,
beat, beat
with the pounding, pounding boom of the drum.

How sweet,
how sweet is my love on the mountains,
how sweetly he falls,
my leader,
from the band,
the holy band,
falls sweetly to the earth,
writhing,
ecstatic,
his fawn-skinned body,
holy,
holy to the god;
hunting,
racing he has killed the goat,
and in joy,
in rapture,
devoured the flesh,

the raw flesh,
bleeding,
of god's holy animal;
and back,
back to the mountains,
back to the mountains he is hurled,
to the mountains of Lydia,
the mountains of Phrygia,
led on,
always,
ever,
by the booming cry,
the Roaring God's shout,
to follow,
evoë!
follow to the mountains,
evoë! evoë!
mountains that flow beneath him,
with milk,
flow white with milk,
white,
flow red with wine,
flow,
flow with the slow thick flow of honey
AND HE IS GOD!
BAKKHOS!
DIONYSOS!
IAKKHOS!
DITHYRAMBOS!
EVIOS!
and his torch flows flame,
held high,
Syrian frankincense,
his pine torch,
and his wand,
his holy wand,
flows flame,
slow-heavy flame as he runs,
dances,

stamps his feet in his own dance,
the god's dance,
his dance,
rousing his dancers,
driving,
goading them on to his dance,
his thick hair flowing like flame as he tosses it,
whirling his wand in ecstatic madness,
shouting them onto their feet,
thundering above their joyful cries:

FIRST BAKKHÊ: *(Sings.)*
On, on, my Bakkhants!
Bright with the gold
of golden Paktolos,
sing praise to Dionysos
to the thunder of his drums!
Dance his dances!
Raise him to glory!
Praise him!
Praise the Lord of Joy
with your Phrygian
cries and incantations,
your ecstatic joy in the god!"

ASIAN BAKKHAI: *(Sing.)*
And the flute shrieks,
shrieks its high-piping tune,
holy to god,
god's holy flute,
shrieking,
shrieking in god's honor,
leading them,
leading, leading,
sweet flute,
onto the mountains,
the sweet mountains,
where the god's holy band,
like foals grazing near their mothers,

leap,
leap joyously with nimble feet,
dancing feet into the light air!
(Music out.)

TEIRESIAS: *(Enters from the side.)* Ooo-ooo! Anyone here? Anyone at the gates? Ooo-ooo! Someone! Anyone! Where's the porter! Who's in charge? Call him! Kadmos! Agenor's son! Call him from the palace! That immigrant Agenor from Sidon who came to Thebes to build her battlements. Call him! It's me. Teiresias. I'm waiting, tell him. He'll know what for. We have a pact, we two old goats, Kadmos and I. We'll do it, we said, and now I'm here, ready to go, withered old limbs and all, dressed in fawn skins, green ivy tied round my wand and crowning my head.

KADMOS: *(Enters from the palace.)* Ah, old friend! I knew it! Knew it was you! I was in the palace when I heard that voice. "That voice," I said to myself, "with such wisdom in it, can only be my old friend Teiresias." But here I am, fawn skin and all, ready to honor the god, dressed for his revels, ready to go. This god? You know? This Dionysos we're all hearing about? Well! He's my daughter's son. It's true. Yes, truly. We must help him. Everything we can. Do our part, you and I, to raise him high in men's eyes! Dionysos! Who has revealed himself to mortals! But where do we go? You're the wise one, old friend, eh? Explain to this withered old cocker, where do we go to join the god's dancers?

    We'll go, you and I, eh? We'll go, tossing our scraggly white manes to the winds. We'll dance all night, we'll leap, we'll whirl, turning, turning, never tiring till our feet fall off! Then all next day we'll pound, pound, pound the earth with our wands! What a joy to forget how old we are!

TEIRESIAS: Me, too, me, too! Ah, Kadmos! Kadmos! Young again! Let's dance again!

KADMOS: Time to go, don't you think? To the mountains? But what if we took a carriage? Hm?

TEIRESIAS: Carriage? Carriage? Never! No, never! That would never do! The god will demand more reverence than that, don't you know!

KADMOS: Well, old Bakkhant, then I'll have to lead the way; lead you like the ancient baby you are.

TEIRESIAS: No need, old friend, Bakkhos will do that.

KADMOS: Where are they? Where are the men? Are no other men of Thebes to dance for Dionysos?

TEIRESIAS: Men of Thebes! Ha! We're the only sane ones here! The men are mad! Stark crazy insane!

KADMOS: Then why are we wasting time? At our age what's there to waste! Here, take my hand.

TEIRESIAS: Yes, yes, I have it. There. Hold tight now. Don't want to lose this old fool, do we?

KADMOS: Fool! That's it! That's it! All fools! That's what they are, these men of Thebes! But I'm no fool. Not me. Not old Kadmos. I'm only a mortal. I don't take any god lightly.

TEIRESIAS: Right you are. Who are we to go around doubting gods? Who exists, who doesn't? Not for me. No, no. I mean, where does that put tradition? You know? Tradition? Our fathers' beliefs, old as time? Nothing can pry those loose for me. Not even wise men, with all their crafty reasoning can ever break their hold on our lives. Leastways not that crazy grandson of yours, that Pentheus. I can just hear them now, the old stick-in-the-muds with their wooly minds, when I twine my head with ivy and go out to dance the god's dance! "Balmy old codger!" they'll say, "and at *his* age! Has he no shame! Vine leaves, indeed!" But this god, this, this, this Dionysos. Tell me, Kadmos, tell me, when did he say that only the young should dance? Hm? That can't be right. No. Cruel! The old, too! And why not? Why not the old, too? No, no! No god ever made such a law. What he wants, this, this Dionysos, this Bakkhos, or whatever it is he's called, he has so many! What he wants is equal honor from all. No one left out. No one. Joy! Joy is all he asks of us!

KADMOS: All right, all right, calm down. Now, I know you're blind as a
bat, you old goat, so let's let *me* be the see-er for once, and—oh
god!—tell you that I see Pentheus coming this way. In a mad rush,
too, in one of his moods. Ekhion's boy, my grandson, the one I gave
my powers to governing Thebes. Just a boy, but what can you do.
And he's moving like a house on fire. I wonder what bee he's got in his
bonnet this time?

PENTHEUS: *(Enters with GUARDS.)* What is this! I demand an answer!
Now! I was out of Thebes when I heard! Some vile eruption of evil
here in the city! Some insanity let loose! Our women lured from
their homes! To frisk in dark nooks in mountain forests in search of
fraudulent ecstasies! Dancing in honor of some upstart divinity! Some
Dionysos, or whatever it is they call him! Possesses women with lewd,
hypnotic spells, or so I've heard! Drinking wine from overflowing
bowls! Hiding in caverns to fuck with lusting males! Sacred Maenad
priestesses they call themselves! Sworn to Bakkhos, they say, but more
at home with Aphroditê, if I have two wits about me!

    Some I've already trapped. Bound and chained in the stables.
The others will be tracked down soon enough. In the mountains.
Once I've locked them in irons in cages, I'll stamp out the vermin of
their obscene orgies!

    And what's this about an intruder? Some newly arrived foreigner
in the city? A wizard sorcerer from Lydia? Curls to his shoulders,
golden, *perfumed!* Cheeks the color of wine! Love spells of Aphroditê
in his eyes! Days and nights he spends with young girls, dangling
before them the obscene *lure* of his orgies. Get him inside these walls,
he'll be done pounding his precious wand and bouncing his curls.
I'll have his head, this stranger who claims Dionysos is a god! Says he's
a god, does he? Sewn into Zeus's thigh? We'll see! Fact is, if anyone is
interested, Dionysos was burned to a crisp along with his mother.
Zeus's lightning punishment for her lie that he was her lover. A man
possessed of such insolence deserves hanging.

    Ah! But here's another miracle! Our ancient seer Teiresias. In
dappled fawn skin, no less. And what's this? Grandfather? Grandfather
Kadmos? Playing the Bakkhant? How can you do this! How can you
make yourself ridiculous! Decked out with your thrashing ivy wand.
Throw it away. You shame me, grandfather! Have you two lost your
minds?

But this is your doing, Teiresias. Not enough gods in Thebes?
You need another? To augment your augurer's business? Larger fees,
hm? All that's saving you now, you doddering fool, is your age. Anything else and you'd be in chains down there in the dungeon with the
Bakkhai. With those who imported these disgusting rites to Thebes.
When the sparkle of wine flows at women's feasts, you know there's
nothing healthy in *those* mysteries.

FIRST BAKKHÊ: This is blasphemy, King Pentheus. You insult the gods,
you insult Kadmos who sowed the dragon's teeth. You're the son of
Ekhion. Are you trying to deny your race?

TEIRESIAS: Give a wise man an honest case to argue and words come easy.
But *your* words, young man, the words that fall easy from *your* tongue,
are neither wise *nor* clever. A man whose strength rests solely in his
self-assurance is a bad citizen. For all his words, he's short on reason.
He's a fool.

This new god you ridicule? There are no words for how great his
fame will be throughout all Hellas. Humankind, young man, has two
great powers. First, the goddess Dêmêter, or whatever you may call
her, earth, perhaps, our source of solid food. And then this god, *this*
god, this Dionysos, son of Semelê. He came later but he matched her
gift when he invented for us the clear liquid juice of the grape. When
we've drunk our fill, it brings an end to sorrow, brings sleep that
drowns the day's cares and worries, the sole, the only remedy for our
distress.

Himself a god, he is poured in honor to the gods, to bring
mankind their blessings. This god is also a prophet. And frenzied
Bakkhic madness inspires prophecy. When the god enters the
possessed like a storm wind, they go mad, raving mad, but they see
the future. And what they see comes true. And Dionysos also helps
the god of War. When an army stands ranged and ready for battle,
they are sometimes struck with panic fear and flee, before raising so
much as a single spear. This madness, too, comes from Dionysos. But
you will see him one day, with his Maenad bands, bounding over the
rocks at Delphi, across the twin peaks of Parnassos, with pine torches,
leaping, whirling, thrashing his Bakkhic wand, great in all of Greece.

Listen to me, Pentheus. Don't mistake that force alone governs
human affairs. And if your mind is sick, don't presume to think

yourself sane. Welcome this god to Thebes. Pour out wine in his honor. Wreathe your head with garlands and dance the Bakkhic dance. As for that matter that causes you so much torment: sex. Oh my boy, Dionysos doesn't suppress lust in a woman. You must look for that in the woman herself, in her nature. Not even at the height of Bakkhic ecstasy will a chaste woman be anything less than chaste. Just think, my boy, the pleasure you take when throngs stand at the gates, magnifying the name of Pentheus. Gods, no less than kings, demand respect. And so, Kadmos and I, for all your scoffing, your insane laughter, will wreathe our heads with ivy, take up our wands, and old and gray as we are, we will dance the god's dance. Two old fools, no doubt, but dance we will, for we have no choice. No logic of yours will persuade me to fight the god. For you are mad, Pentheus, cruelly mad, and no drug can cure your sickness, though a drug must surely have caused it.

FIRST BAKKHÊ: Apollo would agree with you, old Teiresias, and you show wisdom in honoring the mighty god Bromios.

KADMOS: Teiresias advises well, my boy. Stay with us. Don't break with tradition. You're all in the air just now, lost your balance. If, as you believe, this is no god, say, at least, that he is. A pious lie that credits Semelê as mother of a god and honors the whole family. And don't forget how your cousin Aktaion died. His man-eating hounds that he himself had raised tore him to bits on the same mountain where the Bakkhai now dance. He boasted he was a greater hunter than Artemis. Don't let that be you, son. Here, let me crown you with this ivy. Join us. Join us in honoring the god.

PENTHEUS: Don't touch me! Get away from me with that crown! Go play at your Bakkhanals, but don't smear your madness off onto me. Teiresias, your instructor in lunacy, will pay for this where it hurts most. Someone! Go! Go quickly! To this old fool's seat of augury. There where he ponders his birds and their droppings. Pry it up for him. Pry it up with crowbars. Heave it over. Smash it. Raze it to the ground. And when you're done, throw his sacred ribbons to the storm winds. This sacrilege will gall him to the core. The rest will patrol the city for this effeminate, this girlish stranger. He infects our women. Some new disease is afoot. It fouls our beds with his "rituals." Track him down. When you've caught him, tie him up and bring him here to me. He'll die the death he deserves. Death by stoning. He will regret having imported his orgies to Thebes. Go!

(Exeunt GUARDS in haste.)

TEIRESIAS: Poor young fool! How little you know the meaning of your words. You were out of your mind before. Now you're raving. Come, Kadmos. Let's go pray for this brutish man, and for the city, that the god will be patient with us. Come with me. You try to hold *me* up, as I will you. And bring your wand, the god's wand. Two old codgers like us mustn't be caught falling on their faces. What a disgrace that would be. We must go now, to serve Dionysos, son of Zeus. Ah, Kadmos, the name Pentheus means "grief." Let's pray the god brings no grief into your house. This is no prophecy, only fact. The fool speaks folly.

(Exeunt KADMOS and TEIRESIAS; then PENTHEUS into the palace.)

(Music. Song. Dance.)

ASIAN BAKKHAI: *(Sing.)*
    Holiness!
    Reverence!
    Queen among gods!
    Lady sweeping the earth's wide breast
    on wings of gold,
    do you hear?
    Do you hear him?
    Pentheus?
    Hear his unholy insolence against the god?
    Bromios?
    Roaring God?
    Son of Semelê?
    Who at his garlanded celebrations
    is named Prince among the most blessed gods!
    Most holy!
    Blessed! Blessed!
    This is his kingdom,
    his gift:

Dancing,
dancing on the mountains,
joining,
as one,
joining in dance,
together,
dance and laughter,
laughter and the shrieking cry of the flute,
laughter and the end of care,
of grief, of sorrow,
when the sparkle,
the lustrous shimmer of the grape
brightens the gods' feast,
when ivy-wreathed dancers drink deep,
deep,
of the god's wine
and are wrapped in the mantle of sleep.

The unchecked tongue of a foolish man,
the anarchic mind of a man who scorns law,
these,
these lead to ruin,
to disaster;
but wisdom,
good sense,
a peaceful life,
a life of reason,
these,
these remain unshaken,
these sustain,
abide,
these hold,
hold our house together.

Far though they are,
the gods,
far, far though the gods may be,
in the distant sky,
they see us still,

the gods,
the affairs, the ways,
the workings of men.

To have much knowledge,
to hide behind cleverness,
to be proud in one's arrogance,
these,
these are not wisdom,
nor thinking thoughts beyond man's limits.
Life is too brief,
too short,
to grasp at things too great,
to fail to see what is at hand, now:
love,
life's sweetness,
human desire.
The other is a road only madmen pursue,
men of evil in search of such glory,
and it leads to ruin.

Let me go,
oh let me, let me go,
to Kypris, to Kypris,
Aphroditê's island,
where the Loves,
the Loves that beguile,
that divert,
that delight men's hearts,
reside.
Or to Paphos,
Paphos where the hundred-mouthed river,
the alien,
the barbaric river,
unfed by rain,
brings harvests of fruits.
To Pieria, take me,
take me to Pieria,
holy slope of Olympos,

Olympos,
where the Muses dwell;
take me there, Bromios,
divine Bromios,
lead me,
lead your Bakkhants,
lead with your dance,
your holy dancing,
dancing and laughter,
there where your rites are free as the wind,
there where your holy ecstasies reign,
there,
there where the Graces dwell
in sweet content,
where honeyed Desire runs free,
runs free,
holy Desire.

Our god, son of Zeus,
rejoices in festivals.
Our god loves peace,
giver of abundance,
defender of young men's lives.
He gives to all,
to rich, to poor,
in equal measure,
to all,
gives wine,
the griefless joy of wine.
But he hates the man who refuses his gifts,
who refuses to fill his days with calm contentment,
refuses to spend his nights with holy pleasure.
He detests the man who thinks himself superior,
detests the man who knows only excess.
Whatever the common man chooses,
whatever the simple man thinks,
the humble, the lowly,
that, that I choose,
that I take as example,
that I will do.

(Enter PENTHEUS from the palace with SOLDIERS; then a contingent of GUARDS leading DIONYSOS.)

(Music out.)

GUARD: Here he is, King Pentheus, hunted and bound, just as you ordered. But the wild beast was tame, tame as a lamb. Held out his wrists, asked to be tied. No bold attempt at running away. No pale fear in those wine-flushed cheeks. Nothing. The prey even smiled. It was easy. Except it made me ashamed, awkward, even; embarrassed is more like it. I said to him: "Stranger, this isn't me doing this. Pentheus sent me, Pentheus's orders. I just carry them out. Don't blame me." Oh! And then those women! The crazed ones? The ones you captured and chained in the stable? They're gone. Clear out of sight. Dancing for their roaring god on the mountain, calling on Bakkhos! Bakkhos! Roaring Bakkhos! The chains on their ankles snapped and dropped off, and the bolts on the doors came loose, fell to the floor, the doors flew open. No human hand had any part in this, sir. This man who's come to Thebes is a man of miracles. But he's your worry now.

PENTHEUS: Release his hands. He's in my net now and not so nimble he'll escape me. Well. You're not unattractive, I see. Smooth, sleek white body; handsome. I'll bet you put women in a whirl. Yes, well, but that's why you've come to Thebes. I look at you and I see you don't wrestle. Oh, yes. I can tell. Hmm. Whatever would you do with all those curls cascading down those ivory, wine-flushed cheeks? But handsome is, I guess, as handsome does. And such fair smooth skin. No harsh sunlight for you. Our beauty prefers the shade for hunting. Aphroditê? So, then, who are you? I see. Nothing? Well, then, where were you born?

DIONYSOS: Ah, an easy one. I have no secrets. You've heard of Tmolos? The flowery mountain?

PENTHEUS: That holds the city of Sardis in its arms.

DIONYSOS: So now you know. I call Lydia home.

PENTHEUS: These orgies of yours, why do you bring them to Greece?

DIONYSOS: Dionysos ordered it. Dionysos? Son of Zeus?

PENTHEUS: Ah, then you have a Zeus who spawns new gods?

DIONYSOS: No, no, *your* Zeus. The Zeus who bedded Semelê.

PENTHEUS: Was it in a dream that he possessed you?

DIONYSOS: No no, face to face; gave me his power.

PENTHEUS: Describe for me these mysteries of yours.

DIONYSOS: How can I do that? To a nonbeliever?

PENTHEUS: And what good are they to those who *do* believe?

DIONYSOS: That's not for you to know. But they're worth it.

PENTHEUS: How very clever you are at making me curious.

DIONYSOS: God's orgies deal cruelly with the nonbeliever.

PENTHEUS: This god you've laid your eyes on. What's he like?

DIONYSOS: You mean what form does he take? He's not choosy.

PENTHEUS: Why do you do that! Never finish a thought!

DIONYSOS: Well, speak sense to a fool, he'll think you a fool.

PENTHEUS: Is Thebes this god's first stop on his whirlwind tour?

DIONYSOS: Oh, no. All Asia dances his dance.

PENTHEUS: Asians are not Greeks! They're barbaric fools!

DIONYSOS: Not in this case. They just see life differently.

PENTHEUS: These orgies, when do you hold them? Day or night?

DIONYSOS: Night, mostly. There's greater solemnity in the dark.

PENTHEUS: Easier to rape women is what you mean!

DIONYSOS: Yes, well, some dig up dirt even in daylight.

PENTHEUS: I'll see to it you pay for your cynic's wit!

DIONYSOS: As the god will pay you for your provocation.

PENTHEUS: Our mystery priest wrestles well with words!

DIONYSOS: How will you punish me? Will it be brutal?

PENTHEUS: The first thing I'll shear are those girlish lovelocks!

DIONYSOS: Careful. My hair is holy. I keep it for god.

PENTHEUS: Then that wand. Give it to me. Now!

DIONYSOS: Take it yourself. It's his, you know—the god's.

PENTHEUS: You're *my* quarry now! You're bound for prison!

DIONYSOS: Yes, but the god will free me whenever I ask.

PENTHEUS: Call him, you and your Bakkhai! I said *call him!*

DIONYSOS: No need. He's here. Now. He sees what I'm suffering.

PENTHEUS: Here? Where? I said where! I see *nothing!*

DIONYSOS: Where I am, Pentheus. There's no sight without faith.

PENTHEUS: Seize him! He's mocking us! Thebes! Me!

DIONYSOS: I'm the sane one. I won't be bound by a madman.

PENTHEUS: Chain him! I'm in command here! *I* command!

DIONYSOS: Command? You can't command your own life. Do you know what you're saying, Pentheus? I doubt it. You don't even know who you are.

PENTHEUS: I am Pentheus, son of Ekhion and Agavê!

DIONYSOS: Pentheus—you will live to repent that name.

PENTHEUS: Take him! Chain him! Lock him in the stable. There he can have all the darkness he wants. You can dance your dances down there in the dark. And I know your kind of dancing. As for your women accomplices in evil, they're mine now. Slaves. I may sell them, or put them to work at my palace looms. I'll have peace, then. No more beating, beating, beating their maddening drums. Bind him!

DIONYSOS: I'll go now, Pentheus. Why stay? But how can I suffer a fate that isn't mine? Not possible, is it? But you outrage Dionysos when you deny him, and he'll have his revenge. Be certain of that. Your ropes punish me. And when you punish me you punish the god.

(Exeunt GUARDS leading DIONYSOS, followed by PENTHEUS.)

(Music. Song. Dance.)

ASIAN BAKKHAI: *(Sing.)*
    Dirkê!
    Queen!
    Blessèd child of Acheloös!
    It was into your waters that
    Zeus dipped his son,
    his infant son,
    our god,
    snatched from Semelê's womb
    and his everlasting flame,
    and nestled him safely
    deep in his thigh,
    calling:

FIRST BAKKHÊ: *(Chants.)*
   "Enter, Dithyrambos!
  Enter, Twice-born,
  my male womb!
  Bakkhos you are,
  and as Bakkhos will be known
  to all of Thebes!"

ASIAN BAKKHAI: *(Sing.)*
   Why, then, blessèd Dirkê,
  why do you reject me,
  why turn from me,
  flowing swiftly past,
  why,
  when I come to dance,
  garlanded with ivy and bryony,
  on your banks,
  do you shun me?
  And yet it will come,
  come soon,
  soon,
  as surely as there is delight,
  as surely as there is pleasure and joy,
  grace,
  in the clusters of Dionysos's vine,
  when the name of Bromios will have meaning for you.

  Rage,
  what rage he shows,
  what rage this earth child,
  Pentheus, shows,
  Pentheus, bred of the dragon's teeth,
  sired of earthborn Ekhion,
  Pentheus, wild-faced monster,
  Pentheus who slanders his human form;
  not a man, but, like the murderous giants,
  dares to do battle with the gods,
  and will dare,
  dare soon,

soon,
to cast me in chains,
the god's servant,
in a dark dungeon,
where now,
even now,
he has thrown my companion,
my fellow dancer,
my leader.

Do you see, Dionysos,
do you see, son of Zeus,
do you see our suffering,
our battle with oppression?
Come, come,
come down from Olympos,
come down, lord,
brandishing,
brandishing your golden wand,
put an end to this man of blood,
end his arrogant,
his insolent reign.

Where are you?
Where are you, Roarer?
On Nysa,
Nysa the nurturer of beasts?
Leading your dancing bands of Maenads?
Leading them on with your whirling wand?
Or coursing the Korykian peaks of Parnassos?
Or are you now there in the forests of Olympos
where Orpheus once, with the sound of his lyre
and the honey-sweet spell of his voice,
summoned trees and wild beasts with his song?

Oh blessèd Pieria,
honored of Dionysos,
he will come,
the god,

he will come with his rites,
come to you with his dances,
his swirling Bakkhants,
pounding their wands,
to dance his Bakkhic dance down your slopes,
and then ford fast-flowing Axios,
and with his Maenads
cross over that father of rivers,
Lydias,
river that brings man wealth and blessing,
and with its loveliest of waters
enriches that land of good horses.

(The voice of DIONYSOS is heard from the palace.)

DIONYSOS: *(Chants.)*
    IOOOOO!
    IOOOOO!
    Bakkhants!
    Listen!
    Bakkhants!
    Bakkhants, hear me!

ASIAN BAKKHAI: *(Chant.)*
    Who!
    Whose voice!
    Whose voice is that!
    Where?
    That voice?
    The god calls me!
    Where is he?

DIONYSOS: *(Chants.)*
    IOOOOO!
    IOOOOO!
    I call again!
    Son of Zeus!
    Son of Semelê!
    Again!

ASIAN BAKKHAI: *(Chant.)*
    IOOOOO!
    IOOOOO!
    Come to us, lord!
    Be with us!
    Come!
    To our revels!
    Master!
    Come!

DIONYSOS: *(Chants.)*
    Poseidon!
    God of Earthquake!
    Be here!
    Heave!
    Heave the world's floor!
    Rumble! Make it
    rumble to its foundations!

ASIAN BAKKHAI: *(Chant.)*
    AIIIIIII!
    AIIIIIII!
    Look! Look!
    The palace!
    Collapsing!
    Shuddering!
    Tumbling!
    The lintels split!
    Columns shatter!
    Dionysos!
    Dionysos is there!
    In the ruins!
    Bromios!
    The Roarer!
    The god in triumph!

DIONYSOS: *(Chants.)*
    Kindle!
    Kindle the lightning bolt's flame!

Burn down!
Burn down the palace of
Pentheus!

ASIAN BAKKHAI: *(Chant.)*
Look there!
Look!
Semelê's tomb!
Flames!
New flames!
How it blazes!
Flames the thunder god
left long ago!

FIRST BAKKHÊ: *(Chants.)*
Maenads!
Down!
Down to the ground!
Quickly!
Quickly!

ASIAN BAKKHAI: *(Chant.)*
He's coming!
He's coming!
Our king!
Our god!
Son of Zeus!
Destroyer of Pentheus's palace!
AIIIIIIIII!

(Enter DIONYSOS from the palace.)

DIONYSOS: *(Speaks.)* Ah! My women! My Bakkhai! My Asian Bakkhants! What frightened you to fall on your faces? Rise! Come! Your fear is over. It was Bakkhos, Bakkhos who shivered the timbers of Pentheus's palace. No more trembling. Come!

FIRST BAKKHÊ: *(Chants.)*
Oh light of our lives!

Our lives are light
when you shout like a god!
We were alone!
Now we're safe.

DIONYSOS: *(Speaks.)* Were you in despair, women, when they led me into
Pentheus's snare? Deep into his dark dungeons?

FIRST BAKKHÊ: *(Chants.)*
In despair!
Lost!
Without you,
what protection do we have?
You, locked in that godless man's jail!
How did you escape?

DIONYSOS: *(Speaks.)* I freed myself. Easily. No effort.

FIRST BAKKHÊ: *(Chants.)*
But he bound your hands,
your arms!

DIONYSOS: *(Speaks.)* Ah! And what a fool I made of him there!
He thought he was tying me, but never touched me. An illusion.
A hallucination. Feeding on his black desires. Down there in the dark
dungeon where he meant to lock me, he sees a bull, mistaking its
body for mine. Panting, heaving for breath, in a rage, sweat spilling
from his steaming flesh, he struggles to tie its legs and hooves.
So great is his effort his teeth draw blood from his lips.
      And I? I sit quietly. Watching. Watching. Very near. But then
Bakkhos comes, comes out of nowhere, revealing himself, shaking the
palace, rocking, rocking, causing flames to shoot up on Semelê's tomb,
his mother's tomb; and seeing it, Pentheus supposes the palace on fire.
But just between us, the only fire is in Pentheus's mind. "Fire," he
screams, running this way and that in a mad panic, "fire, bring water,
the river!" All in vain. There was so much confusion. But he leaves his
fire fighting, suspecting that I've escaped, and off he sets on the chase,
hacking his way through the palace with his murderous dark sword.
Oh, and he gets what he's after. For Roaring Bromios conjures a

phantom in the courtyard. At least I think so, it's only a guess.
A shining, luminous phantom of—who else? Me!

Well, once Pentheus catches sight of this, he leaps at his prey
like a madman, lunging, stabbing at the shimmering form in front of
him, thinking it's me he's slaughtering. But Bakkhos wasn't finished
with him yet! To top it off, he reduces the palace to rubble, down into
dust it falls; this foolish man's reward for jailing me. Too spent to
continue the fight, he drops his sword and collapses in a daze: a
man, nothing more, just a man who tried to battle a god. The
entertainment complete, I walk out here to you, without a care in the
world for poor Pentheus.

But are those boots I hear? Tramping through the courtyard?
He's bound to be here soon, heaving with arrogant contempt. But I'll
keep a cool head on my shoulders; it behooves a wise man to practice
self-control.

(Music out.)

PENTHEUS: *(Enters from the palace with GUARDS.)* Horror! Horror! Escaped! The stranger! I had him in chains! In there! ÉA! ÉA! You! Here!
The gate! What are you doing! How did you escape!

DIONYSOS: Quiet, there. Quiet, Pentheus. Easy does it.

PENTHEUS: How, how, how did you escape your chains?

DIONYSOS: Didn't I say I'd be freed? Next time, listen.

PENTHEUS: I can't keep up with your strangeness! Who freed you!

DIONYSOS: The Very One whose gift to man is wine.

PENTHEUS: Guards! Surround the city! Seal off the gates!

DIONYSOS: Now, Pentheus, since when can gods not leap walls?

PENTHEUS: Clever! Clever! But not where it counts! Not there!

DIONYSOS: Not so, Pentheus. Clever where it counts the most. But don't listen to me, listen to him; he comes from the mountain with news for you. And don't worry about us; we'll be here waiting when you've finished. We're here to stay.

HERDSMAN: *(Enters.)* Pentheus, King of Thebes, I've come from Kithairon.

PENTHEUS: Say it! This "urgent" news of yours!

HERDSMAN: I've seen those holy women of Thebes, sir. The sacred Bakkhai who ran from the city, barefoot, half-naked in their frenzy, swift as flights of spears. I'm here, sir, come down from high Kithairon, to tell you and the whole city what amazing things they're doing, those women, things even greater than miracles. But I need to know, sir, should I speak freely, or should I trim my tale? I'm afraid of your temper, sir, your royal rage.

PENTHEUS: Speak freely. Whatever your story, I won't hurt you. The more terrible the things you tell me, the more terrible will be the punishment of that man there. All their vileness comes from him.

HERDSMAN: Yes, sir. Well, you see, sir, my cattle were climbing the steep rocky terrain to the high meadows to graze. The sun had just risen, the chill burning off the mountain pastures, when suddenly I see them, all three of them, all three bands of dancing women.

Autonoê led the first, the second your mother Agavê, and Ino the third. They were fast asleep, lying where exhaustion had dropped them; some leaning back against pine boughs, others resting their heads on pillows of oak leaves on the forest floor. Carelessly, perhaps, but modestly. Wine, yes, but not drunk, not as you say, sir, not driven to frenzy by shrieking flutes, not searching for sex on the mountain.

Suddenly, your mother hears the lowing of cattle, and in a single leap stands upright among the sleeping Bakkhai, shrieking a holy ritual shriek to wake them. In a single movement, shaking the sleep from their eyes, they spring to their feet, old women and young, sir, girls not yet married; a sight of such ordered beauty, sir! They first shake free their hair to flow down their backs; and those whose fawn-skin straps had slipped in the night refasten them. But then, then I saw a sight that stole my breath! Around their dappled

fawn-skin waists are snakes that curl upward and lick their cheeks!
I saw women, new mothers, who had left behind their babies, whose
breasts ached, relieve themselves by suckling young gazelles or wild
wolf cubs with their milk. On their heads they wear wreaths of ivy,
bryony, and oak leaves. One of them seizes a wand and strikes a rock:
an icy stream leaps out. Another plunges her wand into the earth: up
springs Bakkhos in a flood of wine. Those eager for milk scratch the
ground with their fingers: milk streams out. And pure honey spurts
from the head of their wands!

If you had been there, Pentheus, if you had seen with your eyes
the miracles these women performed, you would have knelt in prayer
to this god you condemn. We herdsmen ended up babbling all at
once, wildly competing with stories of the strange and wonderful
things we'd seen them do. Then one of the men, a vagrant, a fast
talker who hangs around town and has a way with words, says:
"You men who live on the high mountains, listen! What do you say
we hunt down Pentheus's mother Agavê, drag her from these Bakkhic
revels and haul her on down to Pentheus? He might even be obliged!"

What he said seemed right at the time, so we lay up an ambush,
crawling under bushes and other covering till we're well hid. Then,
as if signaled from some unseen source, the women raise high their
whirling wands and follow with them into headlong twirling,
spinning, reeling, crying out to Iakkhos! Bromios! Child of Zeus!
Roaring God! As one voice! And all the mountain and all its wild
creatures join in the Bakkhic dance, god-possessed, and all things
move with them as they move!

When Agavê comes leaping past me, I spring out to take her,
except she's howling now at the top of her lungs: "Sisters! My stalking
hounds! We're being hunted! These men! Follow me! We'll rout them
with our wands!"

If we hadn't run, run hard, they'd have torn us apart. With bare
hands, no weapons, they charge into the grazing cattle. One girl holds
in her hands the widespread legs of a young heifer with tight udders,
shrieking as she tries to tear it apart. Others rip full-grown cows into
pieces, tossing limbs and severed ribs and hooves every which way to
be caught up by the boughs of trees where they hang smeared with
gore, dripping blood, ragged flesh hanging from firs. Bulls, arrogant,
anger mounting in their horns, are tripped and wrestled to the earth
and dragged by the soft hands of young girls. So many, you can't

count! And stripped of their flesh faster than you can blink your royal eyes, sir!

Then off they set, flying, they run so fast, soaring out over the plains of the Asopos, grazing in their flight the wheat fields of Thebes, till they swoop down like an invading army on the foothill villages of Hysia and Erythra below Kithairon's massif! And there they wreak such havoc, plundering, everything upside down, carting off children from their homes, and what they throw on their backs stays put, unstrapped, even bronze and iron. They carry fire in their soft hair, these women, where it sparkles and flashes but never burns. Enraged by the plundering Bakkhants, the people take up arms and move against them.

What happened then, sir, was terrible and strange to see. The men's sharp-pointed spears draw no blood, but the wands the women hurl do great damage, making the men turn and run in panic. Men defeated by women! Oh, a god is with them! The women then returned to the place where the god had made the spring gush from the earth and they washed away the blood, and snakes licked the drops from their cheeks. Who this god is, master, I don't know, but welcome him to Thebes; he has great power in other things as well. They also say it was he who gave us wine that eases heartache. Lose wine and we lose sexual love and every other pleasure.

FIRST BAKKHÊ: I'm afraid to speak freely in front of a tyrant, sir; I'm trembling; but I'll say it: there is no god greater than Dionysos.

PENTHEUS: Fire! Fire! Raging! Too close, too close! This Bakkhic insolence pounds at our gates! Act now or all Greece reviles us! Captain of the Guard! To the Êlektran Gate! Fast! Bring on the heavy infantry! Our fastest horsemen! Now! Shields! Lances! Every man who makes a bowstring hum! We march against the Bakkhai! This has gone too far! We've endured enough from these women!

(Exeunt CAPTAIN OF THE GUARD with his men; then the HERDSMAN.)

DIONYSOS: You listen, Pentheus, but you fail to learn. You haven't treated me well, but I'll warn you again. Don't take up arms against a god. Be at peace. Bromios won't have it. Don't drive his women from the mountain that rings with the joy of his cry.

PENTHEUS: You! No preaching! You've escaped your dungeon! You're free! Don't tempt me, I'll do it again!

DIONYSOS: In your shoes, I'd sacrifice to him rather than kick against the pricks; a man battling a god.

PENTHEUS: Oh, I'll sacrifice to him, all right. The blood of his women. The women I'll slaughter. Kithairon will stream with their blood.

DIONYSOS: You'll be routed. All of you. What a disgrace. Bronze shields turned aside by the wands of women.

PENTHEUS: Where do I grip this stranger for a fall! How do I pin him! One way or the other he has his way!

DIONYSOS: Friend, there's still time to make peace.

PENTHEUS: Peace? How? By being a slave to my slaves?

DIONYSOS: I'll lead your women back home without weapons.

PENTHEUS: Yes, I know! Another of your "clever" tricks!

DIONYSOS: Trick? What trick? When my arts can save you?

PENTHEUS: You conspire with these women to save your rites!

DIONYSOS: Conspire? Yes. Except that I conspire with the god.

PENTHEUS: Bring out my armor! And *you! Stop talking!*

DIONYSOS: Wait! Would you like to see them there on the mountain?

PENTHEUS: I would even give gold to see that sight!

DIONYSOS: Ah! Suddenly we're all in a passion, are we?

PENTHEUS: Well—not if they were drunk, I wouldn't.

DIONYSOS: But you'd still enjoy it, even if it pained you?

PENTHEUS: Yes. In secret, hiding under the pines.

DIONYSOS: Yes, but they'll track you down, hidden or not.

PENTHEUS: Out in the open, then. That's a good point.

DIONYSOS: Ready, then, are we? All set to be led?

PENTHEUS: Yes. Let's not waste time. This is torture.

DIONYSOS: Your body needs the protection of a linen dress.

PENTHEUS: Linen dress? I'm a man! Why change my sex?

DIONYSOS: Yes, but you're a dead duck if they see you're a man.

PENTHEUS: Ah! Another good point. How clever you are.

DIONYSOS: Dionysos himself taught me this.

PENTHEUS: How do we put your advice into action?

DIONYSOS: We'll just go inside and you'll let me dress you.

PENTHEUS: No, no, not a dress! I'd be ashamed!

DIONYSOS: Lost our passion to see, have we? Pity!

PENTHEUS: Well, then, well, I guess. What kind of dress?

DIONYSOS: You'll even wear a wig. With long curls.

PENTHEUS: Yes? I see. And then? What next? Hm?

DIONYSOS: Skirts to the feet and a net to hold your curls.

PENTHEUS: Curls. Yes. Anything else? That all, then?

DIONYSOS: Not quite. A wand for your hand and a dappled fawn skin.

PENTHEUS: No! I can't! Not a dress! *No!*

DIONYSOS: Blood will flow on Kithairon if you fight the Bakkhai.

PENTHEUS: Right. Yes. First we'll reconnoiter.

DIONYSOS: It's always better than hunting evil with evil.

PENTHEUS: Alright, but how will I get through the city unseen?

DIONYSOS: No problem. The streets are deserted. I'll lead the way.

PENTHEUS: Anything, just so the Bakkhai don't mock me. Let's go in. I'll decide on the best strategy.

DIONYSOS: Whatever you decide, Pentheus, I'm ready.

PENTHEUS: Yes, I think I'll go in now. When I come out, I'll either be with my men—or take your advice. *(Exit into palace)*

DIONYSOS: Women! Our fish has taken the lure! Fast in our net! He'll see the Bakkhai, and lose his life! Dionysos! It's in your hands now! I feel you near! I sense you! Give this man what he deserves! But make him a little more mad, some dizzy fantasy, set his mind reeling. In his right mind he'll never dress in women's dress. With the urging of some small delirium, he'll fight to get it on. PENTHEUS LAUGHINGSTOCK OF THEBES! That's how they'll see him, these Thebans, as I march him off through Thebes, looking every inch the cunt! Just payment for all the shit he shoveled at us!
　　I'll go in now and dress him. He'll wear finery on his way to Hades. And his mother will help. Tear him limb from limb. And so farewell. Then he'll know the son of Zeus. Dionysos. Cruelest of the gods to man. And the sweetest. *(Exit into palace.)*
(Music. Song. Dance.)

ASIAN BAKKHAI: *(Sing.)*
When,
when will I again,
when again will I dance,
ever dance the nightlong dances,
white foot stomping in Bakkhic revelry,
barefoot sweeping the meadow's cool grass,
when again,
when,
will I toss,
toss my head,
toss back my head,
throat bared,
hair,
hair flowing,
streaming in flight,
ecstatic abandon,
whirling,
whirling in the dark-sweet dew of heaven,
like a fawn frisking in the meadow's green joy,
freed of the huntsman urging his hounds,
the terrible chase,
the racing pack,
beyond the watchers,
bounding,
bounding over nets,
well-woven,
dashing, straining,
swift as the wind gusting through passes,
bounding over water meadows,
rejoicing in nature freed of men
and in the soft green shimmer of the forest?

What is wisdom?
What?
Or what fairer gift can the gods give
than to rule the enemy with a powerful fist?
Honor is always a prize to be sought.

The gods advance slowly,
slowly,
but they advance,
advance surely;
seeming never to happen,
it happens,
the gods' power over men,
men who are foolish,
for the gods will chastise them,
chastise for their foolishness,
arrogant men,
men who honor brutality,
whose mad delusion leads them,
guides them,
to dishonor the gods.
But the gods have time,
time on their side,
time to wait,
slow-stepping time,
and cunning,
devious,
they lie in wait for the impious man,
the man without gods,
they put him at ease,
and then, then,
with a vengeance,
hunt him down,
hunt, hunt,
hunt him down.
The foolish man breaks Nature's law,
the ancient law,
longstanding custom,
which says:
Honor all the gods.
It costs so little,
so little,
this honor;
whatever it is,
whatever divinity is,

whatever,
it is power.

What is wisdom?
What?
Or what fairer gift can the gods give
than to rule the enemy with a powerful fist?
Honor is always a prize to be sought.

There is the happiness of the sailor,
tossed by the sea,
who has safely come to port;
there is the happiness of the man
who has triumphed over toil;
the happiness of one outstripping another
in the race for prosperity and power;
and for countless others there are countless hopes,
some fulfilled, some denied;
but of all that I call truly blessed,
the most blessed of all is the man whose life,
day by day,
is happy.

(Music out.)

DIONYSOS: *(Enters from the palace.)* You! Pentheus! Come out! Come out,
you pervert, so eager to see what you shouldn't! Spying on your
mother and her women! You! Pentheus! It's you I want! Let's see you!
A woman! A crazed female! A Bakkhant! *(Enter PENTHEUS from the
palace followed by a MALE SLAVE.)* Well, now, what have we here! A
dead ringer for a daughter of Kadmos!

PENTHEUS:

I see   see two suns
burning   burning   burning
and Thebes   Thebes   seven gates
double   double   and you
you are a bull   leading me   there!
AI!   AI!   horns!

horns!   were you   always a beast?
you are one   now!   a bull!

DIONYSOS: It's the god you see. Friendly now. With us. Now you see as
you ought.

PENTHEUS: Tell me? How do I look? Like Ino? Or more like my mother?
Hm?

DIONYSOS: Two peas in a pod aren't more like. Oh mercy! A naughty
curl's come loose! Here, let me tuck it back in its snood.

PENTHEUS: Inside, I was dancing, practicing, you know? Like a true
Bakkhant. It shook out then, surely. Let me show you.

DIONYSOS: There, there, there! Hold still, now. I'm your maid, you see.
We'll teach this rowdy curl to behave.

PENTHEUS: Oh, yes, please! You're in command now.

DIONYSOS: There! That's better! Oh, but now your sash is undone. The
pleats aren't hanging straight at the ankles.

PENTHEUS: What a bother! I can see. There on the right. Oh! But on the
left it couldn't be better. See?

DIONYSOS: We'll soon be bosom buddies, Pentheus, when you see the
Bakkhai on their best behavior.

PENTHEUS: Oh dear! Now how do I hold this wand! Like so? Hm? Right
or left hand?

DIONYSOS: The right, yes, and advance it now with each right step. My,
how you've changed!

PENTHEUS: I feel I could carry all of Kithairon, its crags and its dancing
women, on these shoulders!

DIONYSOS: Indeed you could! Before, your mind was sick, but now it's just as I want it.

PENTHEUS: Will we need a crowbar? Or will my hands do to tear up the peaks arm and shoulder?

DIONYSOS: Now, now! None of that! No destroying the shrines of the nymphs! And surely not the haunts where Pan does his piping.

PENTHEUS: Right! Brute force to conquer women? Who needs it! I'll hide in a fir tree.

DIONYSOS: You'll hide, yes! And just the right place for a Peeping-Tom Maenad-watcher like you!

PENTHEUS: Oh, I can see them now in their thickets, pumping away, naked as jaybirds!

DIONYSOS: Ah, the very sight you came to see! Unless, of course, they see you first.

PENTHEUS: Take me through Thebes! Through the streets of Thebes! Now! Show them the man to dare this dangerous deed!

DIONYSOS: The weight of Thebes is already on your shoulders. Yours alone. The ordeal that awaits you is uniquely yours, Pentheus. Come, I'll take you safely. Another will bring you back.

PENTHEUS: My mother!

DIONYSOS: An example for all,

PENTHEUS: It's why I've come!

DIONYSOS: you will ride home

PENTHEUS: Ah! How regal!

DIONYSOS: in your mother's arms.

PENTHEUS: You're determined to spoil me!

DIONYSOS: Spoil you? Oh, in my way, I suppose.

PENTHEUS: And I'll have what I deserve!

DIONYSOS: What a remarkable man you are! Remarkable, indeed!
And the fate you will meet will be no less remarkable! It will lift you
towering to the heavens! *(Invoking.)* Agavê! Hear! Hear me, daughters
of Kadmos! Spread wide your arms! I bring you this boy for his grand
ordeal. Bromios and I will be the victors. The rest the event will reveal.

(Exeunt PENTHEUS and DIONYSOS, followed by the MALE SLAVE.)

(Music. Song. Dance.)

ASIAN BAKKHAI: *(Sing.)*
Now,
now,
to the mountains,
now to the mountains,
follow him,
now,
now,
hounds of Madness from Lyssa's pack,
hounds of Frenzy,
to Kadmos's daughters,
where they dance,
where they dance,
dance,
in their furious revels;
goad them,
sting them,
plunge them into madness,
the daughters of Kadmos,
sting them to fury against the maniac spy,
the frenzied spy,
this boy who hides in the clothes of a woman.
His mother will see him first as he spies,

spies from a smooth stone cliff or treetop.
"Maenads," she will cry:

FIRST BAKKHÊ: *(Sings.)*
    "Maenads!
    Who is this?
    Who?
    Who is this
    come to spy?
    Come to the mountains
    to spy on our revels?
    The mountains!
    The mountains!
    To spy on the mountain
    dancers of Kadmos?
    What creature bore him?
    No woman!
    No woman's blood bore him!
    Some lioness!
    Some Lydian Gorgon!
    Some monster of darkness!"

ASIAN BAKKHAI: *(Sing.)*
    Come, Vengeance, come!
    Vengeance, come!
    Now!
    So all may see!
    Vengeance with sword drawn!
    Butchering Vengeance!
    Sword through the throat!
    To slaughter,
    slaughter the godless,
    the lawless,
    slaughter,
    slaughter,
    the unrighteous earthborn
    offspring of Ekhion!

    He tries,

that rebel,
that lawless man,
to rage against your mysteries,
Bakkhos,
rage against your mother's rites,
and in his madness,
in his fit of delusion,
he struggles insanely,
in a frenzy,
to conquer what cannot be conquered.
But judgments about the gods,
false judgments,
are answered by none but death,
and death accepts no evasions.
To give the gods their due is best,
accept mortality and live a quiet,
a peaceful life.
I do not grudge the wise their wisdom;
but my joy is to hunt what is noble,
what is manifest,
to let my life flow toward beauty,
to revere those great values that lead,
day and night,
to goodness and purity,
rejecting those customs that lie outside justice,
to honor the gods

Come, Vengeance, come!
Vengeance, come!
Now!
So all may see!
Vengeance with sword drawn!
Butchering Vengeance!
Sword through the throat!
To slaughter,
slaughter the godless,
the lawless,
slaughter,
slaughter,

the unrighteous earthborn
offspring of Ekhion!

Bakkhos!
Appear!
Roarer!
Appear!
Show us now the grand beast you are!
A BULL!
A SNAKE WITH A THOUSAND HEADS!
A LION IN FLAMES!
Show us!
Show us!
Go, Bakkhos!
Bakkhos, go!
Go where your Maenads dance in your honor!
Now be the HUNTER,
now, now,
hunt HIM,
the would-be hunter,
and smiling,
oh, smiling,
noose his neck,
smiling,
trip him up,
smiling,
pull him down,
smiling down,
down,
to fall among the deadly herd of your Maenads!

(Music out.)

MALE SLAVE: *(Enters.)* Oh house once so blessed in all Hellas! House
descended from old Kadmos who sowed in this soil the dragon's
earthborn harvest, I who am only a slave weep for you now!

FIRST BAKKHÊ: What news have you brought from the Bakkhai?

MALE SLAVE: Pentheus, the son of Ekhion, is dead.

FIRST BAKKHÊ: Bromios! Lord! Your godhead is revealed!

MALE SLAVE: How can you rejoice at my master's fate?

FIRST BAKKHÊ: Now I will shout my barbaric joy! I was an alien here, a stranger, and I was chained like a slave! But now, now I'm free of that fear!

MALE SLAVE: No, there are still men in Thebes who will—

FIRST BAKKHÊ: Men! Let them make their threats! Dionysos! Dionysos rules me! Not Thebes!

MALE SLAVE: I understand, but how can you rejoice at so evil a disaster?

FIRST BAKKHÊ: No, it was your master who was evil! But tell me, tell me how he died!

MALE SLAVE: The three of us set out, Pentheus and I, and the stranger who was to guide us to these mysteries. We passed the last of the farms beyond the city and forded the Asopos. Then we began the steep ascent to Kithairon's rocky heights.

When we arrived, we came to a halt in a grassy glen, knowing we couldn't be far. We were silent, moved without sound across soft grass, wanting to see without being seen. And then we saw. Down a gorge with dizzying cliffs on either side. A valley watered by many streams and shaded by dark pines. There we saw them, the Maenads, sitting, sitting in an open glade, busy with pleasant tasks. Some wove fresh ivy-leaf crowns to top their damaged wands. Others, like fillies, freed of the painted yoke, sang Bakkhic songs in answer to one another.

But Pentheus was in agony to see the women. "Stranger," he said, "I can't see them, can't see from where we stand, can't make out these licentious Maenads! But from the top of that fir tree at the edge I could see without obstruction their obscene antics."

That's when it happened. That's when this miracle that so amazed me happened. The stranger reaches far into the sky, seizes the topmost, heaven-piercing branch of the towering fir, and guides it down, down, down to the dark earth, till it bends like a taut bow, or a rim of wood forced to the shape of a wheel. He, the stranger, took that mountain fir and with his hands pulled it down till it made a circle. This was the work of no mortal man. Then, seating Pentheus on the top branches, he gently lets it rise, that young tree, his hands firm around the trunk, holding it steady not to unseat the rider. Up it towered, sheer to the sheer heaven, with my master on its back. But high as he rode, he still could not see the Maenads, though they saw him, coming into sight on his lofty perch.

At that moment the stranger disappears, and a voice sounds from deep in the sky. Dionysos it must have been, the god, and cries in a roar: "Women! He's here! I've brought him! The man who mocks us! You, me, our rites! Revenge!"

As the voice spoke, all at once, a shaft of holy light bound together heaven and earth with its radiance. Everything hushed, all nature, sky above, forest below, all leaves stilled, no cry of wild creatures. Nothing. No sound. Silence.

The Maenads, who had not heard the voice clearly, leapt to their feet, standing still, and searched the woods with their eyes. And again the voice roared, commanding. And recognizing the Bakkhic god, the daughters of Kadmos took off like a flock of speeding doves.

Agavê his mother, her sisters, all the Bakkhants, swarming across the glade and the torrenting streams, leaping over jagged rocks and boulders, up the sheer side of the cliff, maddened with the breath the god blew into them. They saw him now, the Bakkhai. Pentheus in his tree. And scrambling up a rock towering opposite him, they pelted him with stones and branches of firs. Some threw wands, but nothing reached him, their aim was dreadful. He was too high, too far above their frenzied passion, treed, poor miserable man, cut off from escape.

Then with the speed of lightning, they stripped off branches of oak and used them to uproot the tree at its base. But, no. Again they failed. At this, Agavê cries out: "Women! Circle the tree! Hands on the trunk! Let us capture the climbing beast or he will reveal the secrets of the god's dances!"

Hands in the thousands lay hold and, as one, wrench the tree free of the earth. And Pentheus, falling from his high perch, down, down, whirling, spinning, one long moan as he falls, smashes to the black earth, knowing his end was near.

His mother as priestess of the slaughter is the first to fall upon him. Ripping the band from his head, and with it the wig, to show her who he is, to stop her killing him, he reaches out to touch her cheek, poor woman, screaming: "Mother! It's me! Pentheus! Your son! Born to the house of Ekhion! I've made mistakes, Mother! I'm your son! Don't kill me!"

But Agavê, foaming at the mouth, her eyes rolling in her head, not in her own mind, possessed utterly by Dionysos, Pentheus's pleas mean nothing to her. Grasping his left arm below the elbow, she digs her foot into his rib cage and pulls the arm loose of its socket. Not of her own strength, but the god's, making her dreadful work an easy task.

Ino went at him from the other side, clawing, ripping off pieces of flesh, while Autonoê and the rest of the pack swarm over him with one long scream, his, with the little breath he has left, and theirs, drowning him out with shrieks of triumph. One bears off an arm, another a foot with the boot still on, and his ribs are laid clean with the flesh stripped away. And all those women, hands thick with his blood, play ball with Pentheus's flesh.

His body now lies scattered across the mountain, parts fallen to the foot of the cliff, parts lying in forest darkness, not easy to gather up. And his head, his piteous head, found by his mother, who thinks it a mountain lion's and has spiked it onto the tip of her wand, she carries home across Kithairon, leaving behind her sisters and the other Maenads, still celebrating.

Crying triumph, she enters the gates of Thebes, enters within our walls, exulting, brandishing her ghastly trophy, calling on Bakkhos, her fellow huntsman, her comrade in the kill, her partner in victory. But the victor's crown he brings her is nothing but tears.

I'll go now, go before she comes home, stay clear away of this calamity. Wisdom is knowing the will of the gods and doing as they ask. There is nothing wiser for man. *(Exit.)*

(Music. Song. Dance.)

ASIAN BAKKHAI: *(Sing.)*
Dance!
Let us dance!
Let us stamp our feet for Bakkhos!

Let us sing!
Sing the calamity of Pentheus!
Pentheus,
spawn of the dragon's seed!
Pentheus who put on woman's dress!
Took in his hand the green shaft of fennel!
Miracle wand!
Wand of death!
Pentheus,
led by a bull to disaster!
To Hades!

Theban Bakkhants!
What a famous song of victory you have made!
Glorious hymn!
Hymn of triumph that ends in wailing,
in mourning,
in tears,
tears!
A fine conquest,
to plunge red hands in the blood of one's child!

(Enter AGAVÊ with the head of Pentheus on a wand; her BAND OF THEBAN MAENADS follows.)

FIRST BAKKHÊ: *(Sings.)*
But I see her,
Agavê,
the mother of Pentheus.
Look at her eyes.
Wild. Wild.
Welcome the revelers of the
Roaring God!

AGAVÊ: *(Sings.)*
Asian women!
Revelers of Bakkhos!

FIRST BAKKHÊ: *(Sings.)*
    What do you want of me?
    É! É!

AGAVÊ: *(Sings.)*
    See what I've brought!
    See! See!
    A tendril!
    Newly cut!
    From the mountains!
    The mountains!
    What a happy kill!
    To decorate our halls!

FIRST BAKKHÊ: *(Sings.)*
    I see it.
    We welcome you.
    Join our revels.

AGAVÊ: *(Sings.)*
    Caught with no net!
    Young whelp
    of a savage lion!
    You can see! See!

FIRST BAKKHÊ: *(Sings.)*
    Where in the wilds?

AGAVÊ: *(Sings.)*
    Kithairon.

FIRST BAKKHÊ: *(Sings.)*
    Kithairon?

AGAVÊ: *(Sings.)*
    Butchered him there.

FIRST BAKKHÊ: *(Sings.)*
    Who struck the first blow?

AGAVÊ: *(Sings.)*
 I did! I! I!

FIRST BAKKHÊ: *(Sings.)*
 Happy Agavê.

AGAVÊ: *(Sings.)*
 Is what they call me!

FIRST BAKKHÊ: *(Sings.)*
 Who helped in the kill?

AGAVÊ: *(Sings.)*
 Kadmos.

FIRST BAKKHÊ: *(Sings.)*
 Kadmos?

AGAVÊ: *(Sings.)*
 Kadmos's daughters,
 laid hands,
 hands on this beast,
 but after, after me!
 Happy killing,
 happy!
 Now, now,
 now let us,
 let us,
 now let us
 share in the feast!

FIRST BAKKHÊ: *(Sings.)*
 Share?
 In the feast?
 Poor woman!

AGAVÊ: *(Sings.)*
 Little bull, little bull,
 he's a young one!

See?
Fresh down on his cheeks,
beneath the crest
of his delicate hair.

FIRST BAKKHÊ: *(Sings.)*
His hair looks like
a beast of the wild.

AGAVÊ: *(Sings.)*
Bakkhos is a skillful hunter;
he whipped the Maenads on
against the beast.

FIRST BAKKHÊ: *(Sings.)*
Our god is a hunter.

AGAVÊ: *(Sings.)*
Do you praise me?

FIRST BAKKHÊ: *(Sings.)*
We praise you.

AGAVÊ: *(Sings.)*
Soon the Thebans

FIRST BAKKHÊ: *(Sings.)*
and your child, Pentheus

AGAVÊ: *(Sings.)*
will praise his mother for

FIRST BAKKHÊ: *(Sings.)*
this savage

AGAVÊ: *(Sings.)*
killing, this

FIRST BAKKHÊ: *(Sings.)*
    this

AGAVÊ: *(Sings.)*
    lion cub

FIRST BAKKHÊ: *(Sings.)*
    a superior

AGAVÊ: *(Sings.)*
    catch

FIRST BAKKHÊ: *(Sings.)*
    superior

AGAVÊ: *(Sings.)*
    catch!

FIRST BAKKHÊ: *(Sings.)*
    Are you proud?

AGAVÊ: *(Sings.)*
    Proud?
    Proud!
    I have done greatness,
    manifest greatness,
    greatness for Thebes!

    (Music out.)

FIRST BAKKHÊ: Show it, then, poor Agavê! Show to all of Thebes the
    victory trophy you have brought!

AGAVÊ: Countrymen! Thebans! Citizens of the fair-towered walls of
    Thebes! Behold my quarry! The beast stalked and hunted by the
    daughters of Kadmos! No javelins, no nets took him! But our fair arms
    and hands! Who now will boast of useless weapons! Our bare hands
    caught and tore this beast limb from limb!

Where is my father? Dear old Kadmos? And my son, my
Pentheus? Find him. He must bring a ladder and climb to the roof
and nail this lion's head to the beam ends, this head I hunted and now
bring home!

*(Enter KADMOS with ATTENDANTS carrying a covered litter with
the remains of Pentheus's body.)*

KADMOS: This way, come, follow, follow me with the sad, dead weight of
the body of Pentheus. Lay him down before the palace.
    I searched and searched, forever it seemed. I found him then in
the glens of Kithairon. Torn, torn, torn. No two pieces in any one
place. But everywhere, everywhere in the trackless wood.
    We had just entered the walls, Teiresias and I, returned from the
Bakkhic dancing, when I heard of my daughters' monstrous deed. I
went back then, back to the mountain, back to find what I could of
the boy, slaughtered at the hands of the Maenads.
    I saw Autonoê there, poor Aktaion's mother, and Ino, in the
thickets, both still stung, pitiable creatures, with the Bakkhic frenzy.
But she, Agavê, someone told me, was on her way here to Thebes,
dancing a Bakkhic step, and I see that it's true, and this is no happy
sight.

AGAVÊ: Father! You can boast now! Boast of having the bravest daughters
of any in all the world! I mean all of us daughters, of course, but most
of all me. I left behind my shuttle and loom and found a far greater
quest! Hunting wild beasts with my bare hands! Look here, here in my
arms, a proof of my valor, to hang high on the beam of your palace!
Take it, hold it in your hands, Father, rejoice in this trophy of my kill!
Invite all your friends to a feast, for you are blessed, blessed by the
deeds we have done!

KADMOS: AIIIIII! This grief is more than I can bear! More than I can
look at! What you have done with your pitiful, wretched hands is
murder. What a noble victim you've slaughtered for the gods, and now
you invite Thebes and me to the feast! Anguish is for us both! First
you, then me! This god has dealt justly with us, but his justice is cruel,
merciless. He was born of our blood, in our own house, but has led us
to ruin.

AGAVÊ: How peevish old age makes men! Old codgers with their scowling faces! I wish my son were a hunter like his mother when he hunts wild beasts with the young men of Thebes. But he's good for only one thing. Fighting against gods. You must scold him, Father. It's your place to do so. Call him, someone. I want him to see my happiness.

KADMOS: If ever you know what you've done, your grief will be merciless, child. And yet if you spend your days in your present mind, you will think you are happy, at least, but it won't be true.

AGAVÊ: Why, Father? What could hurt me now?

KADMOS: First, my dear, turn your eyes to the sky.

AGAVÊ: Yes. But why are you asking me to do this?

KADMOS: The sky—is it the same? Or has it changed?

AGAVÊ: Brighter, yes, Father. With a holier light.

KADMOS: And the soaring feeling inside you, has it stopped?

AGAVÊ: I don't—yes, it's clearing. My mind's not the same.

KADMOS: Try with all your strength. Can you answer a question?

AGAVÊ: Yes—but I've—forgotten what we said.

KADMOS: Whose house was it took you in as a bride?

AGAVÊ: You gave me to Ekhion—dragon-born, they say.

KADMOS: Yes, and who was the son born to you there?

AGAVÊ: Pentheus. His father and I made love.

KADMOS: Yes. Now the head. Whose face do you see?

AGAVÊ: A lion's—? Yes? My fellow hunters told me—?

KADMOS: Look squarely at it now. One look will tell you.

AGAVÊ: What? Oh, no! No! What is this? What?

KADMOS: Look closely. There. Let the truth come closer.

AGAVÊ: Grief—grief—deep grief is what I see!

KADMOS: Does it—tell me—does it still look like a lion?

AGAVÊ: Noooo! Noooo! It's Pentheus! Here in my arms!

KADMOS: Yes, my dear, I mourned him before *you* knew.

AGAVÊ: Nooo! Nooo! Who killed him? Why here in my arms?

KADMOS: Damn you, savage truth, you took your time!

AGAVÊ: Say it! Say it! Before my heart bursts!

KADMOS: You killed him. You and your sisters. Killed Pentheus.

AGAVÊ: Where did he die? At home here? Where?

KADMOS: Where his own dogs tore Aktaion to pieces.

AGAVÊ: Kithairon? But why was Pentheus on Kithairon?

KADMOS: To bring scorn upon the god and your Bakkhic rites.

AGAVÊ: But *we*—*we*—what were *we* doing there?

KADMOS: You were mad, the whole city frenzied with Bakkhos.

AGAVÊ: Dionysos destroyed us. How clearly I see that.

KADMOS: For insults done him. You denied his godhead.

AGAVÊ: My son, my son's body, where is it, Father?

KADMOS: There on the litter. It was a terrible search.

AGAVÊ: Why did he have to suffer for my crime?

KADMOS: He was like you, my dear. Like you, he blasphemed the god.
And for this the god has ruined us all. You, this boy, the house, me, in
a single, terrible blow. I now have no male heir, and what is worse is
seeing this flower of your womb, poor woman, put to a miserable and
shameful death. He was our house's light, our hope, our future.
Dear boy, you held us together. Dear daughter's child, how they
feared you. You were a terror in the land. But no one who knew your
nature dared outrage this old man, for you would make him pay for it,
and they knew that well. But now I'm to be an exile, stripped of
honors, I, the great Kadmos, who sowed the race of Thebans, reaping
the grandest harvest of all. I loved you most, my dear, sweet child, and
even in death will hold you most dearly loved.
Who, now, will tug me by the beard, call me "grandfather" and
throw his arms around me in a great hug, saying: "Who's giving you
trouble, old man? Tell me, I'll teach the bully a thing or two!" But
what am I now? Nothing. And you are destroyed. And your mother
has all our pity. And her sisters their misery. Who scorns the gods
now? If so, look at this pitiable boy, and see if you believe.

FIRST BAKKHÊ: I grieve for you, Kadmos. This boy's punishment is
deserved, but your grief is far too harsh.

AGAVÊ: Father, where is his body? His sweet body? I want to see it.

KADMOS: There, daughter. Over there.

AGAVÊ: Are his limbs put decently together?

KADMOS: No. Uncover the body. Let her see him.

AGAVÊ: Oh Father, how can I touch him? How? With polluted hands?
The hands that killed him? Oh Father, how my life has changed in
one disastrous day.
Dear sweet boy. Let me kiss your body. Let me kiss it, kiss it.
Help me, Father. Help me lay out his body. He was so beautiful, so

strong, so powerful, so beautiful. Help me find his proper shape again. Let us put him right.

I made you once, child, I make you once again. There, there, there. Strong legs, round arms, such fine, fine muscles.

Father, give me his head. It belongs here, where I can kiss it, yes, as I kissed you when you were a child. Sweet face, gentle, gentle mouth.

KADMOS: My dear, you mustn't. Come.

AGAVÊ: No. Let me cover him. No one must see. Never again.

(DIONYSOS appears on the roof of the palace.)

DIONYSOS: I am Dionysos, son of Zeus, born of Semelê here in Thebes in a burst of lightning. I am the god come back now to the city that slighted me, fought me, denied me. I offered you everything, and you turned against me. But now you will know me for the god I am, and for the power that I hold over you. I see your city shake in fear, but your repentance comes too late. The lowest of you all was Pentheus, whose torn body lies there. Not only did he scorn me, he put me in chains, he imprisoned me. He now pays the only way possible: a just death, death at his mother's hands, a death of dishonor. It pleased me to see it. In refusing to know me, he refused to know himself. He died as blind as he lived.

And Dionysos now tells you your future. Suffering, suffering and more suffering. Banishment, slavery, pain: exile from Thebes, never again to lay eyes on your city. You and your sisters, Agavê, must pay for your crime. Your pollution is monstrous and defiles the graves of your fathers.

You, Kadmos, I will change to a great serpent, as I will also your wife, Harmonia, daughter of Arês, won by you even though you are mortal. As serpents you will both drive an oxcart leading a barbarian horde as the oracle foretold. And you will lay waste countless numbers of cities with your killer army. But when you come to Apollo's shrine at Delphi, when you have destroyed and crushed it into oblivion, you and your hordes will turn once more to Thebes, and a tragic return it will be. You, Kadmos, you and Harmonia, Arês will spare, establishing you in the Islands of the Blest. This is his decree, Dionysos, born of

no mortal father, but of Zeus. If you had learned wisdom, known true
sanity when you had the chance but refused, Dionysos would now and
forever be fighting in your defense, and you would be happy.

KADMOS: Forgive us, Dionysos, for having wronged you.

DIONYSOS: Too late. When you should have known, you refused.

KADMOS: We know that, but your revenge is too harsh.

DIONYSOS: I am a god and you dishonored me.

KADMOS: Gods must not be like men in their anger.

DIONYSOS: My father Zeus ordained this long ago.

AGAVÊ: It's settled, Father; our fate is banishment.

DIONYSOS: Then why do you delay necessity?

KADMOS: Ah, child, we have arrived at our final evil, you, your sisters, my
ancient self. Old and rejected, I will live among Barbarians, a hated
exile. And then the oracle: as wild and savage serpents my wife and
I will lead mongrel Barbarian hordes against Hellene cities, and
spearsmen against our land's most sacred shrines. I will never find
release from this curse, never sail the downward-plunging Acheron to
find peace in its endless night.

AGAVÊ: Dear, dear Father, we will never meet in exile.

KADMOS: Why are you throwing your arms around me, child, like a
young swan protecting its drone of a father?

AGAVÊ: Because there is no one to help me now, no one to tell me where
to turn in exile.

KADMOS: I can't help you, my dear. I don't know.

(Music. Song. Dance.)

AGAVÊ: *(Chants.)*
> I leave here,
> leave my city,
> my land,
> an outcast, never again
> to see my home,
> never to see the house
> I entered as a bride.
> A life without love.
> Misfortune will trail me
> wherever I go.
> Farewell.

KADMOS: *(Chants.)*
> Go, child,
> find some place
> to hide, some—

AGAVÊ: *(Chants.)*
> I mourn for you, Father—

KADMOS: *(Chants.)*
> And I for you;
> and for your sisters.

AGAVÊ: *(Chants.)*
> Dionysos brought down
> this terrible doom
> on your house.

DIONYSOS: *(Chants.)*
> It was *I* who suffered!
> Suffered at *your* hands!
> My name was unknown,
> unhonored in Thebes!

AGAVÊ: *(Chants.)*
> Father, farewell.

KADMOS: *(Chants.)*
    Farewell, my dear,
    my poor, dear child,
    though faring well
    will not be easy.

AGAVÊ: *(Chants.)*
    Friends, women,
    take me,
    take me away,
    away to find my unhappy sisters,
    pitiless sisters in endless exile.
    Never, never, never again,
    never, will I see
    unholy, slaughtering,
    murderous Kithairon!
    And never will
    Kithairon see me!
    I will never again
    look on god's dedicated wand!
    Never be reminded!
    Never!
    Let that be the matter
    of other Bakkhants!

*

IPHIGENEIA IN AULIS

(ΙΦΙΓΕΝΕΙΑ Η ΕΝ ΑΥΛΙΔΙ)

CHARACTERS

AGAMEMNON *King of Argos and the allied Greek commander*
OLD MAN *slave of Agamemnon and Klytaimnêstra*
MENELAOS *king of Sparta and Agamemnon's brother*
KLYTAIMNÊSTRA *wife of Agamemnon*
IPHIGENEIA *daughter of Agamemnon and Klytaimnêstra*
ORESTÊS *infant son of Agamemnon and Klytaimnêstra*
ACHILLEUS *leader of the Myrmidons*
SLAVE *of Klytaimnêstra*
SOLDIER *from the Greek army*
CHORUS OF YOUNG WOMEN OF CHALKIS
FIRST YOUNG WOMAN *chorus leader*
SOLDIERS, GUARDS, SLAVE ATTENDANTS

IPHIGENEIA IN AULIS

Before dawn.
Aulis on the island of Euboia.
The harbor.
Outside the war tent of Agamemnon.
Enter AGAMEMNON pacing indecisively.
Music.

AGAMEMNON: *(Chants.)*
> Come out, old man, in front of the tent.

OLD MAN: *(Chants.)*
> I'm coming, coming, general.
> What is it, my king?
> Some new plan?

AGAMEMNON: *(Chants.)*
> I'm waiting!

(Enter the OLD MAN from the tent.)

OLD MAN: *(Chants.)*
> And I'm hurrying, fast as can be.
> And wide awake, too.
> The curse of old men
> whose eyes won't stay shut.

AGAMEMNON: *(Chants.)*
> What's that star sailing the night sky?

OLD MAN: *(Chants.)*
> Sirius, master.

AGAMEMNON: *(Chants.)*
> What a blazer!

OLD MAN: *(Chants.)*
     Chasing down the seven Pleiades.

AGAMEMNON: *(Chants.)*
     Still riding high.

OLD MAN: *(Chants.)*
     Dog star. Dog days.

AGAMEMNON: *(Chants.)*
     Nothing moving. No sound.
     No birds, no sea. All still.
     Winds along the Euripos moving silently.

OLD MAN: *(Chants.)*
     Then why are you up, general?
     Back and forth in front of your tent all night.
     Not a voice stirring yet in Aulis.
     The guards standing like statues on the walls.
     Let's go in.

AGAMEMNON: *(Chants.)*
     Old man, I envy you, I do.
     I envy any man who slips through life
     unnoticed, without fame. It's men
     with power and authority I don't envy.

OLD MAN: *(Chants.)*
     But they're the ones who live the good life.

AGAMEMNON: *(Chants.)*
     Good? That?
     No! It's a trap! It's deadly!
     Honors don't come easy.
     Sweet as honey at first,
     till you taste the poison.
     Glory is pain to the man who wins it.

First the gods lay in wait to destroy you,
then men, never-satisfied men,
always changing, rip your heart out.

OLD MAN: *(Chants.)*
No, no, I'm sorry, Agamemnon,
sorry to hear my leader, my king,
talk like that. You're the son of Atreus, master,
and he didn't put you in this world
to live a life of carefree happiness.
No. You're a man. You must expect pain
as well as joy, like it or not.
The gods see to that if no one else.

But look here. You've lit your lamp,
you've written a letter.
That one there, there in your hand.
Then you rub out what you've written,
write it again, then rub it out once more.
And the seal!
One minute on, one minute off,
then throw it to the ground,
tears flooding your eyes,
a river of tears.

These are the acts of a madman, master,
a man loosing his reason out of despair.
What is it?
What makes you so unhappy?

Oh my king, I'm a loyal servant,
I keep secrets, you know that.
And I've been with you since you married.
Came with the bride, with Klytaimnêstra,
from the house of Tyndareos,
part of the dowry. You remember?
And served you well, if I say so myself.

(Music out.)

AGAMEMNON: Lêda the daughter of Thestios had three daughters: Phoibê, my wife Klytaimnêstra, and Helen. Helen, being the most beautiful, had every wellborn, wealthy young man in Greece for a suitor. So jealous were they of each other that they threatened violence, murder, even, if they failed to win her, throwing her father Tyndareos into a quandary, it seemed so hopeless. Should he or shouldn't he marry her off? Then the idea struck him. Each suitor would swear an oath, all of them together, clasping hands, burnt offerings, wine libations, everything, solemn, that whoever married Helen, all the rest would come to his defense. If anyone seduced or abducted her, keeping her husband from her bed, they would chase him down, no matter who he was, Greek or Barbarian, and turn his city to rubble. But once they had sworn, Tyndareos showed how really cunning he was. He left the choice of a husband up to Helen, saying: "Let the sweet winds of love guide her desire!" And so it did. And there's the misery of it. Her love made the worst possible choice. Menelaos. My brother.

Time passed. Then one day out of the East there came to Sparta a man, Paris, who had once judged Aphroditê the loveliest of goddesses, a Trojan, son of King Priam, dazzling in richly embroidered barbarian robes, stitched and trimmed in gold, with opulent jewels. A beautiful man. He came as friend, but left an enemy. For Paris loved Helen, and Helen, Paris, and one day, Menelaos being away, Paris stole off with Helen back to Troy and its pleasant pastures.

Frantic, goaded to madness by the insult, Menelaos roared through Greece reminding suitors of their pledge. And come they did, like flies to the honey pot. Scrambling to arms, mail clanking, weapons newly honed, and ships a thousand strong lined up in the bay. Something to do.

So here we are at Aulis of the narrow straits. And who to lead them, who as commander-in-chief, but yours truly? An honor I'd gladly refuse. But they voted me in. He was, after all, my brother. Well.

Once assembled and mustered, the wind took off, died down, died altogether. Nothing moving. Most of all not us. No ship, no sail. We applied to Kalchas, our resident prophet. "We'd have a wind," he said, "at the cost of a sacrifice." "To whom?" we asked. "To Artemis," he replied, "goddess of the region." That sacrifice, it turned out, was my own daughter, Iphigeneia. This and this alone, according to

Kalchas, would send our ships' sails bellying onward to Troy, and the city would fall before us.

Once I'd heard, I called Talthybios the herald. "Sound the trumpet," I said, "sound it, and tell them to break camp! We're going home! I won't be guilty of killing my own daughter!" Who should come then but Menelaos? To "reason" with me, urging, coaxing, wheedling, sweet talking, to do this terrible thing. I finally wrote my wife to bring her to Aulis, our daughter. I had arranged, I said, her wedding to great Achilleus. I went on to praise him, his honor, reputation, worth, saying he refused to sail with us to Troy unless he could send back home to his seat in Pythia a bride from our family. I lied, of course, to persuade her of my story, so she'd send the girl. Of all of us, only Kalchas, Odysseus and Menelaos knew.

But what I did was wrong, and now I'm undoing it. This letter you see me sealing and unsealing under cover of darkness, old man, take it now, take it and hurry to Argos. But wait, first I'll read it to you. You're a loyal servant, loyal to my wife and me.

OLD MAN: Yes, read it. That way my words and yours will agree.

(Music.)

AGAMEMNON: *(Sings.)*
"Klytaimnêstra,
this letter cancels the last you received from me.
Do not send your daughter to Aulis.
The wind has died, no waves strike the shore
the sea is so calm. We'll find
a better time for our daughter's wedding."

OLD MAN: *(Sings.)*
But what of Achilleus?
When he hears he has no bride,
he'll raise a storm in the camp
against you and your wife.
What will you tell him?

AGAMEMNON: *(Sings.)*
We've used his name is all.

He knows nothing, nothing of a wedding,
a bride, a plan, my willingness
to give him my child in marriage.

OLD MAN: *(Sings.)*
You're playing with fire, my lord.
It frightens me. To bring your daughter here
for the Greeks to slaughter is a dangerous move,
and then to pretend it's all for her marriage
to Achilleus. I'm appalled.

AGAMEMNON: *(Sings.)*
OIMOIIIIIII!
I'm loosing my mind! You're right!
My world reeling around me,
heading me straight to my ruin!
AIIIIIII!
Go! Hurry! Run!
Forget your old legs!

OLD MAN: *(Sings.)*
I'm going, master.

AGAMEMNON: *(Sings.)*
No stopping at springs to rest or sleep.

OLD MAN: *(Sings.)*
You needn't tell me.

AGAMEMNON: *(Sings.)*
Check every fork in the road. No chariot
gets past you with my daughter in it
bringing her to Aulis.

OLD MAN: *(Sings.)*
Master, I will.

AGAMEMNON: *(Sings.)*
If she's left home, and you meet her carriage on the way,

turn them back, turn them, even if you take the reins
yourself, turn them back to the safety of Mykenê's
walls the Cyclopes built.

OLD MAN: *(Sings.)*
> But how will they trust me?
> Why should they believe me
> since you sent for them to Aulis?

AGAMEMNON: *(Sings.)*
> The seal on the letter. They'll know it. Keep it safe.
> Go now. Day is breaking, the sun's chariot
> brings fire to the sky. Go.
> You have a duty. You can save me.

(Exit the OLD MAN.)

All men know pain, all men know sorrow.
Every man has bitterness waiting somewhere.

*(Exit AGAMEMNON into the tent and enter the CHORUS OF
YOUNG WOMEN OF CHALKIS.)*

(Music. Song. Dance.)

YOUNG WOMEN OF CHALKIS: *(Sing.)*
> I have crossed the narrow straits of Euripos
> to sandy Aulis,
> to sandy-shored Aulis,
> Aulis by the sea.
> My city is Chalkis,
> Chalkis where Arethousa's waters
> well from the earth and leaping headlong
> run down to the sea.
> I have come to see them,
> the army,
> the Greeks,
> proud Greeks,
> heroes,

to see them and their pine-prowed ships,
their wing-oared,
deep-sea ships a thousand strong,
ships manned by heroes headed for Troy.
Menelaos of the firebrand hair and
noble Agamemnon lead them in battle
to win back Helen,
beautiful Helen.
Love goddess Aphroditê gave her to Paris,
shepherd prince Paris,
a gift,
when beside the sparkling spring
she entered in strife with Athêna and Hera,
and won the prize for beauty.
And leaving his meadows and mountains behind,
Paris stole her,
Paris stole Helen from her home
beside the reedy Eurotas.

I hurry through the sacred grove of Artemis
where victims die,
are slaughtered,
in sacrifice to the goddess.
And running,
I blush,
my cheeks like fire,
burning with the feverish shyness
of a young wife's desire to see at last
the manly defense of the massed forces,
shields and armor and war tents,
and men,
strong men,
in their bare-legged beauty,
and horseflesh sweating with exertion.
I see the two Aiases,
the son of Oïleus,
and Telamon's son,
the pride of Salamis.
And Protesilaos and Palamêdes,

Poseidon's grandson,
sit together over a game of draughts,
lost in some difficult move.
And there is Diomêdes
showing his muscles at discus,
with Mêrionês,
Arês' son,
beside him,
watching a marvel among men.
And Odysseus,
Laërtês' son,
from his mountainous island,
and Nireus,
the most beautiful of all the Greeks.

And then Achilleus,
beautiful Achilleus,
Achilleus whose feet are swift as the wind,
Thetis's son,
reared by Cheiron,
racing against a four-horse chariot,
along the beach in full battle armor,
across the sands,
fleet-footed hero Achilleus,
racing hard on the curved track,
lap after lap,
straining for victory.
The charioteer shouted at his beautiful horses,
bridles and bits chased with gold;
the yoked pair,
dappled with gray in white manes,
the trace horses bays with dappled fetlocks.
Pherês' grandson Eumêlos goaded them on,
urging, shouting,
faster, faster,
trace horses hugging the curves,
but Achilleus, running in all his armor,
never lagged,
never fell behind the rail and the axles.

(Enter MENELAOS and the OLD MAN.)

(Music out)

OLD MAN: Menelaos, stop! You have no right!

MENELAOS: Get away from me! You're too loyal to your master!

OLD MAN: There are some might think that a virtue!

MENELAOS: I'll show you what it means to meddle!

OLD MAN: You shouldn't have broken the seal on that letter!

MENELAOS: And you had no right to have such a letter! A threat to every Greek life here!

OLD MAN: Argue that with others! Give it back!

MENELAOS: I won't!

OLD MAN: Then I won't let go!

MENELAOS: I'll bloody your head for your insolence!

OLD MAN: Do it! It's an honor to die for my master!

MENELAOS: Big words for a slave! Let go!

OLD MAN: Master! Help! Help! He stole your letter! We're being robbed! Help!

AGAMEMNON: *(Enters from the tent.)* Here! What's the meaning of this! Brawling?

MENELAOS: I have a better right to be heard than he!

AGAMEMNON: *(After waving the OLD MAN into the tent.)* What's the quarrel, Menelaos? Why this violence?

MENELAOS: I'll tell you! Just first look me in the eye!

AGAMEMNON: Look you in the eye? Do you think I'm afraid? I'm a son of Atreus.

MENELAOS: All right! This letter! This is treason!

AGAMEMNON: That letter—give it back to me.

MENELAOS: Not till every Greek here knows what it says!

AGAMEMNON: Really? You broke the seal? Then you know what you have no business to know.

MENELAOS: Oh, I broke the seal, all right. And you're the one to suffer for this betrayal.

AGAMEMNON: How did you find the old man? Gods, the impudence!

MENELAOS: I was watching for your daughter's arrival.

AGAMEMNON: Who gave you that right? Who are you to meddle in my affairs? You impudent bastard!

MENELAOS: I'm not your slave! I do as I choose!

AGAMEMNON: Bastard! It's my family! I'll do as I like!

MENELAOS: No, you're not to be trusted. You're steady as a mudslide.

AGAMEMNON: How clever you are with your slanderous, slippery tongue.

MENELAOS: And you with your unsteady, wavering mind? How difficult it must be to be just and open, especially to friends. But here are a few questions. Just don't turn a tantrum and storm away. I won't be too hard on you.
    You remember, do you, how you lusted for command of the forces at Troy? You pretended reluctance, but ambition burned at your

core. How humble you presented yourself. You sought out every man's hand. You threw wide your doors to any comer. You accosted any- and everyone, no matter their station, drew them into talk whether they wanted it or not. Everything about you was congeniality in your bid for the big promotion in the open market. Lovely, lovely power, lovely life! But once you'd snared it, once power was in your grip, you whistled a different tune. No more Mr. Friendly to one-time friends. "Who did you say? Never heard of him!" Ah, the new man! "Wants to see me, you say? Tell him I'm busy." Not an easy man to get to.

An honest man, Agamemnon, doesn't change when he changes station. He stays steady as a rock. Especially now when he has the means to help people most. This is my first complaint; the first bone of contention. But there's more. You then led the allied armies here to Aulis, and your luck bottoms out. Including you and your self-importance. No wind. With no wind we don't sail. Then the men start banging their shields and raising a racket to turn back home and not waste more fucking time on this nonsense. At that you're nearly paralyzed. Commander of a thousand ships and unable to blanket the plains of Troy with his valiant spearsmen! So who do you send for? Me. "What do I do, Menelaos?" you moan. "Help me think— a plan—anything!" Anything, that is, that can save your face from losing your command, and with it your precious glory!

Then up speaks Kalchas in the midst of a ritual: "Sacrifice your child to Artemis, Agamemnon, and the winds will come!"

Your heart leaps up at that, I can tell you. You couldn't agree fast enough, rushing off to your tent to write—willingly, I must stress— to your wife to bring your daughter here to Aulis to marry Achilleus. All a pretext, of course—but your precious glory was safe.

Now you've changed your mind, it seems. The same spot, the same sky, but a new message. No longer to be the killer of your daughter. Well, you're not the first. Thousands of men have clambered and scratched their way to power, and then, all at once, in the blink of an eye, it's over and they're back to zero.

Sometimes the people are at fault, too ignorant to know what's good for them. But often the fault lies in the man himself, unable to keep the city's good in view. Most of all, though, my grief is for Greece. It was a grand thing we set out to do. Now the savage barbarian, those nobodies, can laugh us to scorn. And all because of you—you and your daughter. No man should lead a city or an army on the basis of his connections. The highest value in a leader of anything is mind.

FIRST YOUNG WOMAN: Brother fighting brother—a terrible thing; words, insults, straining to violence.

AGAMEMNON: It's my turn now to criticize you. The only difference, I'll be briefer and a bit more restrained; no huffing and puffing, no bulging, bloodshot eyes, no reeling off barefaced lies. Brother to brother should be a respectful exchange, sensible, plainspoken. Good men are considerate of one another.

So, tell me, what's your problem? Are you burning for a virtuous wife? Can't help you there, I'm afraid. You made an awful mess with the one you had. Am I, who have no complaint to speak of, to pay through the nose for your foolish blunders? I don't think so. Nor is it my new-won distinction that's bugging you. The only thing on your mind is a woman in your arms; a beauty at that. Discretion and honor go hang. But, then, a degenerate man toadies to degenerate pleasures. And if I happen to make a mistake, and later take measures to correct it, does that make me a madman? Again, I don't think so. Divine Justice unloaded you of a bad wife, and all you can think of now is to get her back. Now, that's madness. And the suitors, all lusting to win the bride, hence their oath to Tyndareos? Madness, too. The only thing leading *them* on was itching crotches.

Make no mistake: Blind Hope brought them to Aulis and not any military might of yours. So take them! Go fight your war! Those men out there are just stupid enough to follow you. But the gods aren't so foolish. They know an honest oath from one got by force. So. I will not kill my child. I see no justice in giving you the satisfaction of punishing your wife, when for me it means a lifetime of remorse for the unspeakable crime committed against my own flesh.

Well, that's about it. That's what I wanted to say. Short. Sweet. To the point. You can take it to heart or not. That's up to you. But as for me, I intend to put my life in proper order!

FIRST YOUNG WOMAN: You've changed your mind, but for the better: refusing to do harm to your child.

MENELAOS: AIIIIIIII! Then I have no friends!

AGAMEMNON: You have, when you don't set out to destroy them!

MENELAOS: I thought we were brothers! When will you show it?

AGAMEMNON: Brothers in sanity, not in madness!

MENELAOS: Brothers share everything, even sorrow!

AGAMEMNON: Than act like a brother, instead of hurting me!

MENELAOS: Your country needs you, now!

AGAMEMNON: But Greece, like you, is infected by some mad god!

MENELAOS: All right, you're the general, strut your peacock's pride! I'll make other plans with other friends. And I know where they are. You've betrayed your own brother.

SOLDIER: *(Entering in haste.)* Agamemnon, king and commander of the allied armies! I've brought them, sir! Iphigeneia your daughter, and your wife Klytaimnêstra! And with them your infant son, Orestês. Your wife said you'd been gone from home for so long, it would please you to see him again.

It was a long journey, sir; difficult, too, but now they're cooling their feet in a nearby stream; the horses, too. After they'd drunk, we set them loose to graze in the green meadow, and I came on ahead so as not to surprise you.

Oh, and by the way, sir, the whole army knows of your daughter's arrival. Word travels fast around here, as you probably know. They're crowding from every direction, pushing, shoving, for a good spot to catch sight of the girl; every man and his brother wants a look. Well, people blessed by fortune are always famous.

But everyone's asking what she's doing here. "Is it a wedding? What's going on? Did the general miss her so much he sent for her?" Others are saying she'll be consecrated to Artemis, goddess of Aulis, to prepare for her coming marriage. "But who's the bridegroom," they say?

We have to get a move on, sir. The sacrificial basket needs preparing. And then you'll lead the procession around the altar. And wreaths for your heads, too. There's to be a wedding feast! Flutes piping! Dancing to make the earth shake with stamping feet! Your daughter will be a happy bride today, sir!

AGAMEMNON: Thank you. You may leave us. Let Fortune take its course and turn out well. *(Exit the SOLDIER.)* OIMIIIIIIII! What do I say? Where do I begin? How do I answer the misery my life has become? I'm fate's victim. My every move outwitted by the cunning of destiny. Life is at least livable if you're born with no advantage—a nobody. And yet they have advantage. They can give way to their grief, they have freedom to speak whatever they please. But the man born with a scepter in his grip, born in the harsh gaze of the public eye, has no such luxury. He has no right to indignity. The slave of the common rabble he rules. The victim of pomp, of circumstance, of decorum. Duties! Obligations! A prison!

I'm ashamed of my tears, ashamed to show my sorrow. And yet my shame is greater for not showing, for I have such cause to shed tears that not to shed them is to make my misery greater.

But what will I tell my wife? How will I face her, greet her, look her in the eye, and not betray the horror behind *these* eyes? Why did she come? Why did she have to, like this, now, unasked? It was bad enough before, now the disaster is unspeakable.

But how could she not—how could she not have come, not have wanted to give her daughter in marriage, her own child, her belovèd, her darling? And in coming she will uncover the depth of my treachery. Oh my child, my poor, dear, innocent child! Innocent? No. Death, it seems, will soon be her bridegroom. Not innocent. How I pity you, my dear! I hear her now: "Father! Why are you killing me? I wish you and everyone you love such a marriage!" Orestês will be there. Barely able to walk, no words yet, he'll scream his inarticulate horror, but my heart will read their meaning.

Oh Priam, what ruin your son has brought me with his lust!

FIRST YOUNG WOMAN: I pity you, though I may be a foreigner and a woman, and these are a king's troubles.

MENELAOS: Brother, give me your hand.

AGAMEMNON: Here. You've won. The loss is mine.

MENELAOS: I swear to you, brother, by Pelops and by his son, our
father, Atreus, that what I am about to say comes from my heart,
unvarnished, unpremeditated, but simply what I feel and think—
no more, no less.

As I watched you just now, and saw tears flowing from your eyes,
your voice faltering, I felt my own tears come and a lump rise in my
throat, and I pitied you. You mustn't kill your child. I'm with you
now. Side by side. No longer your enemy. I take back everything I
said, everything. I support you. There is no justice allows your child to
die for my sake. No justice that allows me to put my interests over
yours. And surely no justice that condemns you to live with your
child's death while my children enjoy the light of day.

What could I possibly need? A wife? I can get one, anyone, every
bit as good as Helen ever was. Is the loss of a brother, whom I should
cherish, worth winning back Helen? An evil bargain at any price! I was
rash just now; I acted like a child. But I've pulled back, looked closely
at the situation, and see now just how terrible a thing it is to kill one's
child. I was overwhelmed by pity, pity for the girl, by the family bond
between her and me, and to think I condemned her to death on the
altar, for me, for my own petty sake, for the sake of my marriage!
What is Helen to her, that dear, sweet, innocent child? No. Let them
go, send them back, the soldiers. Back to where they belong. Away
from Aulis.

And no more tears, Agamemnon. No more tears, brother, do
you hear? Your tears bring on mine. And whatever the oracles may say
regarding your daughter, it's your concern, not mine. I make my share
over to you. I want no part of it. "What's happened to all his threats?"
I hear you thinking. Love is what's happened. Love for a brother. Is
that so unusual? No, just a change in heart for the better.

FIRST YOUNG WOMAN: Those are noble words. Worthy of Tantalos,
son of Zeus. You do your ancestors proud.

AGAMEMNON: Thank you, Menelaos. I never expected to hear such
words from you. You do yourself honor; it shows your true nature.
Conflict sometimes arises between brothers over a woman or even a
throne. I despise such feuds. But I have come to a place where I have
no choice, locked in by Fate and Necessity. Blood. Blood is the only
way. Her blood. My daughter's.

MENELAOS: Why? Who can force you to kill her?

AGAMEMNON: The allied forces of the entire Greek army.

MENELAOS: Not if you've sent her back to Argos.

AGAMEMNON: I could do that, yes. But it would come out.

MENELAOS: Why are you in such fear of the mob?

AGAMEMNON: Kalchas will spread the word, be sure—the prophecy.

MENELAOS: The dead don't talk. That's easily arranged.

AGAMEMNON: Then there's that other. Aren't you afraid?

MENELAOS: Who? Tell me. Then I'll know.

AGAMEMNON: The slimy son of Sisyphos. He knows it all.

MENELAOS: Odysseus? He can't touch us. He's nobody.

AGAMEMNON: But he's cunning. He sides with the mob.

MENELAOS: He suffers from a disease: Ambition.

AGAMEMNON: Can't you see him now, circled by the assembled armies, spinning out the tale: what Kalchas said, what I promised—to sacrifice my daughter—and then reneged on it, betraying even myself, and them. He'll have the whole army on his side, telling them to kill us, you and me, and then slaughter the child! And what if I escape to Argos? What good would that do? They'd descend on the city, raze it to the ground, even the invincible walls built by the Cyclopes. You see where this puts me. How do I survive? How do I live through this nightmare? Why have the gods done this to me?

   I want you to do one thing for me, Menelaos. When you make your way through the troops, be certain that Klytaimnêstra knows nothing till I've handed over our daughter to the god of the dead.

That way at least I'll endure my torment with the fewest tears possible.
And you, too, women of Chalkis, I ask for your silence.

(Exeunt AGAMEMNON to his tent and MENELAOS to his camp.)

(Music. Song. Dance.)

YOUNG WOMEN OF CHALKIS: *(Sing.)*
Great is Aphroditê,
goddess of love,
and great is her power,
and they who know her in moderation are blest.
Touched lightly by love,
not burned in a sea of passion,
of lust,
that drives men mad,
is a blissful state.
When Eros,
blond Eros,
lets fly his arrows of love and desire,
there is one that brings rapture,
the other ruin and confusion.
From this one,
Kypris,
goddess Aphroditê,
from this one,
loveliest of immortals,
protect me,
protect my house and bed.
Let love lie gently on me,
let love come kindly.
Let me know Aphroditê purely,
not in a rage of despair.

Many are the ways of man,
many are man's natures,
but one thing is set,
one thing is known and clear as day,
and that is kindness and goodness of soul,

that is the noble,
and that is nurtured by teaching what is right,
and knowing,
and that leads in the end to virtue.
Modesty is wisdom,
leading us down the proper path and
knowing it as beautiful.
And out of beauty comes honor
and a life of unending fame.
To pursue virtue is a noble thing.
In women it is sheltered,
to keep love pure at home;
in men it is discipline in its countless forms,
and discipline makes great cities.

You came,
Paris,
to the slopes of Mount Ida,
to Ida where they reared you to tend your cattle,
herds of white heifers,
playing on your reed-pipe barbarous tunes,
aping the Phrygian pipe of Olympos.
And then they came,
the goddesses came,
all three,
and while the cattle grazed,
the heavy-uddered cattle,
the goddesses revealed their charms,
and you judged whose beauty was greatest.
Your choice was madness,
and madness led you to Greece,
to Helen's palace,
her ivory palace,
and there you saw Helen,
and Helen saw you,
and she received your love gift,
and you received hers,
and it is love has brought strife and armies and Greeks
in their proud ships to tear down Troy.

(Enter KLYTAIMNÊSTRA, IPHIGENEIA, and the infant ORESTÊS in a horse-drawn carriage. Another carriage follows with SLAVE ATTENDANTS and piled high with wedding gifts.)

YOUNG WOMEN OF CHALKIS: *(Chant.)*
> They're here!
> Look!
> The great ones!
> Iphigeneia,
> Agamemnon's princess daughter.
> And Klytaimnêstra,
> queen,
> daughter of Tyndareos.
> How great,
> how great is their family!
> Illustrious house!
> The great,
> the fortunate,
> are like gods to mere mortals.

FIRST YOUNG WOMAN: *(Chants.)*
> Let us wait here, women.
> Let us greet the queen
> as she steps from her chariot.
> Don't let her stumble.
> Give her your hands.
> Give them gently.

YOUNG WOMEN OF CHALKIS: *(Chant.)*
> Gently.
> Gently.
> Gently.

FIRST YOUNG WOMAN: *(Chants.)*
> Down to the firm earth.
> Wish them well.
> Agamemnon's child must not be afraid.
> We, too, are strangers.
> Welcome to the strangers from Argos.

(Music out.)

KLYTAIMNÊSTRA: I thank you, thank you for your words. How kindly
spoken. I will take them as a good omen. I come here bringing my
daughter to her destiny, to a marriage that I hope will be happy.
(To the SLAVE ATTENDANTS.) Come, unload these gifts from the
carriage. Wedding gifts for the bride. Her dowry. Carry them into the
tent carefully and set them down. *(To IPHIGENIA.)* Come, daughter.
Down from the carriage. Help her, women, help her dainty feet onto
the hard earth. Take her on your arms and let her down gently. And
someone do the same for me? Oh but first the baby. Take him.
Now your arm. Thank you. That's better. You've saved me from an
unsightly descent. And someone see to the horses. They frighten easily
when no one is there to comfort them. Here, I'll take him now.
This is Orestês. Agamemnon's son. Still a baby. Asleep, my sweet?
The carriage lulled him, I think. No, there, he's awake. It's your sister's
wedding, dear one, you must be happy for her. And for yourself. You,
who were born a king's son, are to have a noble kinsman for a brother.
The son of a sea nymph and as godlike as his ancestors the gods. You'll
see. Now sit here at my feet, child. And you come, too, Iphigeneia.
Stand beside your mother and show these women how much I have to
be happy for. But here comes your father, my dear. Say something.

(Enter AGAMEMNON from the tent.)

IPHIGENEIA: Oh Mother, I'm sorry, don't be angry if I run from you.
I want to be the first to hold him! Oh Father, I've missed you so!

KLYTAIMNÊSTRA: My lord and revered king, Agamemnon, great joy
of my life, you summoned us here to Aulis, and we are come, your
obedient servants.

IPHIGENEIA: I want to hug you so badly, Father! I just want to look
at you!

KLYTAIMNÊSTRA: It's only natural, child. Of all the children I bore your
father, you always loved him most.

IPHIGENEIA: I'm so happy to see you, Father! It's been so long!

AGAMEMNON: And I'm happy, too, my dear. What can I say?

IPHIGENEIA: Dear, dear, Father! Thank you for bringing me here!

AGAMEMNON: Perhaps, my child. I don't know. We'll see.

IPHIGENEIA: But why do you look so troubled? How sad your eyes are.

AGAMEMNON: A king and army commander has much on his mind.

IPHIGENEIA: But I want you to forget them. Be with me now.

AGAMEMNON: I am, my dear, I am—nowhere else.

IPHIGENEIA: Then smooth away that frown and be happy for me.

AGAMEMNON: All right. There. How's that? I couldn't be happier.

IPHIGENEIA: And yet I see tears pouring from your eyes.

AGAMEMNON: Don't try to understand. It would make me feel worse.

IPHIGENEIA: Well, then, I'll talk nonsense to make you laugh!

AGAMEMNON: Oh god, how can I bear this!—There's a good girl.

IPHIGENEIA: Stay at home with me, Father, with your children.

AGAMEMNON: I want it so much it tears my heart apart.

IPHIGENEIA: Then curse the war! Curse Menelaos's ills!

AGAMEMNON: What has already ruined me will ruin others.

IPHIGENEIA: Why have you been stranded so long in this bay?

AGAMEMNON: Something must happen before we're allowed to sail.

IPHIGENEIA: Father, where is this famous town of Troy?

AGAMEMNON: Where Paris lives. Paris who should never have been born.

IPHIGENEIA: Will you be going far when you leave me?

AGAMEMNON: Far? Yes. But we'll meet again, my child.

IPHIGENEIA: If only it were proper for me to sail with you!

AGAMEMNON: You, too, have a long voyage, and you'll think of your father.

IPHIGENEIA: Will Mother come with me, or will I travel alone?

AGAMEMNON: Alone, all alone, no mother, no father.

IPHIGENEIA: Do you mean you've found me another home, Father?

AGAMEMNON: No more questions. You're a girl. You can't know everything.

IPHIGENEIA: Hurry back to me soon, Father, when you're done at Troy.

AGAMEMNON: There's a sacrifice I must first make here in Aulis.

IPHIGENEIA: Yes, with holy rites. Have you planned it out?

AGAMEMNON: You'll see. You'll have a place by the lustral water.

IPHIGENEIA: And dance for you, Father, around the altar?

AGAMEMNON: How I envy your blessèd ignorance! Go inside now. It's better that young girls not be seen. But kiss me. Give me your hand. Your journey will take you from your father for a long time. Sweet body, dear cheeks, blonde head, what a weight of sorrow Troy and Helen have laid on you! No, I mustn't touch you anymore. It makes my tears flow. Go in. *(Exit IPHIGENEIA into the tent.)* Forgive me, Klytaimnêstra, for this display of a father's grief at what should be a happy moment. I'm about to hand over my daughter to Achilleus to have as his bride. And then I think of all the pain and anxiety of raising her and this parting, it tears at my heart. It's not easy for a father.

KLYTAIMNÊSTRA: I know. I feel it, too. The same pain, the same anxiety of loss. I'll know it no less than you when I lead my daughter out into the sound of wedding hymns. I understand. But time heals. Time dries tears. We'll get used to it. But tell me now of this young husband. I know his name, but not the man. Not his family. Who are they? Where are they from? I want to know more.

AGAMEMNON: Asopos had a daughter. Aigina.

KLYTAIMNÊSTRA: Who married whom? God or a mortal?

AGAMEMNON: Zeus. Their son was Aiakos, King of Oinone.

KLYTAIMNÊSTRA: And who was the son of Aiakos?

AGAMEMNON: Pêleus, who married Thetis, the sea god's daughter.

KLYTAIMNÊSTRA: Did Zeus give her, or did Pêleus take her despite him?

AGAMEMNON: Zeus betrothed them and gave the bride in marriage.

KLYTAIMNÊSTRA: And where were they married? Beneath the deep blue sea?

AGAMEMNON: At the foot of Mount Pêlion, where Cheiron lives.

KLYTAIMNÊSTRA: Cheiron, yes, that's where the centaurs play.

AGAMEMNON: And all the gods came to their wedding feast.

KLYTAIMNÊSTRA: Who raised Achilleus, Thetis or his father?

AGAMEMNON: No, Cheiron. To keep him free of the evils of men.

KLYTAIMNÊSTRA: A wise teacher, and an even wiser father.

AGAMEMNON: And this is the man who will be your daughter's husband.

KLYTAIMNÊSTRA: Excellent, I must say. Where is he from?

AGAMEMNON: Phthia, on the banks of the Apidanos.

KLYTAIMNÊSTRA: Is that where he'll take our daughter?

AGAMEMNON: That must be the business of the one who wins her.

KLYTAIMNÊSTRA: I wish them both well. When is the wedding?

AGAMEMNON: When the moon is full.

KLYTAIMNÊSTRA: Have you sacrificed to the goddess for the girl?

AGAMEMNON: I will. I was occupied with that when you came.

KLYTAIMNÊSTRA: And following that we hold the wedding feast?

AGAMEMNON: Yes, after the sacrifice.

KLYTAIMNÊSTRA: And where will I hold the women's banquet?

AGAMEMNON: Here beside the sterns of the high ships.

KLYTAIMNÊSTRA: By the tackle and stinking fish? Whatever you say.

AGAMEMNON: You know what you must do. I wish you'd do it.

KLYTAIMNÊSTRA: Do? Do what? I do everything you say.

AGAMEMNON: I'll stay here in Aulis with the bridegroom, while—

KLYTAIMNÊSTRA: While? While what? Where will I be? A mother has duties—

AGAMEMNON: While you go back to Argos and see to your daughters.

KLYTAIMNÊSTRA: And abandon my child? But who will raise the bridal torch?

AGAMEMNON: The fire will be lit, you can trust me.

KLYTAIMNÊSTRA: This is against custom. It demands seriousness.

AGAMEMNON: An army camp is not the place for a woman!

KLYTAIMNÊSTRA: It's a mother's right to give her children in marriage!

AGAMEMNON: It's a mother's duty to look after her daughters!

KLYTAIMNÊSTRA: They are being seen to in the women's quarters!

AGAMEMNON: Do as I say!

KLYTAIMNÊSTRA: No! No, by the sovereign goddess who reigns in Argos! Very well, husband, we each have our tasks, and much to do. You have much to arrange outside the tent, and I'll see to matter inside. My daughter will have a proper wedding. *(Exit into tent.)*

AGAMEMNON: Will nothing go right? I try and I try and I fail. I try to spare her the sight of my onerous duty, and it comes to nothing. I plot, I contrive, I deceive even those I love most—and nothing. I must go to Kalchas to arrange the sacrifice just as the goddess demands. This deed that revolts me. This deed that will be an agony to all Greece. A wise man has a wife who listens to him, or no wife at all. *(Exit.)*

(Music. Song. Dance.)

YOUNG WOMEN OF CHALKIS: *(Sing.)*
They will sail now,
sail,
the Greeks set sail,
in their proud ships,
to where Simoïs's swirling waters spin silver,
Greeks,

armed Greeks,
with their fleets,
their weapons,
their spears and pikes,
to the land Apollo holds dear,
the plains of Troy,
the citadel of Ilion,
where Kassandra tosses her sun-bright hair,
crowned in laurel,
gripped by the god,
by Apollo's might,
Apollo who drives her reeling, spinning,
into unknown time,
to see the unknown.

On Troy's proud towers,
on her circling walls,
Trojans will watch as the war god nears,
war god Arês,
with his sturdy bronze shield,
Arês,
in his gleaming battle gear of bronze.
And with him,
in his wake,
the pine-winged ships,
ships sped on by bellied sails,
plow the seas,
nearing the silvery streams of Simoïs.
War god and Greeks coming,
coming,
to win back Helen,
sister of the sky-twin Dioskouroi,
sons of Zeus,
Helen,
to be won by the clashing bronze shields,
by the deadly spears of Argive warriors.

War god Arês will circle Pergamos,
the Phrygians' city,

girdle her battlements,
her stone-built towers,
with war,
slaughter and war,
with blood,
death,
destruction,
and Priam's head will be hacked,
and every Trojan warrior butchered,
every house be brought low.
Then Troy's women,
then Priam's wife,
will weep hot tears,
and Zeus's daughter will know tears,
bitter tears,
for deserting her husband.

I hope never,
never to see,
I hope my children,
my children's children,
will never behold so dark a day
as will fall on those Lydian women,
wives resplendent in gold,
the women of Troy,
as they sit at their looms,
among themselves,
wailing:

FIRST YOUNG WOMAN: *(Sings.)*
    "What man will rip me from my native soil,
    my ruined city, like a flower uprooted,
    and drag me by my flowing hair?"

YOUNG WOMEN OF CHALKIS: *(Sing.)*
    It is to you,
    Helen,
    to you, daughter of the long-necked swan,

they owe their fate,
these women,
if the story is more than a fable,
that Zeus came to Lêda as a great-winged bird.
Or is it a lying tale without truth,
diversion dreamed up by poets?

(Music out.)

ACHILLEUS: *(Enters.)* Is General Agamemnon anywhere near? If not, where can I find him? Will one of you slaves go after him, and tell him that Pêleus's son Achilleus is at his tent, waiting to see him. *(Exit a SLAVE.)* I'm afraid I have a complaint, you see. We've been here beside the Euripos for a long while, and it's not the same for all of us. Those who are unmarried and without families have abandoned our houses with no protection. Others, men who are married, have wives and children at home. It's odd, but the passion for this war that has swept Greece must be the work of some god. How else to explain it?

But all things considered, I feel it's only right to have my say on the way things stand. Anyone else who wants to is free to speak for himself. Well. When I left Pharsalos and my father Pêleus, I didn't expect to be wasting my time here beside the Euripos doing nothing, waiting for a breath of wind to blow up. Besides, I have my men to deal with, my Myrmidons. They're forever pestering me with questions. "How much longer, Achilleus? All we do is sit here counting off days! When do we sail for Troy? Do something! If not, then lead us home, and stop waiting for the sons of Atreus to act!"

KLYTAIMNÊSTRA: *(Enters from the tent.)* Achilleus, son of Thetis, I heard your voice from inside the tent, and have come out to greet you.

ACHILLEUS: And who is this beautiful woman? So gracious! So charming!

KLYTAIMNÊSTRA: We've never met; there's no way you could know me. But I thank you for your courtesy.

ACHILLEUS: Who are you? Why have you come? This is no place for a woman. Fenced in with men in armor, weapons, shields!

KLYTAIMNÊSTRA: I'm Klytaimnêstra, daughter of Lêda. Agamemnon's wife.

ACHILLEUS: Brief and to the point. But, dear lady, I shouldn't be seen talking with a woman.

KLYTAIMNÊSTRA: Wait! Don't run off! Don't be frightened. Give me your right hand. Here's mine. A happy prologue to a happy marriage.

ACHILLEUS: What must I—? Touch your hand? But how could I face Agamemnon having touched what I should not!

KLYTAIMNÊSTRA: Should not? But, son of Thetis, you're marrying my daughter!

ACHILLEUS: Marrying your—? But—! I don't understand! How do I answer this? Is this some delusion?

KLYTAIMNÊSTRA: I'm sorry, I've offended you. I know that men are shy when it comes to talk of marriage and new relatives.

ACHILLEUS: Kind lady, I never courted your daughter. Nor have the sons of Atreus mentioned marriage.

KLYTAIMNÊSTRA: If what you say is true, I don't understand either. I can well imagine how shocking my words must be. Yours are as shocking to me.

ACHILLEUS: Yes, but we can work this out, I'm sure. I suspect we've both been equally misled.

KLYTAIMNÊSTRA: Who would have done this to me? This outrage? I'm here to arrange a marriage, but there is no marriage. Except in my mind, it seems. I'm deeply ashamed.

ACHILLEUS: Perhaps we're both being made fools of. I think we'd do best to ignore it. It's not important.

KLYTAIMNÊSTRA: I'm sorry. I have to leave now. I can't face you, I'm so humiliated. I've been made out to be a liar.

ACHILLEUS: Good-bye, then. I'll go in to see your husband.

OLD MAN: *(Calls from the half-opened entrance to the tent.)* Achilleus, son of Thetis! Stop! Wait! It's you I'm calling! And you, daughter of Lêda! Please!

ACHILLEUS: Who is that? Why are you hiding? He sounds terrified.

OLD MAN: I'm a slave. It's true, so why not say it. It's all fortune dealt me.

ACHILLEUS: A slave? Whose? Not mine. We keep our property apart— Agamemnon and I.

OLD MAN: No, that lady's slave. The lady there with you. Her father gave me to her once.

ACHILLEUS: All right, I'm here. Why did you stop me?

OLD MAN: Is it just the two of you there? No one else?

ACHILLEUS: Yes, only the two of us. Come out.

OLD MAN: It's happened, what I feared! I pray fortune spare those I want to save! *(Enters from the tent.)*

ACHILLEUS: Your message, old man.

KLYTAIMNÊSTRA: You're safe. I'll see to that. Tell us.

OLD MAN: I'm a friend, lady, to you and your children.

KLYTAIMNÊSTRA: I know you for an old slave of my house.

OLD MAN: And came to Argos as part of your dowry.

KLYTAIMNÊSTRA: And have been with me ever since.

OLD MAN: A friend to you, but less a friend to your husband.

KLYTAIMNÊSTRA: Why are you hesitating?

OLD MAN: Your daughter, mistress. Your husband is going to kill her.

KLYTAIMNÊSTRA: What? How dare you! You're mad!

OLD MAN: With his own hand. A knife in her white throat.

KLYTAIMNÊSTRA: Stop! Stop, I can't bear it! Is my husband insane?

OLD MAN: Just not where you and your child are concerned.

KLYTAIMNÊSTRA: What demon could drive him to such a horror?

OLD MAN: An oracle, according to Kalchas. So the fleet can sail.

KLYTAIMNÊSTRA: Sail where? How can he do this, how can he kill her?

OLD MAN: To Troy, for Menelaos to win back Helen.

KLYTAIMNÊSTRA: And for that he kills my daughter?

OLD MAN: He's sacrificing her to Artemis.

KLYTAIMNÊSTRA: And the false marriage that brought me here?

OLD MAN: He knew you'd accept it.

KLYTAIMNÊSTRA: I've delivered her to death, and her mother, too.

OLD MAN: I pity you both. This is dreadful.

KLYTAIMNÊSTRA: I'm lost. Only tears are left me.

OLD MAN: Let them come. It's a bad blow.

KLYTAIMNÊSTRA: Where did you learn this?

OLD MAN: He sent me with a second letter.

KLYTAIMNÊSTRA: Telling me to bring the girl to her death?

OLD MAN: Warning you not to. He was in his right mind then.

KLYTAIMNÊSTRA: But why didn't you deliver it?

OLD MAN: Menelaos took it. He caused all this.

KLYTAIMNÊSTRA: Achilleus, do you hear this?

ACHILLEUS: I hear of your cruel suffering, and the insult to me.

KLYTAIMNÊSTRA: They're killing my child. The marriage was the snare.
Son of Thetis, I'm only a mortal and your mother is a goddess, so I
feel no shame in falling at your knees. What good is pride now? She's
my child. She's all that matters. What else can I do but fight for her?
(To ACHILLEUS.) Son of great Thetis, save me, save my girl in our
misery, the same girl who was meant to be your wife, though it was all
a cruel joke—but even so. I decked her out in garlands of flowers for
you. I brought her here to become your bride. But all I've done is
bring her to her death.

    The shame and dishonor will be yours, Achilleus, if you fail to
defend her. You may not have been her husband, but you were called
her husband; the dear husband of my poor, unfortunate girl. I implore
you by your chin, by your strong right arm, by your goddess
mother—I implore you by your name, for it is your name that has
destroyed me, the same name that should have defended me.

    I have no altar to flee to as a refuge, only your knees. I have no
friend to help. You've heard of Agamemnon's vicious cruelty, how he
stops at nothing. And here I am, a woman, in a camp of unruly men
ready to commit any evil. If you have the boldness to stretch your
hand out over me, then we're saved. If not, we're lost.

FIRST YOUNG WOMAN: Motherhood is a powerful magic that possesses
all mothers. They will risk any danger for the sake a child.

ACHILLEUS: Pride rises in me and urges me on. And yet I learned moderation from my master, moderation in grief and triumph, for such men live a life of balance and reason. I admit, there are times when not to be wise is a pleasure, but there are also times when good judgment is the best course.

I was raised in the house of Cheiron the centaur, that most holy of men. He taught me always to be honest and straight dealing in all I did. So as long as the sons of Atreus lead us justly, I'll follow; but let them lead us badly, I'll refuse. Whatever happens, whether here or in Troy, I will be my own man, my nature free and uncommitted, and in doing so honor Arês, war god, the best I'm able. As for you, who have been so cruelly treated by those who are nearest to you, I will show you as much pity and fight for you as roundly as a soldier's duty permits. More than that I cannot do.

Your daughter, who has been referred to as my bride, I assure you will never be slaughtered by her father. I won't allow it. I will not permit myself to be used dishonorably by him or anyone. For if I do, my name will be your daughter's executioner as surely as if it had wielded the knife itself. Your husband may be the cause of this, but my body is the one would be polluted if your child dies because of my name. The brutality of the use they've put her to appalls me, an outrage so monstrous it beggars imagination. If he has his way, I would be ranked the lowest of cowards in the entire Greek army, a nothing, and Menelaos a hero. I would no longer be the son of Pêleus, but the whelp of some ravening demon if your husband is allowed to use my name to do his killing. I swear by my grandfather Nêreus, sea god, and my mother Thetis, King Agamemnon will lay no hand, not a finger, on your daughter, not even to graze her gown.

Let their prophet Kalchas begin the sacrifice with his barley and lustral water and he'll regret it. What is a seer anyway but a man who mouths a single truth in a pack of lies, and that's only when he's lucky. When luck deserts him, he's forgotten. I say this not because of the marriage. There are countless girls who want to share my bed. But I've been misused brutally by King Agamemnon, and the insult stings. I won't have it. If he wanted to use my name as a lure to trap the girl, he should have asked. After all, it was mainly because of me you agreed to bring your daughter.

If use of my name had sped our ships to Troy, I'd have lent it. Why not? We're all Greeks. We have a common interest, we're all in the same war. Why should I have refused? As it is, these generals regard me as a nobody, indifferent whether I'm treated with honor or ignored. Let anyone try to take your daughter from me and this sword will do more than mirror his reflection.

So, be calm. I realize I appeared at a difficult time like some all-powerful god, even though I'm not one. But I assure you, to save the girl, I will become one.

FIRST YOUNG WOMAN: Every word you've said, son of Pêleus, is worthy of the great sea goddess, your mother. Her words live in you.

KLYTAIMNÊSTRA: Dear man, how can I ever find words to praise you that are neither too much nor too meager, and so offend you one way or the other? Men worthy of praise hate those who praise them to excess. It shames me to drag you into my sufferings when they have nothing to do with you. And yet, when a good man comes to the aid of someone even remote from him, whose troubles are none of his own, his is a noble action. I ask for your pity only because my troubles are pitiable.

First I thought you would be my daughter's bridegroom, and so my son. But that proved an empty hope. And now my daughter's death may serve as an evil omen for your own marriage whenever it comes, and that you must guard against. Everything you said, from first to last, was nobly said. If you decide to save her, my child will be saved. Would it please you if she came here to embrace your knees as a suppliant? This isn't the way of a young girl, of course, but she'll come if you wish, with dignity and humble modesty. And yet, if my own supplication can move you to pity, I'd rather we didn't call her. She's shy, you see. But modesty is worth honoring in any form.

ACHILLEUS: No, don't bring her out. Better not to invite ignorant gossip. Soldiers crammed together, away from home and domestic cares, revel in malicious slander and back-biting filth. Supplicate me or not, it comes out the same. My greatest concern is to save you from disaster. You may rest assured of one thing: I don't lie. And if I do, if I deceive you, then may *I* die. If I live, she lives; if she dies, I die.

KLYTAIMNÊSTRA: Fortune bless you for caring for the unfortunate.

ACHILLEUS: Listen to me. We have to plan.

KLYTAIMNÊSTRA: Listen? You're my only hope.

ACHILLEUS: We'll persuade her father to see reason.

KLYTAIMNÊSTRA: He's a coward, he's afraid of the army.

ACHILLEUS: Talk to him. Beat down his arguments.

KLYTAIMNÊSTRA: That's cold comfort. Tell me what to do.

ACHILLEUS: Reason with him first, convince him not to kill the child. If
he refuses, then come to me. But only then. For if you persuade him
yourself, there will be no need for my involvement. You'll be safe, as
will your daughter. This way there will be no rift between us,
Agamemnon and me, we remain friends, and the army will have no
cause for censure. I'd have pulled it off by reason rather than force.
This way, things would turn out well for all of you, even without my
help.

KLYTAIMNÊSTRA: How wisely you see these matters. I'll do as you say.
But what if I don't succeed? Where will I find you? Where shall I
come searching for you in my misery?

ACHILLEUS: I'll be there when you need me. Above all, you mustn't be
seen rushing through the troops frantically searching me out. Do
nothing to disgrace your father's house. Tyndareos was a great man in
Greece, don't shame his honor.

KLYTAIMNÊSTRA: Whatever you say. I trust you. If there are gods, you'll
be rewarded. If not, then what does any of this matter?

(*Exeunt KLYTAIMNÊSTRA and the OLD MAN into the tent and
ACHILLEUS to his camp.*)

(*Music. Song. Dance.*)

YOUNG WOMEN OF CHALKIS: (*Sing.*)
    What songs they sang,
    what joyous songs,

at the marriage of Peleus on Pêlion,
songs sung to the Libyan flute,
to the dance-loving lyre,
the shrill pipe of the reeds,
when the Muses, the Muses came dancing,
dancing, stomping,
stomping in sandals of gold,
dancing,
rejoicing to the feast of the gods,
and their voices rang out through the groves and glens,
through the centaurs' mountain home,
rang in praise of Thetis and the son of Aiakos.
And there,
drawing wine from golden bowls,
Dardanos's son,
the favorite, loved plaything of Zeus's bed,
nubile Ganymede,
Phrygian Ganymede,
while on the shore,
along the bright sands,
the fifty Nereïds in celebration,
Nêreus's daughters danced their whirling,
weaving dance.

And then came the centaurs,
man-horse centaurs,
riding, thudding from their forest home,
their heads crowned with fresh leaves,
sporting pine spears,
riding,
rushing to Bakkhos's wine bowl.
And they cried aloud:

FIRST YOUNG WOMAN: *(Sings.)*
   "Daughter of Nêreus, Thetis, goddess,
   your son will be great, a mighty man,
   a light, a beacon to all of Thessaly.
   Cheiron knows, Cheiron, wise centaur,
   Cheiron reads Apollo's oracles.

He will come one day leading his Myrmidons,
armed with spear and great bronze shield,
armed himself in war gear of gold,
fashioned by Hephaistos, fire god,
his mother's gift, Thetis's gift to her warrior son
who will set Troy's citadel ablaze."

YOUNG WOMEN OF CHALKIS: *(Sing.)*
And the gods in celebration,
in joy,
blessed the marriage of the firstborn Nereïd
and Aiakos's son.

Your head, Iphigeneia,
your radiant hair,
the Greeks will crown like the head of a heifer,
a spotted heifer led down from the mountains,
an unstained heifer led down to the sacrifice,
down to the altar,
and there the knife will pierce your throat,
and your blood will wash the goddess's altar.
But you were not raised to the tune of the pipe,
the shepherd's tune,
nor to the whistle of the vigilant herdsman
guarding his flocks.
You were raised up at your mother's side,
one day to be the bride of a great man's son.
Where is modesty,
where is virtue,
now blasphemy rules,
now anarchy leads,
and lawlessness wins the day?
Where is fear of the gods
when the gods are dismissed?

(Enter KLYTAIMNÊSTRA from the tent.)

(Music out.)

KLYTAIMNÊSTRA: *(Enters from tent.)* Where could he be? I've come out looking for him. He went out some time ago and hasn't returned. My daughter has learned, poor child, that her father plans to kill her. She's shaken to the core with sobbing and tears. Ah, but here he comes. He'll soon stand convicted of planning an evil act against his child.

AGAMEMNON: *(Enters.)* Ah, daughter of Lêda, how convenient to find you here. I have matters to discuss. Better if the bride doesn't hear.

KLYTAIMNÊSTRA: And what would these matters be?

AGAMEMNON: No—call her from the tent. Say her father wants her. The lustral waters are prepared, as is the barley to cast into the flame. The cattle stand ready, too, that must spill their dark blood to Artemis before the marriage.

KLYTAIMNÊSTRA: What honeyed words, husband. But there are no words vile enough for your plan. *(Calling into the tent.)* Come out, child, come out to your father, since you already know his intention. And bring Orestês. Wrap him in your robe. *(IPHIGENEIA enters from the tent carrying ORESTÊS.)* Here she is, the obedient daughter. Very well. Now I'll speak for us both.

AGAMEMNON: Child, why are you weeping? Where's that smile I know? Why are you hiding your face with your robe, your eyes cast down?

KLYTAIMNÊSTRA: Where do I begin? Where do I start my tale of misery and distress? It is bitter grief throughout: beginning, middle, end.

AGAMEMNON: What is it? What? Why are you all looking at me with such pain and distress?

KLYTAIMNÊSTRA: Husband, try to be honorable for once, and answer like a man.

AGAMEMNON: You have no cause to speak to me that way. Ask your question.

KLYTAIMNÊSTRA: Is it your intention to kill our daughter?

AGAMEMNON: How dare you! These vile suspicions!

KLYTAIMNÊSTRA: Answer the question.

AGAMEMNON: Ask a reasonable question, I'll answer!

KLYTAIMNÊSTRA: Answer. This is the one I'm asking.

AGAMEMNON: Oh gods! Why is everything against me?

KLYTAIMNÊSTRA: And against me—and her! All three of us!

AGAMEMNON: How have you been wronged?

KLYTAIMNÊSTRA: How can you ask that? Have you lost your mind?

AGAMEMNON: And so I'm ruined. I've been betrayed.

KLYTAIMNÊSTRA: I know it all. Everything. I know what you're about to do. Your silence alone condemns you. Don't waste your breath.

AGAMEMNON: No more words. Why add lies that only enlarge my disgrace?

KLYTAIMNÊSTRA: You'll listen to me now. And no more riddles, no more words doubling back and back on themselves, but just plain talk—the truth.

   In the first place, you married me by force, against my will, by murdering my first husband, Tantalos. And you tore my baby from my breast and dashed its brains out on the floor with your heel. And then my brothers came, two sons of Zeus, on their glistening horses, to war against you. They saved me from you. But you crawled, tail between your legs, to beg protection from my old father, Tyndareos, and he rescued you. So I was your wife, again. I reconciled myself to you, to your house, I was an irreproachable wife, as you yourself can bear witness. In matters of sex, I made few demands, but was always compliant. I saw to it that your house grew in wealth and influence, so that when you entered it you did so joyously, and when leaving, you left with pride and satisfaction. Good wives are rare. Bad ones are no trouble to find. I also bore you this son, after first giving birth to three daughters, and now you're taking one of them from me, cruelly depriving me.

How would you answer if someone asked why you're killing her? No. I'll answer for you. So that Menelaos can have back his precious Helen. The life of an innocent child for the life of a whore. Buying back what we loathe with what we love most.

Think about this for once. You go off to your war. Sail away. To Troy. For years. What do I do? In a house empty of one part of my heart? What do I do when I see her special places, where she stood, where she sat, her girl's room, empty? What? Alone with endless grieving and a broken heart, moaning laments for her who will never return. "He killed you, dear child, the father who gave you life, killed you. He held the knife." What a motive for hatred you will have left behind in your house. But you'll return. And the deserved welcome you will receive from me and my children will be no cause for surprise. By everything that's holy, don't force me to betray you and my duty to you by betraying me.

Tell me. What prayers will fall from your lips when you kill her? What blessing will you call down on yourself as you butcher your child? A homecoming to match the shame of your setting out? And what am I to pray for? A blessing on your head? When the world calls down blessings on murderers, the whole world is mad, including the gods. And when you come home to Argos, will you sweep your children up in your arms and kiss them? No. Heaven won't allow it. And which of your children will even dare look at you, terrified that the one you kiss you will also kill? Has any of this ever crossed your mind? Or is your mind fixed on one thing only? Parading around with your scepter and playing the general.

As general, you should have addressed your men with *these* words: "Men of Argos! You want to sail to Troy, you say! Then let us draw lots and see whose daughter will die!" There would have been justice in such words, as there was no justice in your choice of your daughter as victim.

And what of Menelaos? This is his war, after all. Why not offer up his own daughter? His own, his dear, beloved Hermionê. A pawn in his game to win back whorish Helen. But no, it's my child who will be ripped from my arms, mine, despite my faithfulness to you, while she who made a sty of her husband's bed will have her daughter safe at home in Sparta, and be happy.

Tell me. Is there anything I've said here that is not true? If not, and if I speak justly and truly, then do not kill your daughter, your daughter and mine. Prove yourself a man of wisdom and judgment.

FIRST YOUNG WOMAN: Listen to her, Agamemnon. Saving a child is a noble act. No one would deny that.

IPHIGENEIA: If I had the gift of Orpheus, Father, a voice whose song had the power to charm even stones to rise up and follow him; if I had words to persuade anyone of anything, I'd use them, I would use all my arts. But my only art at this moment is my tears. I offer them to you. I press my body against your knees like a torn suppliant's branch, the body that this woman once bore you. Don't send me to death before my time, Father. It's sweet to see day's holy light. Don't force me to face the gloom in Death's Dark Kingdom.

I was the first to call you father, the first you called your child; the first to sit on your knees and hug and kiss you and be hugged and kissed by you. And you'd say to me: "Will I see you living and happy in your husband's house, a sight to make your old father rejoice?" And I would answer, reaching to touch your chin, as I do now: "And you, Father? What will I do for you when you are old? You'll come and be welcome in my house, and I'll look after you, and nurse you in your age, for all the dear, sweet things you've done for me." I remember, remember it all, but you've forgotten and now want to kill me.

Father, in the name of Pelops and your father Atreus and my mother here suffering an agony worse than at my birth, don't do it. What have Paris and Helen to do with me, or I with them? Why should Paris's coming to Sparta mean my death? Look at me. No, in my eyes. Kiss me. At least I'll have that to remember as I'm dying, if you refuse to listen. (AGAMEMNON and IPHIGENEIA kiss. IPHIGENEIA takes ORESTÊS from KLYTAIMNÊSTRA.) Little brother, too small to be any help to your friends, weep with me, cry out to your father not to kill your sister. You see? Even babies sense the injustice of life. He has no words, but still he pleads with you. Be merciful. Pity me. Don't kill me. Both of us beg you, our hands at your chin, your dears, one just a baby, the other a grown girl. Well. A few words can say it all. The light of the dear sun was made for life,

and in death there is nothing. Only a madman longs for death.
The life of a dog is better than a noble death.

FIRST YOUNG WOMAN: Cruel Helen, this is your doing. You and your
shameful love have caused the deadly struggle between the sons of
Atreus and their children.

AGAMEMNON: I know what is pitiable, and I know what is not. I love
my children. I would be a madman if I didn't. It is as terrible, wife, to
do what I must do, as not to do it, but do it I must, I have no choice.
Look around you, child. A vast army, an armada of warships, men
heavy in bronze mail and weapons, all Greeks, all Hellenes, from every
part of the land. And they can't sail, can't sail to Ilion, can't pull down
the famous towers of Troy, unless I offer you up as sacrifice, as the
prophet Kalchas says the gods demand.

Some fierce mad lust has seized the army to sail at once to the
barbarian's land and end this rape of Greek wives. And if they don't
sail, if I refuse to sacrifice you, they will come to Argos, they will kill
us all, my girls back home, the three of you, me.

I'm no slave to Menelaos, it's not his will I'm made to
accomplish, no, but the will of Greece. It's Greece has made me its
slave. It's Greece has expunged my will. Necessity is my master. Greece
must be free. And if you and I can make it so, child, then we must.
As Greeks we must not be subject to barbarians, but defend ourselves
against the plunder and rape of Greek wives by brute force. *(Exit.)*

(Music. Song. Dance.)

KLYTAIMNÊSTRA: *(Chants.)*
  Oh child, daughter!
  Women, her death destroys me.
  Your father, child,
  your father has deserted you
  and leaves you to die.

IPHIGENEIA: *(Chants.)*
  The same sad song of misery serves us both.
  The sound, the song of weeping.
  The sun's sweet light,

the light of day,
are no longer mine.

(Sings.)

IOOOO!
IOOOO!
Oh unhappy snowbound valley of Phrygia,
unhappy slopes of Ida,
Ida where once Priam, Troy's king,
cast out his son, the tender baby, Paris,
Paris torn rudely from his mother's breast,
Paris left to die, Priam's child,
known in time, known in Troy at his return,
as the son of Ida, Paris of Ida,
left to die on Ida's slopes.

If only, oh, if only that herdsman
had never found, never raised him,
Paris of Ida,
to tend his oxen on Ida's slopes,
to tend his herds in meadows,
lush meadows where waters sparkle, and
springs gush bright from the earth,
fountains of the Nymphs, meadows
alive with flowers, where roses and hyacinths
grow to be gathered by goddesses.

It was here one day that Athêna came,
and devious Aphroditê, and Hera and
Hermês, messenger of Zeus.
Aphroditê, proud of the lust she wakens,
Athêna, proud of her martial spear, and
Hera proud of Zeus's bed.
These three came,
came for a judgment,
a deadly judgment,
a contest in beauty that meant my death,
but for the Greeks glory and renown.

And this, this is the offering to Artemis,
the sacrifice,
my life for a wind to Troy.

Oh Mother, he has left me,
my father has left me,
deserted, betrayed me.
And Helen, cursed Helen,
I curse you, curse you, Helen
who has cost me my life,
killed by my father, my
ungodly father, by my
father's ungodly knife.

And I curse you, Aulis,
for your welcoming bay,
safe harbor for the bronze-beaked ships,
proud fleet speeding the Greeks to Troy.
And Zeus I curse for winds of no help;
Zeus and his treasury of winds:
for one a fair wind to billow his sails;
for another a stern wind to drop his sails;
some set sail, and some make port.
Others are cursed with waiting, waiting.
I pity, how I pity our race and its distress,
we, we whose life is but a day.
Life and distress, life and its sufferings,
are our fate.
I curse the sufferings Tyndareos's daughter
put upon our race!

(Music out.)

FIRST YOUNG WOMAN: I pity you for your cruel fate; nothing you
    have done deserves it.

IPHIGENEIA: Mother! Mother, there are men coming!

KLYTAIMNÊSTRA: And Achilleus, child, son of the sea goddess, Achilleus, in whose name you came here.

IPHIGENEIA: I want to hide, Mother. Open the doors.

KLYTAIMNÊSTRA: But, child, why?

IPHIGENEIA: I'm ashamed to see him.

KLYTAIMNÊSTRA: Why?

IPHIGENEIA: The marriage. This doomed, hopeless marriage.

KLYTAIMNÊSTRA: This is no time for delicacy. Stay. Don't be shy. We do what we can.

(Sounds of shouting offstage. Enter ACHILLEUS followed by SLAVE ATTENDANTS carrying his armor and weapons.)

ACHILLEUS: Unhappy daughter of Lêda—

KLYTAIMNÊSTRA: Yes, unhappy—

ACHILLEUS: The Greeks. They're shouting. Terrible things.

KLYTAIMNÊSTRA: About what?

ACHILLEUS: Your daughter.

KLYTAIMNÊSTRA: I know what's coming.

ACHILLEUS: They demand she be slaughtered.

KLYTAIMNÊSTRA: And no one defends her?

ACHILLEUS: They're shouting about me, too.

KLYTAIMNÊSTRA: What? Tell me.

ACHILLEUS: "Stone him to death!"

KLYTAIMNÊSTRA: For defending my daughter?

ACHILLEUS: For that.

KLYTAIMNÊSTRA: Who would dare such a thing?

ACHILLEUS: Every Greek out there.

KLYTAIMNÊSTRA: And your own men? Your Myrmidons?

ACHILLEUS: They were the first to turn on me.

KLYTAIMNÊSTRA: Dear child, we're lost.

ACHILLEUS: They called me the slave of my hoped-for marriage.

KLYTAIMNÊSTRA: And how did you answer?

ACHILLEUS: That they were not to kill my bride.

KLYTAIMNÊSTRA: And you were right.

ACHILLEUS: That Agamemnon had promised her.

KLYTAIMNÊSTRA: And had her brought from Argos.

ACHILLEUS: The force of their shouts drowned me out.

KLYTAIMNÊSTRA: A mob is a monstrous thing.

ACHILLEUS: I'll defend you all the same.

KLYTAIMNÊSTRA: Against the whole army? Single-handed?

ACHILLEUS: Do you see these men with my armor?

KLYTAIMNÊSTRA: Bless you, but—

ACHILLEUS: I'll earn that blessing.

KLYTAIMNÊSTRA: Will my daughter not be sacrificed?

ACHILLEUS: Not without my consent.

KLYTAIMNÊSTRA: Will they come to take her?

ACHILLEUS: Hordes of them, led on by Odysseus.

KLYTAIMNÊSTRA: On orders or by his own choice?

ACHILLEUS: The men chose him, but he was pleased.

KLYTAIMNÊSTRA: A vile man to do a vile thing.

ACHILLEUS: I'll stop him.

KLYTAIMNÊSTRA: Will he drag her away by force?

ACHILLEUS: By her golden hair.

KLYTAIMNÊSTRA: What will I do?

ACHILLEUS: Hang on. Don't let go of her.

KLYTAIMNÊSTRA: That's all? And she won't die?

ACHILLEUS: The least we can expect is a struggle.

IPHIGENEIA: Mother, listen to me; listen to me, both of you. You,
Mother, are angry with your husband. But that shouldn't be; it makes
no sense: it's no easy task to fight the inevitable. And it's right we
thank this stranger for his generous and courageous heart. But we
must also consider his reputation, and do nothing to tarnish that. It
would do us no good, and might even bring him to harm. Listen to
me now, Mother, and the way I've worked things out, for I've thought
about it carefully.

I have made up my mind to die. But to die in glory. I've put behind me all petty considerations, all meanness of spirit. If you come to see it my way, Mother, you'll see how right I am. All of Greece, all of Greece in its greatness, looks to me. It depends on me whether the ships sail and whether Troy is destroyed. It is for me to see that in future our women are safe from abduction by barbarians. And the way to that is to make Troy pay for Paris's cruel rape of Helen. My death can accomplish all this. And with it I will be known as the one who gave Greece her freedom, and my name will be blessed for all time.

It isn't right for me to cling too dearly to life. You gave me life not only for your sake, but for the sake of Greece, for the common good. Countless thousands of men have strapped on their shields, countless thousands have taken up oars, ready, every one of them, to fight, to die, for a Greece cruelly wronged. Am I to destroy all that? Is my single life so important? How could I answer them if this were to happen? But there's something more.

How can it be right for this man to battle the whole Greek army and die for the sake of a woman? It's more important that one man live in light than ten thousand women. And if Artemis demands that I be sacrificed, I'm only mortal, who am I to oppose the goddess? That must never happen. My life belongs to Greece. Offer me up, then, kill me, and bring down Troy. That will be my monument. That will be my marriage, my children, and my glory for all time.

Greeks were destined to rule, Mother, not to serve, but to rule others, other countries, other people; to be ruled by others would be to make slaves of Greeks; and Greeks were born to be free.

FIRST YOUNG WOMAN: Young woman, who could find fault in you? You play your part nobly. It is destiny and the goddess are to blame.

ACHILLEUS: Daughter of Agamemnon, if I won you for my wife, I would know that some god chose to make me happy. I envy Greece. You belong to Greece and Greece to you, and both are blessed. Your words are noble and worthy of your land. You have recognized that the gods are stronger and given up your struggle. You have made a virtue of Necessity.

The more I know you, the more I see your nobility and greatness of spirit, the more I long to have you as my bride. I want you to live. I want to save you. I want to take you home, to serve you. And with

Thetis as my witness, I swear that I will be grieved if I fail to do battle for you against every man of the Greeks. Death—death is a terrible thing.

IPHIGENEIA: What I say now I say in fear of no one. Helen's beauty has stirred up enough strife, and will cause battles and murders because of her body. But as for you, stranger, promise me you will kill no one, nor be killed yourself, for the sake of me. Allow me to save Greece if that is my mission.

ACHILLEUS: What a noble spirit! It puts me to shame. What more can I say? You've chosen, and chosen from a courageous heart. Why should a man not confess it? And yet, it may be, you'll think differently. So listen to my plan.

I'll place my arms close by the altar. I refuse to let you die. And when the knife is at your throat, if you think differently than you do at this moment, accept my offer. I won't let you die because of one reckless impulse. I'm going to the goddess's temple now with these arms, and wait till you come.

(Exeunt ACHILLEUS and his SLAVE ATTENDANTS.)

IPHIGENEIA: Mother, why these tears?

KLYTAIMNÊSTRA: This sorrow in my heart.

IPHIGENEIA: Don't make me a coward. Do as I say.

KLYTAIMNÊSTRA: I won't fail you.

IPHIGENEIA: Don't cut your hair or dress in mourning.

KLYTAIMNÊSTRA: But I'll have lost you.

IPHIGENEIA: No. I'll be saved. My name is your glory.

KLYTAIMNÊSTRA: But how can I not mourn you?

IPHIGENEIA: Not one tear. I won't have a grave.

KLYTAIMNÊSTRA: But we mourn the dead, not the tomb.

IPHIGENEIA: The goddess's altar will be my tomb.

KLYTAIMNÊSTRA: Yes, I'll do as you say.

IPHIGENEIA: I'm happy. I'll have saved Greece.

KLYTAIMNÊSTRA: What shall I tell your sisters?

IPHIGENEIA: Good-bye. And raise up Orestês to splendid manhood.

KLYTAIMNÊSTRA: Hug him now. The last time.

IPHIGENEIA: Sweet boy, you helped the best you could.

KLYTAIMNÊSTRA: What can I do to please you in Argos?

IPHIGENEIA: Don't hate Father. He's your husband.

KLYTAIMNÊSTRA: He'll run a fearful race because of you.

IPHIGENEIA: He had no choice. He killed me to save Greece.

KLYTAIMNÊSTRA: He killed you by treachery. Cowardice unworthy of Atreus.

(Enter several SLAVE ATTENDANTS.)

IPHIGENEIA: Will someone lead me there before they drag me?

KLYTAIMNÊSTRA: I'll be with you.

IPHIGENEIA: No, that wouldn't be right.

KLYTAIMNÊSTRA: Holding tight to your robes.

IPHIGENEIA: No, Mother, please. Please stay here. It's better for both of

us. Father's slaves will lead me to the meadow where I'm to be
slaughtered.

KLYTAIMNÊSTRA: Child, you're not going—?

IPHIGENEIA: Never to come back.

KLYTAIMNÊSTRA: Leaving your mother?

IPHIGENEIA: Yes, with hope in my heart.

KLYTAIMNÊSTRA: No. Don't leave me—

IPHIGENEIA: There must be no tears. And you, young women, raise a
hymn of rejoicing to Artemis, a song in praise of my fate to virgin
Artemis, Zeus's daughter. Let there be silence throughout the camp.
    Take up the baskets, begin the sacrifice. Let the fire blaze high
with barleycorns. Father will lead the procession from left to right
around the altar. I come bringing salvation, salvation to Greece, and
victory. Lead me.

*(One of the SLAVE ATTENDANTS takes her hand and begins to lead
IPHIGENEIA off.)*

(Music. Song. Dance.)

IPHIGENEIA: *(Sings.)*
    Lead the destroyer, the conqueror of Troy,
    I who will tear down the towers of Ilion.
    Bring me, bring me garlands,
    garlands to wreath my head.
    And water, streams of water,
    purifying waters.
    Dance your dances, women,
    dance for Artemis around her temple,
    dance, dance around her altar,
    virgin Artemis, blessèd Artemis,
    dance in honor of Artemis.

With my blood I will wash away,
wash, if I must, wash the oracle out of our path.

Dear, dear Mother, dearest of mothers,
I can give you no tears, no tears.
Tears are not meant for the altar of Artemis,
not meant for holy rites.

Sing, women, sing in praise of Artemis,
whose temple looks eastward to Chalkis,
to Chalkis across the strait,
where warships wait in the narrows of Aulis,
and men burn, burn for a wind
to begin the end,
the destruction, the fall of Troy,
because of me.
Oh Argos that bore me!
Mykenê, my home!

FIRST YOUNG WOMAN: *(Sings.)*
    Sing praise to the city,
    the Cyclopes-built city.
    Praise to the city of Perseus.

IPHIGENEIA: *(Sings.)*
    You raised me to be a beacon of hope.
    My death is a light in the darkness.

FIRST YOUNG WOMAN: *(Sings.)*
    And you, you will be our glory for ever.

IPHIGENEIA: *(Sings.)*
    Bright radiance of Zeus, farewell.
    Great star of day that lights the earth, farewell.
    Another destiny is mine, another life.
    Farewell dear light, dear light I love.

*(Exeunt IPHIGENEIA with the SLAVE ATTENDANTS and
KLYTAIMNÊSTRA, carrying ORESTÊS, enters the tent.)*

FIRST YOUNG WOMAN: *(Chants.)*
IOOOO! IOOOO!
Blessings on you, sacker of Troy.
Blessings on you who will level Troy's towers.
She lowers her head for the victim's garlands;
she bows her head for streams of holy waters.
She walks to the altar,
she walks to the slaughter,
to shed her blood, her blood to the goddess,
blood that will flow at the thrust of the knife
in her lovely throat.

Your father awaits you with purifying waters,
the army awaits you to set sail for Troy.
But let us praise Artemis,
goddess, queen, daughter of Zeus,
and beg her to turn this defeat to victory,
this death to triumph.

Great Artemis who delights in this human slaughter,
send them on,
send them to Troy,
the army to Troy,
to deceitful, treacherous Troy,
and there let Agamemnon crown Greek spears
with victory, garlands of triumph,
and to his own glory win undying fame.

(Music out.)

SLAVE ATTENDANT: *(Enters.)* Daughter of Tendareos, Klytaimnêstra, come out of the tent, I have news.

KLYTAIMNÊSTRA: *(Enters from tent carrying ORESTÊS.)* I heard your voice. Here I am. Please, please don't bring me a worse disaster than that I already bear. I can't endure it.

SLAVE ATTENDANT: It's your daughter. A miracle has happened. Something strange and wonderful.

KLYTAIMNÊSTRA: Tell me.

SLAVE ATTENDANT: Belovèd queen and mistress, I'll tell you everything
as I saw it, unless words fail me in the reeling confusion of my mind.

When we arrived with your daughter at the grove sacred to
Artemis, and the meadow sprinkled with blossoms, the army of the
Greeks rushed to us, men pressing tightly all around, crowding,
shoving, shoulders colliding, yelling their excitement.

When King Agamemnon saw her approaching through the grove
to the place where she was to die, he groaned from deep inside him,
turned aside his head to hide his tears and covered his face with his
robe. Coming up close to her father, she said to him: "Father, I've
come. I gladly give my body as a sacrifice for my country and for all of
Greece. Lead me to the altar if this is my destiny. I pray that what I do
here will make you prosper, will give you success, and bring you safely
to your homes after a splendid victory. But no Greek must lay a hand
on me. I offer up my neck to your knife, here, now, proudly and in
silence."

Those were her words, and the entire army marveled at the girl's
nobility and heroism. Then Talthybios, whose office it was, called for a
reverent silence from the army, and the prophet Kalchas drew from its
sheath a whetted knife, placed it in a gold-worked basket, and
crowned the girl with a garland.

Then the son of Peleus, Achilleus, took in his hand the basket
and the lustral water and, sprinkling the altar, circled it, intoning:
"Goddess Artemis, daughter of Zeus and slayer of wild beasts, goddess
of the moon's great light in the darkness, hear our prayer. Accept this
sacrifice which the army of the Greeks and King Agamemnon offer to
you: undefiled blood from the throat of a beautiful virgin. Grant, now,
that our ships may safely set sail and our weapons destroy the looming
towers of Troy." The sons of Atreus and the assembled army of the
Greeks stood silent, looking at the ground, as the priest, praying, took
up the knife and looked for the place to strike.

My soul was so heavy with anguish that I stood there, my eyes
cast to the ground. And then it happened. The greatest of wonders.
We all heard the thud of the blow, but what had happened to her?
The girl was nowhere to be seen. She had vanished. The priest and the
entire army cried out, echoing each other, at the miracle sent by some
god. There on the ground, there in front of our scarcely believing eyes,

lay a deer, gasping, a vast and glorious animal whose blood washed across the goddess's altar.

Kalchas then, his face radiant with joy and relief, shouted out: "Commanders of the allied armies of Greece! Behold this victim, laid by the goddess at her altar in place of the girl, this wild deer of the mountains! She happily accepts this sacrifice rather than pollute her altar with noble blood, and promises a favoring wind on the voyage to Troy! Let every man lift up his spirits and board the ships, for today we leave the hollow bay of Aulis and sail out across the Aegean!" When the fire god's flames had burned the victim to ashes, Kalchas raised a suitable prayer to bring the army back safely.

Agamemnon has sent me to tell you of the good fortune the gods have given him, and the undying glory he has won among the Greeks. I was there. I saw it. There can be no doubt: your daughter was taken up to join the gods. So you must end your grief and set aside your anger against your husband. No man knows what the gods intend, but those they love, they protect. On this same day your daughter died and was brought to life again.

FIRST YOUNG WOMAN: How glad I am for you, lady. Your daughter is alive and living among the gods.

(Music. Song. Dance.)

KLYTAIMNÊSTRA: *(Chants.)*
Oh my child, what god has stolen you away?
How am I to speak your name and know you will hear?
How do I know, how,
how can I be sure this is not some lie,
some evil tale made up to end
my cruel grief and mourning for you?

FIRST YOUNG WOMAN: *(Chants.)*
Look! Agamemnon!
Come to tell you the same story.

AGAMEMNON: *(Enters.)* Wife, our daughter has given us reason to rejoice. She's with the gods. Now take this young calf of a son of mine and turn back home. The army will sail soon. Good-bye. It will be a

long time before my next greeting. Word travels slowly from Troy. I
wish you well in all things.

FIRST YOUNG WOMAN: *(Chants.)*
    Sail safely and with joy, son of Atreus,
    to the land of the Trojans,
    and safely and joyously home again
    when you have loaded your proud ships
    with plunder from Troy.

(Exeunt AGAMEMNON, then the CHORUS.)

(KLYTAIMNÊSTRA remains standing silently holding ORESTÊS.)

*

RHESOS

(ΡΗΣΟΣ)

CHARACTERS

HÊKTOR *crown prince of Troy, Trojan commander-in-chief*
AENEAS *Trojan leader, cousin of Hêktor*
DOLON *youthful Trojan soldier*
RHESOS *king of Thrace.*
ODYSSEUS *Greek chief, king of Ithaka*
DIOMÊDES *Greek chief, crown prince of Argos*
ATHÊNA *goddess*
PARIS *brother of Hêktor*
CHARIOTEER *of Rhesos*
SHEPHERD
MUSE *mother of Rhesos*
CHORUS OF TROJAN SENTRIES
FIRST TROJAN SENTRY *chorus leader*
TROJAN SOLDIERS, ATTENDANTS, GUARDS

RHESOS

Late night.
Hêktor's Trojan encampment on the plains outside Troy.
HÊKTOR sleeps on a bed of leaves on the ground.
Other sleeping TROJAN SOLDIERS surround him.
Enter the CHORUS OF TROJAN SENTRIES in search of HÊKTOR.
Music.

FIRST TROJAN SENTRY: *(Chants.)*
    He's here somewhere!
    Find him, men!

SECOND TROJAN SENTRY: *(Chants.)*
    Hêktor, sir.

THIRD TROJAN SENTRY: *(Chants.)*
    I'll look over there!

SECOND TROJAN SENTRY: *(Chants.)*
    Hêktor!

FIRST TROJAN SENTRY: *(Chants.)*
    What is this?
    Nobody guarding the king?

THIRD TROJAN SENTRY: *(Chants.)*
    Not a guard in sight!

FIRST TROJAN SENTRY: *(Chants.)*
    Every one of them! Asleep!

SECOND TROJAN SENTRY: *(Chants.)*
    Hêktor, sir! There's news, sir!

THIRD TROJAN SENTRY: *(Chants.)*
    Over there! Look! I see him!

THIRD TROJAN SENTRY: *(Chants; shaking HÊKTOR.)*
  Wake up! Sir! Hêktor!

HÊKTOR: *(Chants.)*
  Who's there?

THIRD TROJAN SENTRY: *(Chants; to the FIRST TROJAN SENTRY.)*
  I can't look at him!
  His eyes were so fierce when he opened them!
  Like the Gorgon face on Athêna's armor!
  You talk to him!

FIRST TROJAN SENTRY: *(Chants.)*
  It's time, sir! Wake up! There's news!

HÊKTOR: *(Chants; rising.)*
  Who are you?

FIRST TROJAN SENTRY: *(Chants.)*
  The fourth night watch, sir!

HÊKTOR: *(Chants.)*
  What's the password?

(The FIRST TROJAN SENTRY whispers in HÊKTOR's ear.)

HÊKTOR: *(Chants.)*
  It's the middle of the night!
  Why did you wake me?
  And I asked who you are!

FIRST TROJAN SENTRY: *(Chants.)*
  Sentries, sir! Don't be afraid, sir!

HÊKTOR: *(Chants.)*
  What's all the confusion?
  You leave your post, you disturb a sleeping camp!
  It's bad enough out here in the night cold—
  a stone's throw from the Greek army—

sleeping in full armor!
And then you come and wake us!

FIRST TROJAN SENTRY: *(Chants.)*
> To arms, Hêktor! We have to arm!
> Send for the allies, warn them!
> "On your feet!" tell them.
> "To arms!" tell them.
> "Cavalrymen, to your horses!"

SECOND TROJAN SENTRY: *(Chants.)*
> Rouse all the command posts, sir!

THIRD TROJAN SENTRY: *(Chants.)*
> The priests in charge of sacrifice!

SECOND TROJAN SENTRY: *(Chants.)*
> The light-armed troops!

THIRD TROJAN SENTRY: *(Chants.)*
> The archers!

(Wakened TROJAN SOLDIERS begin to gather in the vicinity to listen.)

HÊKTOR: *(Chants.)*
> First you tell me there's nothing to fear,
> then you run shaking, terror struck, rousing the army,
> ready to sound the alarm, shouting orders at me!
> What is all this?
> If you came to report, report!
> And this time make some sense of it!

FIRST TROJAN SENTRY: *(Chants.)*
> The Greeks, sir!
> They've set thousands of fires alight, sir,
> lighting up the night.

THIRD TROJAN SENTRY: *(Chants.)*
> The mooring lines of their ships

are alive in the firelight.
The whole army, in an uproar,
has surrounded Agamemnon's tent, sir,
demanding some new pronouncement.

SECOND TROJAN SENTRY: *(Chants.)*
Never before have these Greeks
been so routed by fright.

FIRST TROJAN SENTRY: *(Chants.)*
Not knowing what might happen, sir,
I came to report, so you'd never say of me
that I had failed you.

(Music out.)

HÊKTOR: No, friend, you've come in good time. You tell us of *your* fear,
but I'd say it's the Greeks who are shivering in their boots. Our
esteemed enemy is planning a major retreat under cover of night.
Or so it seems. They'll wade out to their ships, sail off in the dark,
and farewell, Troy! At least that's what these fires in the night tell me.
(More TROJAN SOLDIERS enter the scene to listen.) For all of my
success in battle today, Fortune now robs me of my lion's feast! I was
ready with this spear to sweep the plain and kill every last man of
them! Then the sun fails me and douses its fires, and along come our
priests and prophets, who read the sign of the gods, warning to wait
for dawn, only then to drive these invaders from the plains of Troy!
Without these meddling seers, I'd never have given up the field, but
fired the Greek ships and slaughtered every man in sight!

It appears now that the Greeks and our prophets don't agree.
Like slaves on the run they take advantage of the night. All right, let's
do it! Wake them! Wake the army! There's no time to lose! If we don't
get them on land, we'll split their backs as they scramble aboard ship
and bloody the ladders with their own gore! And those we capture,
we'll chain and teach respect for Troy's earth as they till the land with
the plowshare, furrow by furrow! Let's go!

FIRST TROJAN SENTRY: Before we know what they're doing? We don't
even know they're running yet.

HÊKTOR: What else can it be? Why the fires?

FIRST TROJAN SENTRY: I don't know. But I have misgivings.

HÊKTOR: If *this* scares you, anything will.

FIRST TROJAN SENTRY: But they've never lit so many before.

HÊKTOR: They've also never been routed like this before.

FIRST TROJAN SENTRY: That was your victory. What comes next?

HÊKTOR: There's only one order in war: arm and fight.

SECOND TROJAN SOLDIER: Here comes Aeneas. It looks like news.

AENEAS: *(Enters with ARMED GUARDS.)* Hêktor, what is the night guard doing here? And why have they disturbed the army's rest?

HÊKTOR: To arms, Aeneas!

AENEAS: Has there been a night attack?

HÊKTOR: Attack? No. They're scrambling for their ships!

AENEAS: You have proof for this?

HÊKTOR: Proof? What proof do I need? Look at the fires, the torches! The sky's ablaze! They're not about to wait for dawn. The fire's to light their ships and help the escape. They'll push off their well-benched vessels and head for home.

AENEAS: And you plan to do what? To arms, you say? And why are *you* armed?

HÊKTOR: To attack them as they board! Am I to let them go? After what they've done to us? This spear of *mine* won't be idle, I assure you! I will not be shamed! I'm not a coward! The god has put them square into our hands, and I won't let them off without a fight!

AENEAS: Hêktor, if only you knew how to plan as well as you fight. But no man masters every art, and yours is fighting, there's no doubting that. Roused by the news of the beacons, you're all hot to get your army on the move and leap over enemy trenches—in the dark, let me remind you. All right, so far so good! Let's suppose you manage to cross them—and the word is, by the way, they're deep as wells—and there's the enemy, not turned tail, as you assume, and scrambling madly board their ships, but face-on, staring you in the eyeballs, spears poised and ready for the attack. What do you think? That you'll defeat them? That you'll arrive back home a flaming hero? My guess is you'll never see Troy again.

And then there's the palisades. How does a retreating army, even Trojans, god knows, manage those stakes in a rout? Not to mention charioteers maneuvering embankments without smashing their axles.

But suppose you make it, suppose you come out on top, victorious. What then? Well, what then is, of course, Achilleus— Achilleus to be reckoned with—Achilleus held in reserve for just such a moment. And take my word for it, he's not about to let you fire their ships, *or* seize Greek captives, which, I suspect, is high on your agenda. He's a powerhouse, that man, a firebrand who'll dare anything, strong as a bull.

No. But I have a better idea. Let's let our Trojans sleep in peace on their shields, away from the grueling task of war, and send out a scout instead, a volunteer, to spy on the enemy camp. And if it's true, and if they're in flight, we'll be after those Greeks in a flash, every man of us. But if those fires are a trap to catch us short, then he'll tell us, our friendly spy, and we'll know and take counsel and act on good advice. Believe me, Hêktor, it's the best we can do.

(Music.)

FIRST TROJAN SENTRY: *(Chants.)*
    He's right, sir. I agree.
    Listen to him.
    Change your mind.

SECOND TROJAN SENTRY: *(Chants.)*
    A general's command should never waver.

THIRD TROJAN SENTRY: *(Chants.)*
> Let's get a man down there now, sir,
> to see what's what,
> spy on the enemy's ships,
> and find out why those fires.

FIRST TROJAN SENTRY: *(Chants.)*
> We need to know, sir.

(Music out.)

HÊKTOR: Good. Since you all agree, I concede the victory to you. *(To the TROJAN SOLDIERS who have continued to gather.)* You, some of you, go to the allies, assure them. They may have heard of our meeting and be troubled by it. *(Several TROJAN SOLDIERS hurry off.)* I'll send out a spy, Aeneas. And if it's some trap they're planning, you'll hear and be called to council. But if they *have* turned tail, and are about to cast off, be ready for an alert. When you hear the trumpets, move out, because I won't wait. I'll attack, and I'll attack now, tonight. Those Greeks and their scudding ships will know I mean business.

AENEAS: No delay now, Hêktor. Send the spy at once. You're thinking straight now. And if the time comes you need me, I'll be at your side.

(Exeunt AENEAS and his ARMED GUARDS.)

HÊKTOR: So. Who among you men is my man? Who's it going to be? Who'll step up for his country when she needs him most? Who will it be to help Troy to victory? Troy's spy? I need a volunteer. Unfortunately, I can't serve my country in everything myself.

(DOLON, a very young man, steps from the crowd of SOLDIERS.)

DOLON: That would be me, sir. Anything for Troy, even my life. I'll make my way down to their ships, learn what their plans are, and be back to report on the double. I accept, sir. Whatever you say.

HÊKTOR: Yes, Dolon, I see now how your name suits you—a wily trickster. And you love your city. So be it! Your father's house is already rich in fame and fortune, now it will be doubly so, thanks to your bravery.

DOLON: Hard work is a good thing, sir; and the harder the work the more fitting the reward. And the better the reward, the greater the pleasure.

HÊKTOR: I agree. Just payment is only fair. Name your price. Anything short of my throne.

DOLON: No, sir, I don't have my eye on power.

HÊKTOR: Then marry a daughter of Priam, and be my brother-in-law.

DOLON: Thanks, but I wouldn't marry above my station.

HÊKTOR: Well, there's always gold, if that's what you want.

DOLON: There's plenty of gold at home, sir, we're very well off.

HÊKTOR: Name any of Troy's treasures and it's yours.

DOLON: I'll take my reward when we've taken prisoners.

HÊKTOR: Anyone but Agamemnon and Menelaos.

DOLON: Kill them. Why should I care about Menelaos?

HÊKTOR: Surely you're not asking me for Aias?

DOLON: Well-born hands like his don't do well in the field.

HÊKTOR: Ah, then it's ransom you want! Name your man.

DOLON: Ransom? No, I told you: we have gold at home.

HÊKTOR: In that case, you'll be the first to choose from the spoils.

DOLON: Nail them up in the temples. They belong to the gods.

HÊKTOR: But what more can you ask? What else is here?

DOLON: The horses of Achilleus, sir. When I stake my life on a roll of the dice by the gods, the reward should be worth it.

HÊKTOR: Ah, now there's a prize I covet myself! We're rivals, after all, Dolon. Rival lovers. I lust for them as deeply as any lover. Immortal steeds from immortal sires, that team will never tire. Poseidon, lord of the sea, broke and tamed them when they were colts, and gave them to Pêleus, who in turn gave them to his impetuous son Achilleus. I've raised your hopes, I see, Dolon, and so I mustn't disappoint them. They're yours, Achilleus's horses, a grand prize for your house.

DOLON: Hêktor, thank you. It's the honest reward courage deserves, and the finest prize in Troy. No hard feelings, sir, I hope? As Troy's greatest warrior, there are many thousands of things for you to delight in.

(HÊKTOR nods and retires to his bed of leaves and sits.)

(Music.)

FIRST TROJAN SENTRY: *(Chants.)*
When you aim high, Dolon, you win big.
And you're aiming high.
Win and you're a great man.

THIRD TROJAN SENTRY: *(Chants.)*
It's a glorious thing you're doing, my friend.
But marrying the king's sister
would have been bold, too.

SECOND TROJAN SENTRY: *(Chants.)*
Justice will reward you
with what heaven ordains, Dolon.
But what men promise is only a promise.

(Music out.)

DOLON: I'm on my way, men. Home first to suit myself up right, then off to the Greek ships.

FIRST TROJAN SENTRY: What will you change into?

DOLON: Something just right for my mission and my wily ways.

FIRST TROJAN SENTRY: Wily! Aha! So, tell us: what will you wear?

DOLON: A wolf skin, what else? I'll cover my back, pull the beast's jaws down tight on my head, fit the paws to my hands, tie its back legs to mine, and lope along like any old wolf to puzzle enemy trackers. Along the trenches and the bows of the ships, I'll keep a low profile, but once I've reached open territory, I'll get to my feet and run like Hades. And that, gentlemen, is what I'll do.

THIRD TROJAN SENTRY: May Hermês, god of wiliness, protect you, Dolon, and bring you back safe and sound.

FIRST TROJAN SENTRY: You know what you're after, man. All you need is luck

DOLON: You don't get rid of me that easily. I'll be back, all right, and lugging the head of Odysseus to prove I made it down to the ships. Or maybe Diomêdes, who knows? What's more, I'll be back before daybreak—my hands slippery with Argive blood.

(Exit DOLON.)

(Music. Song. Dance.)

TROJAN SENTRIES: *(Sing.)*
    Lord of Thymbra,
    lord of Delos and Lykia,
    Apollo,
    bright one,
    son of Zeus,
    come with your bow,
    come,
    come in the night,
    lead him,
    lead Dolon,

lead,
lead this man,
preserve him,
guide him,
stand strong for Troy's children,
fight with Troy,
with the sons of Troy,
you,
all-powerful god,
who built Troy's walls!

Bring him, Apollo, to the fleet of the Greeks,
bring him, bring Dolon, unseen but seeing,
then back once more to his father's hearth,
back to the altars of his father's home.
And when our king, our ruler, Hêktor,
has destroyed Greek strength,
and all the Greek war might,
let Dolon mount proudly Pêleus's chariot,
drawn by the deathless team,
the gift of Poseidon, god of the sea.

(Music out.)

FIRST TROJAN SENTRY: He's a good man, Dolon. Braver than most of
us. Who else offered to take on this mission?

THIRD TROJAN SENTRY: Right, I admire his courage. There aren't
many brave enough when a city's tossed on a stormy sea.

SECOND TROJAN SENTRY: Dolon's a hero, all right, but bravery's not
dead in Troy. That I'll never believe. And I spit on the ally who refuses
to fight beside me!

FIRST TROJAN SENTRY: I can just see him, pacing along on all fours in
that wolf skin of his!

SECOND TROJAN SENTRY: What a sight that must be!

FIRST TROJAN SENTRY: I wonder what prize he'll stab first? He won't waste time. Not him. By all the gods, I hope it's Menelaos!

THIRD TROJAN SENTRY: And I hope it's that bastard Agamemnon! What a trophy his head would be to lay in Helen's lap!

SECOND TROJAN SENTRY: That I'd really like to see! He's the one began it all, with that fleet of a thousand ships he sailed to Troy!

FIRST TROJAN SENTRY: "Here's your brother-in-law, Helen! Give him a peck!"

(The men howl with laughter.)

(Enter a SHEPHERD. HÊKTOR rises and comes forward.)

SHEPHERD: King Hêktor, sir, may I always bring news to my royal masters as good as what I bring to you now!

HÊKTOR: What boors these country yokels are. You may not have noticed, but your "royal masters" are at war. And here you come reporting on the state of your flocks. You know, I presume, my house or my father's palace? All right, then, choose one or the other and take your information there.

SHEPHERD: We shepherds are yokels, sir, no denying it. But, still, the news I bring is good.

HÊKTOR: Man, we're at war! Do you understand?

SHEPHERD: Yes, sir, and that's why I'm here. War. A man has come, a friend of yours, leading a vast force to be an ally.

HÊKTOR: And what country did he empty to bring me this vast force?

SHEPHERD: Thrace, sir. His father's name is Strymon.

HÊKTOR: Rhesos? What are you saying? Rhesos on Trojan soil? Now? Here?

SHEPHERD: You have it, sir. Saved me half of what I came to say.

HÊKTOR: But why approach through the mountains and not the plains?

SHEPHERD: I can't say for sure, sir, but I can guess. It's no small thing marching an army through the night, when it's rumored the plains are crawling with enemy troops. I'd say he took the turn through the mountains so as not to run smack into them Greeks, sir. We country folk live high up on Ida, as you know, where it turns to rock. And, well, in the night, we heard a terrible noise coming through the oak woods where wolves and other beasts run wild. It was him, sir, coming along with great loud shouts and clamor in the night, except we didn't know it was him, and it scared us half to death. Well—we was so panic struck we rounded up and drove your flocks on up to high country, thinking the Greeks had come to plunder your livestock and wreck the pens. And then I heard a language that wasn't Greek, and so we weren't afraid after that.

    I took a stand in the road and asked the king's scouts in Thracian who their general was, whose son is he, this man coming as an ally to Troy and Troy's people. When I heard everything I wanted to hear, I just stood there, relieved. And then I saw him, Rhesos, tall in his horse-drawn chariot, like a god. A yoke beam looking like a balance, all of gold, joined the necks of his two young mares that were whiter even than sun on snow. On his shoulder was a blazing shield of beaten gold. Bronze Gorgons, like that on Athêna's breastplate, are bound to the frontlet shields on the horses' foreheads, and the harness fitted out with bells that clang the sound of fear like an alarm.

    Sir, I couldn't count the numbers of their men even with an abacus, there was so many, more even than you could imagine— horsemen, infantry, archers, division after division, on and on they came like they'd never stop—and behind them hordes of naked warriors in long Thracian cloaks. This is the man who comes as Troy's ally. Whether he runs for his life or fights him, not even Achilleus can escape death.

FIRST TROJAN SENTRY: When the gods stand firm for a city, its downward fortune can be reversed.

HÊKTOR: Now that I've won the day with this spear, and Zeus is on our side, all kinds of friends, it seems, by the hordes, will be flocking round us. Well, we have no use for them. What good are they to us now? Where were they when war god Arês battered our ship of state, blasting and tearing our sails to rags? Rhesos showed then what a friend he was to Troy. He's come for the victory feast without having helped the huntsmen run down the game.

SECOND TROJAN SENTRY: You're right, sir; it's not much of a friendship.

FIRST TROJAN SENTRY: And yet, if he can help, why not welcome him?

HÊKTOR: We've kept Troy standing this long, we'll continue. We're enough.

FIRST TROJAN SENTRY: Are you confident, sir, this enemy has been defeated?

HÊKTOR: God's dawn will prove how true that is.

THIRD TROJAN SENTRY: Beware of the future: the gods can change their minds.

HÊKTOR: I hate it when "friends" come too late to help "friends"! But he's here now, let him stay. Just not as an ally. As a guest, at the guests' table. Troy owes this man nothing.

FIRST TROJAN SENTRY: Reject an ally, sir, and he can turn hostile.

SHEPHERD: Just the sight of their numbers would terrify the Greeks.

HÊKTOR: *(To the FIRST TROJAN SENTRY.)* Your advice is good. *(To the SHEPHERD.)* And you have kept your eyes open as you should.
In view of this shepherd's report, let him come, let golden-armored Rhesos come as an ally. *(Exit.)*
(HÊKTOR paces at the rear.)

(Music. Song. Dance.)

TROJAN SENTRIES: *(Sing.)*

Adrasteia,
Nemesis,
Necessity,
daughter of Zeus,
guard my lips from ill-spoken words,
for now, now,
I will say,
I will say,
what my heart prompts me,
what my soul takes joy in expressing.
Rhesos, son of Strymon,
river god's son,
you have come,
have come,
come at last, come so late,
to the friendly god's courtyard,
sent by your Pierian mother, the Muse,
and the river of fine bridges.

Strymon begot you, river god Strymon,
swirling crystal waters in her virginal folds,
planted the seed of youth and glory,
the seed of you, Rhesos, driving now,
driving your dappled mares,
you who come like Zeus Light Bringer.
Oh Phrygia, my land, land of my fathers,
now, now with god's blessing,
we can sing, rejoice, for in him, in Rhesos,
Zeus has come to us, Zeus Deliverer!

Will ancient Troy again see the rowdy
daylong revel of lovers and friends,
where the lyre is plucked,
and melodies rise,
and flowing cups in contest never cease,
left to right,
circling, circling,

minds reeling and lovers singing,
carousing away the endless night,
when the sons of Atreus have left our shores
and sailed back home to distant Sparta?
Oh Rhesos, Rhesos,
brother, friend,
make it, make it happen,
with your hand and spear,
before you leave us!
Oh Rhesos, come,
come raise your shield,
your golden shield,
flash its gleam in the eyes of Achilleus,
its golden glare,
urge on your horses,
drive them, prod them,
lay on the goad,
and with a swift thrust
toss your double-pronged javelin!
No one, none, who dares to resist you,
will dance again on the plains of Argos,
but lie here on Phrygian soil,
a welcome weight leveled by a Thracian spear,
to molder in the arms of Earth's embrace.

(Enter RHESOS in his chariot with great ceremony, accompanied by a splendid RETINUE.)

FIRST TROJAN SENTRY: *(Chants.)*
He has come, he has come, the great king!
The lion cub Thrace has reared has arrived!
The image of royalty and majesty!
Behold his grand body bound in gold!
Hear the bells, their boastful clamor
clanging on his shield!
A god has come, great Troy, a god, god Arês,
stallion son of Strymon and the Muse,
a god to inspire you!

(Music out.)

RHESOS: I salute you, Hêktor, noble son of a noble father, and this land's lord! True I have arrived at the eleventh hour, as they say, but I rejoice to see you so fully in charge and so near the enemy's encampment. We have only now to make rubble of their walls and set the hulls of their ships afire.

HÊKTOR: Rhesos, son of a Muse and the River Strymon, I'm a lover of truth, and I prefer speaking the truth whatever the occasion. I also speak plainly and without flourish. I countenance no deception. And I am no diplomat. That said, I say this. It is long past due for your arrival, much too long; we could have used your might in our struggle. But you ignored us, you looked the other way, while we were beaten down by the force of the Greek invader. We might have fallen, for all you cared. And don't blame your friends, saying they never called on you, seeking your help. How many Trojan heralds, how many embassies approached you to beg for your help in our defense? Was there a special gift you longed for that we failed to send? Despite our kindred race, our one blood—we are both of Barbarian stock— you betrayed us to the enemy Greeks.

    What were you but one of many petty rulers, when I came to raise you to the throne of Thrace? In Pangaion and Paionia I fought face to face with brave and violent Thracian chiefs, broke their lines of shields, deposed them, enslaved them, and led them, leashed, to you, now their king.

    There's much you owe us. But you scorn your friends and come to relieve them in their agonized distress only when it's too late. Others, unrelated in any way, came long ago, many of them now resting beneath our earth—what a sign of loyalty they present!—while others, still, remain, in arms, foot soldiers, cavalry, withstanding the cruel cold blasts of winds and the parching heat of the heavens, that god of flame—unlike you, in your luxurious beds, and raising endless toasts to—friendship.

    So, there is Hêktor's mind, if you care to know, and Hêktor in his grievance declares you guilty.

RHESOS: I'm no different from you, Hêktor, no different a man. I waste no words, I speak to the point, and I, too, am no diplomat. The enormity of my grief cannot be measured, my shame, my discontent, at not having arrived in your country. I had come as far as the shore of the Euxine Sea to ferry across my Thracian army to Troy, when the neighboring Scythians attacked me. The ground there was thick with Scythian and Thracian blood. It was this kept me from arriving as Troy's ally. But once I had destroyed the enemy and taken their children hostage, I set on them a tax as tribute to be delivered annually.

That done, I crossed the straits of the Thracian Bosporos by ship, and marched my army the rest of the way on foot. Nor was I, as you claim, drinking endless toasts, nor lying abed in golden chambers, but enduring the icy raw blasts of the sea that froze this soldier's cloak as I wrapped it round me on eternally sleepless nights. I may arrive late, as you say, but at least I'm here, and still in good time.

It's ten years now, day after hopeless day, you've played at the random dice game of war with these Greeks, and what have you achieved short of nothing? Give me one single day of sunlight and I will have destroyed their fortifications, set flaming their fleet, and killed every Greek among them. At dawn of the day following, your interminable troubles behind you, I will leave Troy and set off for home.

And, no, not a single Trojan need raise a shield. I'll see to these Greeks and their braggart boasting myself, when I crush them into oblivion—at the eleventh hour.

(Music.)

FIRST TROJAN SENTRY: *(Chants.)*
Your words are welcome, Rhesos.

THIRD TROJAN SENTRY: *(Chants.)*
Welcome, yes, Rhesos,
you come from Zeus.

SECOND TROJAN SENTRY: *(Chants.)*
A friend, Rhesos, you
come as a friend to Troy.

THIRD SOLDIER: *(Chants.)*
> I pray that Zeus may guard you from Envy
> if your words offend either gods or men.

FIRST TROJAN SENTRY: *(Chants.)*
> No Argive hero has arrived here greater than you.

THIRD TROJAN SENTRY: *(Chants.)*
> Achilleus could never survive your spear.

SECOND TROJAN SENTRY: *(Chants.)*
> Nor could Aias endure it.

FIRST TROJAN SENTRY: *(Chants.)*
> I pray, my lord, to see the new day dawn,
> when your spear hand is bloodied
> with redeeming our Trojan dead!

> *(Music out.)*

RHESOS: My absence was too long, Hêktor, but now I will set things right. And I pray that Nemesis approve my words. Once we have liberated Troy, and you have selected for the gods the choicest of the spoils, together we will march on Greece and root it out with our spears, ravage the land, and teach it what it means to suffer as you have.

HÊKTOR: If only I could escape these present evils and rule a Troy as secure as in the past, I would give thanks to the gods with all my heart. But this thought of yours of invading the Greeks, it's not as easily done as said.

RHESOS: Isn't it said that the best of the Greeks are at Troy?

HÊKTOR: The best? Yes. And they're great enough for me.

RHESOS: Well, then, once we've killed them, the rest is easy.

HÊKTOR: Look too far into the future, you lose sight of the present.

RHESOS: You seem content to suffer and not to react.

HÊKTOR: I'm content with the power I have. Troy's big enough. All right, now, choose: right wing, left wing, or center in the allied lines. It's up to you.

RHESOS: I want to fight alone, Hêktor. But I understand. It would shame you not to join in the attack on their ships—after all the years you've struggled for this. I agree. Just station me face to face with Achilleus and his army.

HÊKTOR: Achilleus—Achilleus won't be there.

RHESOS: But everyone knows he sailed to Troy.

HÊKTOR: He did. And he's here. But his rage at the generals keeps him from fighting.

RHESOS: Then who is their second greatest?

HÊKTOR: I'd say Aias is his equal in every way. And then there's Tydeus's son, Diomêdes. Their loudest and most cunning is Odysseus. His spirit's brave enough, but he's done us more damage than anyone else. In the dead of night, he stole from its temple the statue of Athêna and carried it back to the Argive ships. Another time, he disguised himself as a miserable beggar in rags and got through our walls, past the sentries, all the while loudly cursing the Greeks. He'd been sent to spy. He got out, too. Killed the sentry and gate guards. He's always seen lurking around Apollo's altar at Thymbra, near the city, watching for his advantage. What a cunning fox he is, always slipping through our fingers.

RHESOS: No man of honor kills his enemy by stealth. He meets him face to face. I will capture this man who lurks in ambush, plotting stratagems like a common thief. I'll impale him, living, at the gate leading from the city, for all to see and for vultures to feast on. This thief who dishonors the temples of the gods will have the death he deserves.

HÊKTOR: Very well. But you must make your camp now. It's still night. I'll show you where you and your army can bivouac. Somewhere apart from the rest. The password is "Phoibos." Remember it and tell it to your troops in case you need anything. *(To the CHORUS OF TROJAN SENTRIES.)* You men take up positions in front of our lines. Keep a sharp lookout for Dolon. If he's all right, he should be nearing the Trojan camp. *(Exeunt HÊKTOR and RHESOS and his RETINUE.)*

(Music.)

FIRST TROJAN SENTRY: *(Chants.)*
    Whose watch is it now?
    Who relieves us?

SECOND TROJAN SENTRY: *(Chants.)*
    Night's first constellations are setting.

THIRD TROJAN SENTRY: *(Chants.)*
    And there are the seven Pleiades rising.

SECOND TROJAN SENTRY: *(Chants.)*
    And Zeus Eagle high in the sky.

FOURTH TROJAN SENTRY: *(Chants.)*
    Wake up! What's the delay?
    Out of your beds! Duty calls!

FIRST TROJAN SENTRY: *(Chants.)*
    Look at the moon!

FIFTH TROJAN SENTRY: *(Chants.)*
    It will be dawn soon.

SECOND TROJAN SENTRY: *(Chants.)*
    And there!
    The star that announces her!

FIRST TROJAN SENTRY: *(Chants.)*
    Who stood the first watch?

SIXTH TROJAN SENTRY: *(Chants.)*
Migdon's son, Koroibos.

SECOND TROJAN SENTRY: *(Chants.)*
Who after that?

THIRD TROJAN SENTRY: *(Chants.)*
The Paionians roused the Kilikians
and the Mysians roused us.

FIFTH TROJAN SENTRY: *(Chants.)*
Then it's time to wake the Lykians.
They drew the fifth watch.

SECOND TROJAN SENTRY: *(Chants.)*
It must be.
No, wait. Listen. I hear it.
The nightingale down by the river.

FIRST TROJAN SENTRY: *(Sings.)*
Sitting in her bloody nest above the Simoïs,
she trills her sad song of many notes.
The bed, the blood, the murder of Itys,
her own son Itys.
"Itys, Itys!" she sings.
"Itys!"

SECOND TROJAN SENTRY: *(Sings.)*
The flocks are grazing now in the high meadows.
I hear the shepherd's piping in the night.

THIRD TROJAN SENTRY: *(Sings.)*
Sweet sleep casts its spell on my eyes.
It falls so gently on their lids at dawn.

SECOND TROJAN SENTRY: *(Chants.)*
Where's Dolon?
He should be back now.

THIRD TROJAN SENTRY: *(Chants.)*
  It frightens me.
  He's been gone a long time.

SECOND TROJAN SENTRY: *(Chants.)*
  Can he have been ambushed and killed?

THIRD TROJAN SENTRY: *(Chants.)*
  Possible.
  It's got me scared.

FIRST TROJAN SENTRY: *(Chants.)*
  Let's go wake the Lykians.
  They drew the dawn watch.

  (Exit the CHORUS OF TROJAN SENTRIES. Enter ODYSSEUS and DIOMÊDES.)

  (Music out.)

ODYSSEUS: Diomêdes? What's that sound? Arms clattering? Or am I
  imagining things?

DIOMÊDES: It's nothing, Odysseus. Harness chains on chariot rails.
  It frightened me, too. But, no, just horse gear jangling.

ODYSSEUS: Don't fall on any sentries in the dark.

DIOMÊDES: Don't worry, I'll step carefully.

ODYSSEUS: In case you wake them, do you know the password?

DIOMÊDES: Yes, "Phoibos," Dolon told me.

ODYSSEUS: They were here, that's for sure. But they're gone now.
  What can it mean?

DIOMÊDES: Dolon said this was Hêktor's camp. It's for him I came.
  To slice his throat!

ODYSSEUS: Could it be a trap? Where else could they be?

DIOMÊDES: That's not impossible.

ODYSSEUS: Yes, Hêktor's a bold one now he's winning.

DIOMÊDES: What do we do now? We've lost our man, and with him our hopes.

ODYSSEUS: We get back to our ships, and fast. There's some god protecting Hêktor. He has luck on his side, and I'd just as soon not tempt it.

DIOMÊDES: What's the rush? Why not Aeneas or Paris? They're the worst of the lot. We can have their heads.

ODYSSEUS: Oh? In the dark, surrounded by the enemy, and not be caught?

DIOMÊDES: Go back to the ships empty-handed? Without a scratch to the enemy? I'd be shamed!

ODYSSEUS: Without a scratch? We killed Dolon, didn't we, that would-be spy in his wolf's pelt? Here's the spoils! *(He holds up the wolf skin.)* Do you expect to rout the whole camp?

DIOMÊDES: I'm convinced. Let's go. Let's hope our luck holds out.

(ATHÊNA appears, visible to the audience, but not to ODYSSEUS and DIOMÊDES.)

ATHÊNA: Where to now, gentlemen? Withdrawing so soon? Leaving behind Trojan lines with a bitter taste in your mouths and grieving hearts? Some god, I know, disallowed you reaping the life of Hêktor or Paris. But haven't you heard? There has come to Troy in grand style, and with untold numbers, a man to stand as an ally to the Trojans. Rhesos. If he lives through this night, neither Achilleus nor Aias with his spear can prevent him from razing your walls to the ground and wreaking destruction on you and your ships. Kill him, kill Rhesos, and you are the victors. Forget Hêktor and that head of his you'd like to take back. His head will be had in good time by another.

ODYSSEUS: Athêna! Mistress! I recognize your voice, that voice I have heard speak to me in times of danger when you have come to protect me, you who are with me always. Tell me now: where has this barbarian been stationed?

ATHÊNA: Nearby, as you will see. Hêktor provided him quarters beyond the camp, where he will sleep till night turns to dawn. Near him you'll find tethered his gleaming Thracian mares, so radiant in the dark a swan's wing on water is not more bright. Kill their master, and lead them off as trophies. Earth has no greater prize.

ODYSSEUS: Choose, Diomêdes. You do the killing and I see to the horses, or let me do it.

DIOMÊDES: I'll do the killing, you tend to the horses. You're a past master at cunning, Odysseus, and a wily trickster. We should do what we do best.

ATHÊNA: Look, I see Paris heading this way. He's heard from some guard a rumor there's an enemy in camp.

DIOMÊDES: Alone or with others?

ATHÊNA: Alone. He's come to report to Hêktor of spies in the camp.

DIOMÊDES: Well, then, shouldn't he be the first to die?

ATHÊNA: You can't do more than destiny allows. Fate doesn't permit it. You're not to be his killer. Go, now. It's for you to bring to Rhesos the death that has been reserved for him. Hurry! As for Paris approaching, I'll pretend I'm his Kyprian ally, Aphroditê, standing near in his every need. I'll speak rotten lies of deceit to him. Don't worry, though he's been near, he's heard nothing.

(Exeunt ODYSSEUS and DIOMÊDES.)

PARIS: *(Enters.)* Hêktor! General! Brother! Wake up, Hêktor! It's time! There are Greeks in camp! Marauders, maybe spies!

ATHÊNA: Never fear, dear Paris, Aphroditê's here to protect you. I think of you a lot, especially in this war. And I can never thank you enough, you know, for your graciousness in giving me the prize. But now I have a gift for *you.* I've brought to Troy in its hour of triumph in the field a man, a friend to Phrygia, a Thracian, son of the singing Muse, a goddess's son whose father is River Strymon.

PARIS: You have always looked kindly on Troy and on me, and I believe the best I ever did for Troy, as well as for myself, was giving you the prize that won us your favor. I've come here looking for Hêktor. Wild rumors are circling the camp. Sentries are saying Greek spies have broken in. One man who says he saw nothing does nothing but talk of them; while another who saw them coming has nothing to say. That's why I've come to wake Hêktor.

ATHÊNA: You've nothing to fear, Paris. The camp is in good hands. Hêktor has gone to show the Thracians to their quarters.

PARIS: I trust you, lady, and so I'll take up my post without any fear.

ATHÊNA: On your way, then. You   know very well I always have your interests at heart. It won't be long till you know the worth of my care for you. *(Exit PARIS.)* *(ATHÊNA calls in her own voice.)* You two! In there! Odysseus, Diomêdes! Give your sharp sword a rest, Odysseus. Rhesos is down! He's dead! We have his horses. But the enemy knows, they're on your trail. Run to the ships! Now! Why are you waiting? Save yourselves! Run! There's a thunderbolt headed straight for you!

(Enter ODYSSEUS and DIOMÊDES chased by the CHORUS OF TROJAN SENTRIES, as ATHÊNA disappears.)

(Music. Song. Dance.)

FIRST TROJAN SENTRY: *(Chants.)*
There they are!
Catch them, men!

SECOND TROJAN SENTRY: *(Chants.)*
    Get them!

THIRD TROJAN SENTRY: *(Chants.)*
    Strike!

SECOND TROJAN SENTRY: *(Chants.)*
    Strike!

FOURTH TROJAN SENTRY: *(Chants.)*
    Strike!

FIRST TROJAN SENTRY: *(Chants.)*
    Run them through!

FIFTH TROJAN SENTRY: *(Chants.)*
    Who are they?

FIRST TROJAN SENTRY: *(Chants.)*
    I never saw them!

THIRD TROJAN SENTRY: *(Chants.)*
    Over here!

SECOND TROJAN SENTRY: *(Chants.)*
    There he is!

FIFTH TROJAN SENTRY: *(Chants.)*
    There!

SIXTH TROJAN SENTRY: *(Chants.)*
    I got one!

FOURTH TROJAN SENTRY: *(Chants.)*
    Me, too!

SECOND TROJAN SENTRY: *(Chants.)*
    Bastards!

FOURTH TROJAN SENTRY: *(Chants.)*
    Thieves!

THIRD TROJAN SENTRY: *(Chants.)*
    Disturbing the camp!

SIXTH TROJAN SENTRY: *(Chants.)*
    Marauders!

FIRST TROJAN SENTRY: *(Chants.)*
    Who are you?
    What's your company?

(Music out.)

ODYSSEUS: None of your business! Touch us and you're dead!

FIRST TROJAN SENTRY: The password! Answer or you've got a spear
    coming out your other side!

ODYSSEUS: No, stop, don't be afraid!

FIRST TROJAN SENTRY: Close in, men! Let's get them!

SECOND TROJAN SENTRY: Did you kill Rhesos?

ODYSSEUS: No, but you could have! Back off!

FIRST TROJAN SENTRY: Not on your life!

ODYSSEUS: Hey, don't kill a friend! We're allies!

FIRST TROJAN SENTRY: Allies? Prove it! The password!

ODYSSEUS: "Phoibos!"

FIRST TROJAN SENTRY: All right, hold off, men! *(To ODYSSEUS.)*
    Where are they? The thieves? Do you know?

ODYSSEUS: Over there somewhere, I think.

FIRST TROJAN SENTRY: Spread out, men!

SEVENTH TROJAN SENTRY: Don't we need help?

FIRST TROJAN SENTRY: Better not to disturb the allies. There's enough
    trouble without an alarm. Let's find them! Now!

*(The CHORUS OF TROJAN SENTRIES rushes off. When they are
gone, ODYSSEUS and DIOMÊDES run off in the other direction.
Music continues, and the CHORUS OF TROJAN SENTRIES reenters
straggling.)*

(Music.)

FIRST TROJAN SENTRY: *(Chants.)*
    Who could he have been?
    Slipped right through my fingers!
    And now he's out there bragging about it!
    We'll never find him now.
    Didn't even get a good look at him in this dark.
    Walked right on through our lines, past our guards.
    How could he have managed a thing like that?

SECOND TROJAN SENTRY: *(Chants.)*
    By sticking to the shadows, that's how,
    even in the dark.
    And being fearless, the ballsy bastard.

THIRD TROJAN SENTRY: *(Chants.)*
    Who is he, I wonder?

FOURTH TROJAN SENTRY: *(Chants.)*
    Probably one of those no-count islanders.

FIFTH TROJAN SENTRY: *(Chants.)*
    A Thessalian, maybe.

SECOND TROJAN SENTRY: *(Chants.)*
    A pirate for sure.

FIFTH TROJAN SENTRY: *(Chants.)*
    They all thieves, the whole lot of them.

SECOND TROJAN SENTRY: *(Chants.)*
    I wonder what god he swears by?

FIRST TROJAN SENTRY: *(Chants.)*
    I'm beginning to think it was Odysseus,
    judging by what he's done in the past.

SIXTH TROJAN SENTRY: *(Chants.)*
    You think so?

FIRST TROJAN SENTRY: *(Chants.)*
    I'd bet my life on it.

SIXTH TROJAN SENTRY: *(Chants.)*
    That one's got balls for sure.
    Given us a real run for our money, he has.

FIRST TROJAN SENTRY: *(Chants.)*
    He's sly. Balls is right. It's not the first time.
    Got right on into Troy once.
    Looked a real mess. Bleary eyed, dressed in rags,
    even smuggled in a sword beneath all those wrappings.
    He crept his way right on in through our gates,
    begging for all he was worth, crust of bread,
    drink of water, like he was dying, like he was
    trying to keep body and soul together.
    The grimy, filthy bastard smelled like a goat.

THIRD TROJAN SENTRY: *(Chants.)*
    Right, I remember.
    Cursing Agamemnon and Menelaos
    like he hated their guts.

FIFTH TROJAN SENTRY: *(Chants.)*
> He deserves to be dead.
> Should have died before
> setting foot on Trojan soil!

FIRST TROJAN SENTRY: *(Chants.)*
> Odysseus or no Odysseus, I'm scared.
> Hêktor'll lay into us for sure. What else?
> We were the ones on watch.

SIXTH TROJAN SENTRY: *(Chants.)*
> So—?

FIRST TROJAN SENTRY: *(Chants.)*
> He'll blame us.

SIXTH TROJAN SENTRY: *(Chants.)*
> For what?

FIRST TROJAN SENTRY: *(Chants.)*
> For letting them get through.

SIXTH TROJAN SENTRY: *(Chants.)*
> Who?

THIRD TROJAN SENTRY: *(Chants.)*
> Whoever it was broke through our lines tonight.

(The voice of Rhesos's CHARIOTEER is heard from off.)

CHARIOTEER: *(Chants from off.)*
> Oh gods, gods!
> Disaster! Disaster!

FIRST TROJAN SENTRY: *(Chants.)*
> Quiet! Get down!
> Someone may be headed for our snare!

CHARIOTEER: *(Chants from off.)*
>   Help! I'm hurt!
>   Oh Rhesos, Rhesos,
>   I curse the day you first saw hateful Troy!
>   This is no end, no proper end to your life!

SECOND TROJAN SENTRY: *(Chants.)*
>   It's one of the allies!

(Enter the CHARIOTEER, a wound in his side, bloody.)

FIRST TROJAN SENTRY: *(Speaks.)* Which are you? Which ally? It's too
dark. I can't see clearly.

CHARIOTEER: *(Chants.)*
>   I need to find one of your chiefs.
>   Where's Hêktor?
>   Asleep on his shield?
>   Someone! I must tell—
>   I must tell what happened—
>   in the night! Someone must
>   know what Thrace has suffered!
>   They came and went—
>   nobody saw—
>   vanished!

FIRST TROJAN SENTRY: *(Chants.)*
>   Some disaster's happened to the Thracians
>   if this man's right.

CHARIOTEER: *(Chants.)*
>   The army is gone—wiped out—
>   the Thracians—
>   the king—killed—
>   by some treacherous hand!
>   AIIII!
>   AIIIIII! AIIII!
>   My wound—agony—the pain—
>   can't stand!

I wish I could die—die!
Oh Rhesos!
No sooner we came as allies to Troy,
and death greets us—
a death of shame—
Rhesos—

FIRST TROJAN SENTRY: *(Chants.)*
It's the Thracian army was hit.
It looks bad.

(He motions for several SENTRIES to go find Hêktor. They exit.)

(Music out.)

CHARIOTEER: A terrible thing has been done, a terrible evil that ends in shame, in disgrace, that makes it doubly evil. To die in glory is one thing, and yet, I think, even such a death is bitter to the one who dies. Can it be otherwise? But at least a good name remains for the glory of his house. But our death is the death of fools, without glory or sense. Hêktor himself led us to where we would camp. He told us the password, and with that the whole army, as one, lay down and slept like dogs we were so tired from our march. Rhesos had understood from Hêktor that you had mastered the field and were all but camping beside the Greeks ships, and so no night guards were posted. In our exhaustion we dropped our armor at our sides and didn't bother with goads over the horses' yokes. We fell to the ground and slept.
But worried about the horses—I mean, I loved them, the beautiful creatures—I woke thinking that at dawn I'd be harnessing them for battle and might not have time to feed them properly. So I get up and feed them extra rations, they deserved it. And then I see something.

Two men, skulking around our camp, prowlers, I think, keeping well to where the darkness is thickest. I was concerned. I made a move toward them. They crouch again and then make off. Foragers, I think, allies, and give it no further thought. I shout at them to stay away from our camp. They say nothing, and I say nothing more. I went back to my bed on the ground and slept.

And then it happened. In my sleep. I had a dream, a vision. I see the two young mares I had raised and drove as I stood besides Rhesos in his chariot—see it so clearly it could have been next to me. Two wolves had mounted the fillies' backs and were riding them, riding, their stiff pricks stabbing, goring them, the mares snorting from flaring nostrils, panting, rearing wildly in their terror. As I run to drive those wild beasts from the fillies, I wake suddenly from my own night terror, and raising my head hear moaning. Men dying, I think to myself. A jet of hot blood strikes me then, and I turn to see my young master close beside me, in the final agonies of death. He wasn't dying easy. I jump to my feet. Where is my spear! Hunting madly for one, there's suddenly beside me a sturdy warrior who plunges deep into my belly with his sword. I know his power from the thrust that plows into my body its bloody furrow. I fall, face down, as they grab the chariot and team, and escape.

AIII! AIIIIII! The pain's too much! I can't stand. I know what happened. I saw. But how those men were killed and who killed them, I can only guess. It was "friends," "friends" who did this. Who else can it be?

FIRST TROJAN SENTRY: Poor man, I know you were his driver, your king, but don't torment yourself. We aren't the guilty ones, it's the enemy, be sure, not friends, the enemy. But here comes Hêktor. He's heard; he'll sympathize with your misfortune.

(Enter HÊKTOR with the SENTRIES who went to find him, along with several other SOLDIERS.)

HÊKTOR: You! Every one of you! What exactly do you call yourselves? Soldiers? Not in my book! You're a disgrace to the army, a disgrace to Troy! It's you who did this, allowed enemy spies to infiltrate our lines, allowed the enemy to massacre the army! And then you allow them to leave as easily as they came! Is that what sentries are for? I'm asking! To lay down on the job? To allow their comrades to be slaughtered, while they're off doing god knows what? You'll pay for this, every one of you!

And where are they now, the enemy, the enemy that wandered off unscathed, without a blow? Having a good laugh at Trojan cowardice is where they're at! Off jeering the incompetence of the Trojan high command—which is me!

Your punishment awaits you, gentlemen. And I swear, with Zeus as my witness, you will die either by the whip or by the headsman's ax

for what you've done. And if I fail to live up to my oath, you may
think of Hêktor as a coward—for Hêktor will be a nothing.

(Music. Song. Dance.)

FIRST TROJAN SENTRY: *(Sings.)*
Sir! No! No!
We came to you, came at once, sir,
to tell you of the fires they'd started,
fires by the Greek ships, sir!

SECOND TROJAN SENTRY: *(Sings.)*
We never shut our eyes, sir!
Never once! We kept them peeled!
Never dozed off once, sir, by Simoïs's stream!

THIRD TROJAN SENTRY: *(Sings.)*
Great king, don't be angered with us!

SECOND TROJAN SENTRY: *(Sings.)*
We're innocent, sir, we did nothing!

FIRST TROJAN SENTRY: *(Sings.)*
Wait, sir, wait awhile!
If later you find we did wrong,
punishes us then, bury us alive
in Troy's sweet earth!

(Music out.)

CHARIOTEER: What are you doing, Hêktor? Threatening your men?
We're all Barbarian here, the same blood, so why try to trap my mind
in your web of words? That's the Greek way. Leave that to them.
But it's you who did this. You alone. And we, we dead and wounded
Thracians, won't settle for anything less. It would take a long and
cunning defense to persuade me you're not guilty of killing your
friends.

It was the horses, the mares, the brilliant team, you coveted. You
lusted for them the way a lover longs. It was for them you begged on

your knees that we come, allies, brothers in blood, for them you killed. We came. And now we're dead. Not even Paris's breach of hospitality equals yours, Hêktor. You, the killer of allies, killer of friends! And don't say it was the Greeks who came to slaughter us. How could even *one* Greek have crossed the Trojan lines and not been seen? You were camped in the vanguard, and so was the entire Phrygian army. What other allies of yours are dead and wounded by these enemies you claim? No, the casualties are ours, all ours, the wounded, the dead, whose eyes are closed and will never again see the light of day.

Let me put it bluntly, Hêktor. It's not the Greeks are to blame. Who could slip through an enemy army in the dark and find the place where Rhesos lay sleeping on the ground—unless, of course, some god directed the killers? The enemy didn't even know Rhesos had arrived. This whole thing smells of a plot.

HÊKTOR: Not once, since the Greek forces landed in Troy, has Troy been without allies, and not once has there been complaint or any discord. Are we now to start with you? Can you really believe that my passion for horses is so great that I would kill friends to get them? It's Odysseus I smell behind this. Who else could have done it? Who else have plotted such a scheme? And, yes, he frightens me. But I'm also troubled for Dolon. Could he and Odysseus have crossed paths, and Odysseus have killed him? He's been gone a long while, and still no sign of him.

CHARIOTEER: What do I know of these Odysseuses of yours! All I know is we're hurt! And no Greeks did it!

HÊKTOR: Think whatever you like, if it's what you want!

CHARIOTEER: Oh god, what I want is to die in my own land!

HÊKTOR: No, no dying. We have enough dead.

CHARIOTEER: Where do I go now that I've lost my master?

HÊKTOR: My own house will see you're healed and cared for.

CHARIOTEER: Care? What care? From a murderer's hands?

HÊKTOR: Will he never give up this lament?

CHARIOTEER: I curse the man who did this! If not you, Hêktor, then he who did. Justice will know.

HÊKTOR: *(To several SOLDIERS.)* Help him to my house; put him to bed. Care for him so we have no more complaints. *(Several SOLDIERS raise the CHARIOTEER to his feet and help him off. To a SOLDIER.)* Go to Priam and the elders on the wall. Tell them, bury the Thracian dead beside the bend in the main road.

(The SOLDIER hurries off.)

(Music.)

FIRST TROJAN SENTRY: *(Chants.)*
   Why is some god reversing Troy's fate,
   Troy's luck, that once was go great?
   Why is Troy's fate to suffer again?
   What disaster will it give birth to?

(The MUSE appears hovering over the scene, in her arms the body of RHESOS.)

SECOND TROJAN SENTRY: *(Chants.)*
   Look, Hêktor, look! There!
   What is this goddess who hovers in the air,
   in her arms the body of Rhesos, dead!
   The sight fills me with fear!

MUSE: *(Speaks.)* Behold me, people of Troy, and have no fear. I am the Muse honored by the wise, one of the sisters, praised by the poets, a mother holding her dear son, dead, in her arms, her child, killed by enemy hands. It was Odysseus, cunning Odysseus, killed him, Odysseus who one day will know the way of Justice.

(Sings.)

I mourn you, my dear, with a song of grief,
a song of sorrow I have sung since you
sailed for Troy on that fateful day.
I held you back, your father begged,
we couldn't hold you.
I mourn you, dear child,
your mother mourns.

FIRST TROJAN SENTRY: *(Speaks.)* I grieve with you, lady, I mourn as
one who is no kin mourns.

MUSE: *(Sings.)*
I curse the grandson of Oineus, Diomêdes!
I curse the son of Laërtês, Odysseus,
who stole my boy, who emptied my life,
the dearest child a mother ever bore!
And I curse Helen,
who betrayed her Greek home for a Phrygian bed!
She killed you at Troy's walls, dear son, and
emptied numberless cities of their bravest.

(Music out.)

MUSE: But it was you, Thamyris, you, both in your life and your death,
who have often wrenched my heart. You were arrogant, and in your
arrogance you went beyond the mark, you slandered the Muses in
their art, and that slander led to the birth of my unfortunate son. It
was when I waded through the water's stream that river god Strymon
drew me to his fertile bed, and so I conceived.

When we had mounted high up the slope of craggy Pangaion,
where the earth is dappled with gold, we Muses competed with pipe
and lyre and song with that great singer of Thrace, the same
Thamyris—and we blinded him, blinded Thamyris, for the slights he
had so often made us.

And when you were born, dear son, ashamed to face my virgin
sisters, I gave you back to your father's watery stream; and he put you
not into the hands of mortals, but to the gentle nursing care of the
nymphs of his springs, who raised you to be king of Thrace and the
first among men.

As long as you stayed in Thrace, defending it even in bloody battle, I never feared for your safety. I warned you only never to go to Troy, for I knew the doom that awaited you there. But Hêktor's endless embassies finally convinced you, and you went to help defend your friends. And yet, in the end, where does the real blame fall? Where but on Athêna? Odysseus? Diomêdes? No. By themselves they could do nothing.

It was you, you, Athêna, you who did this dreadful deed. And did you think I could be forever blinded to it? And is this our reward? Is this how you reward us, the Muses who honor your city over all others with our art and our presence in your land? And Orpheus, blood cousin to this man you have killed, revealed to your city in the glow of torch-lit processions the mysteries too sacred for words. And who instructed Musaios, your great, your revered Athenian who exceeded all other poets? Apollo, myself, and my sisters. And this is our reward. My son, dead in my arms, and bitter tears. I will sing my own dirge.

FIRST TROJAN SENTRY: He was wrong, then, Hêktor, the charioteer who slandered us with Rhesos's death.

HÊKTOR: I knew it. It took no prophet's tongue to tell of Odysseus's cunning in this man's death. Odysseus deals in death. *(To the MUSE.)* I had no choice, lady. None. When I saw the Greek encampment here on the plains of Troy, I knew I had no choice but to send out heralds to plead with friends and allies to come to Troy's rescue. And that's what I did. Rhesos was under an obligation to help, and he came. And his death is a loss I will feel forever. In his honor I will build a great tomb, and will burn together with his body a multitude of splendid robes. He proved himself a friend. He came to our defense. Cruel fortune tripped him up. We mourn him.

MUSE: He will not descend to the black plain of death. This much I will implore from the Bride below, daughter of Dêmêter, goddess of fertile fields, that she will return his soul from the dead. This much she will grant, for she owes me a sign that she honors the family of Orpheus. Rhesos will be to me as one who is dead, never again to see the light of day, never again meet me, or see my face. He will lie deep in the earth, concealed in caverns laced with veins of silver, at once a man and a god, living and deathless, like the prophet of Bakkhos beneath the rocky horn of Pangaion, a god honored by all who understand.

I will bear more lightly now the grief of the sea goddess; for her son, too, must die. We sisters will first sing our dirge for you, my son, then later for Achilleus on Thetis's day of sorrow. Athêna who killed you, cannot save him. Apollo's unerring arrow waits in his quiver.

I weep for the sorrow of mothers, the sorrow of mortals! Be wise, live childless, and you will never bury your children! *(She vanishes.)*

SECOND TROJAN SENTRY: His mother will see to Rhesos's burial, sir.

THIRD TROJAN SENTRY: It's dawn, sir. The sun will soon be up.

FIRST TROJAN SENTRY: It's time to make plans, sir. Decisions—

HÊKTOR: Right. Get the allies on the move. Armed for battle. Teams hitched. When the trumpets sound, with lighted torches we'll cross their trenches, take their walls, and set their ships ablaze. We'll conquer these arrogant Greeks as surely as the sun's rays light the new day and herald a new day of freedom for Troy!
(Music. Song. Dance.)

FIRST TROJAN SENTRY: *(Chants.)*
Do as he says!

THIRD TROJAN SENTRY: *(Chants.)*
To arms!
SECOND TROJAN SENTRY: *(Chants.)*
Get the allies moving!

THIRD TROJAN SENTRY: *(Chants.)*
Pass it along!

SECOND TROJAN SENTRY: *(Chants.)*
Let's go!

FIRST TROJAN SENTRY: *(Chants.)*
Who knows? Some god may
join our side and bring us victory.

*

ACHAIANS: another designation for Greeks or Hellenes.

ACHERON: a river in northern Greece, which, because it ran underground in several places, was believed to be the river that led to the underworld, the sunless realm of the dead presided over by Hades, lord of the dead.

ACHILLEUS: greatest of the Greek warriors in the war at Troy; killed Hêktor; was killed by Paris.

ADRASTEIA: personification of retribution; means: what cannot be escaped from.

ADRASTOS: king of Argos; leader of the Seven against Thebes.

AENEAS: cousin of Hêktor; led Trojan refugees after the war; founded Rome.

AGAMEMNON: king of Mykenê; brother of Menelaos; leader of the Greeks against Troy; husband of Klytaimnêstra; killed by his wife.

AGAVÊ: daughter of Kadmos; mother of Pentheus.

AGENOR: king of Tyre; father of Kadmos and Europa.

AIAKOS: king of Aigina; judge of souls; keeper of the keys of Hades.

AIAS: son of Telamon; cousin of Achilleus; greatest Greek warrior after Achilleus; killed himself when denied the arms of Achilleus.

AIAS: son of Oïleus; Greek commander at Troy; known as the lesser Aias.

AIGISTHOS: son of Thyestes; lover of Klytaimnêstra; helped in the murder of Agamemnon; killed by Orestês.

AIGINA: nymph; daughter of river-god Asopos.

AITOLIA: Greek region between Phokis and Acarnania.

AKTAION: son of Autonoê; cousin of Pentheus; torn apart by his own dogs for spying on Artemis bathing.

ALPHEIOS: river in Greece; site of the temple of Zeus at Olympia.

AMPHIARAÖS: Argive prophet and warrior; foresaw that all but Adrastos would die in the assault of the Seven against Thebes; when fleeing the field of battle, Zeus sent a thunderbolt to open the earth and swallow him and his chariot.

AMPHION: Theban hero who with Zêthos built the walls of Thebes with the playing of his lyre.

ANTIGONÊ: daughter of Oedipus and Iokastê; sister of Ismênê, Eteoklês and Polyneikês.

APHRODITÊ: goddess of sexual love, beauty and fertility; wife of Hephaistos and lover of Arês; said to have been born out of the sea foam;

also known as Kypris after the island that was the seat of her cult; one of the three goddesses in the beauty competition judged by Paris, to win which she offered Helen as a bribe to Paris, thus inciting the Trojan War.

APIDANOS: river in Thessaly.

APOLLO: born on Delos; one of the twelve Olympian gods; symbol of light, youth, beauty; synonymous with music, poetry, medicine, and prophecy; his temple of oracular prophecy at Delphi in central Greece was the most famous in the ancient world; twin brother of Artemis; archer renowned for his unfailing aim.

ARÊS: god of war unpopular among the Greeks; son of Zeus and Hera; lover of Aphroditê and probably father of Eros.

ARETHOUSA: a spring at Chalkis.

ARGIVE: Homeric name for any Greek; a native of Argos; of or pertaining to ancient Argos.

ARGOS: ancient city in southeastern Greece in the northeastern Peloponnesos; also a region in which the city is situated.

ARTEMIS: daughter of Zeus and Hera; twin sister of Apollo; virgin huntress associated with wild places and animals; primitive birth goddess; known as an archer.

ASOPOS: one of the rivers at Thebes.

ATALANTA: Arkadian huntress; mother of Parthenopaios.

ATHÊNA: daughter of Zeus, who sprang fully armed from his head; goddess of wisdom, skills, and warfare; chief defender of the Greeks at Troy; particular defender of Odysseus; in competition with Poseidon, who produced the horse, she won the favor of Athens by producing the olive tree, considered the more valuable, and for which she was made patron of Athens, her namesake.

ATREUS: king of Mykenê; father of Agamemnon and Menelaos; brother of Thyestes.

ATTIKA: peninsula of southeastern Greece; in ancient times a region dominated by Athens, its chief city.

AULIS: port in Boiotia where the Greek fleet gathered to sail to Troy.

AUTONOÊ: daughter of Kadmos; sister of Agavê.

BAKKHAI: women worshipers of Dionysos.

BAKKHOS: also known as Dionysos.

BAKTRIA: mountainous region of Central Asia.

BOIOTIA: country north of Attika.

BROMIOS: another name for Dionysos; means roarer.

CASTALIA: scared spring near Delphi on Mount Parnassos.

CHALKIS: principal city of Euboia.

CHEIRON: centaur; lives in a cave on Mount Pelion; tutor to many Greek heroes, including Achilleus.

DAIMON: spirit of divine power; may be evil.

DANAANS: another name for Greeks or Hellenes.

DANAOS: father of fifty daughters who fled from marriage to their Egyptian cousins.

DARDANOS: ancestor of Priam; founded Troy.

DELOS: island in the Aegean; birthplace of Apollo and Artemis.

DELPHI: Greek city on the southern slopes of Mount Parnassos; site of the most famous oracle of Apollo; in the Greek world considered the world-navel.

DÊMÊTER: Greek corn goddess; associated with fertility; a mother goddess; mother of Persephonê.

DESIRE: a handsome youth who appears on vases in association with Dionysos; personification of the sensual aspect of Dionysos.

DIOMÊDES: king of the Bistones in Thrace; killed in combat with Heraklês over his four-horse team of man-eating horses.

DIONYSOS: god of divine inspiration and the release of mass emotion; associated with wine, fruitfulness, and vegetation; son of Zeus and Semelê; leader of the Bakkhai; bestower of ecstasy; worshipped in a cult centered around orgiastic rites and veiled in great mystery; also known as Iakkhos and Bakkhos.

DIOSKOUROI: the twins Kastor and Polydeukês; sons of Zeus (or Tyndareos) by Lêda; deified by Zeus; brothers of Helen and Klytaimnêstra.

DIRKÊ: one of the two major rivers near Thebes.

DITHYRAMBOS: a cult epithet of Dionysos.

DODONA: city in Epirus with a temple to Zeus.

DOLON: youthful Trojan spy.

ECHIDNA: daimon of earth; symbolizes the power of earth; gave birth to the Sphinx.

EKHION: father of Pentheus; one of the Sown Men.

ÊLEKTRA: daughter of Agamemnon and Klytaimnêstra; brother of Orestês.

ÊLEKTRAN GATE: one of Thebes' seven gates.

ELEUSIS: town in Attika fourteen miles west of Athens; site in classical times of a mystical religious festival, the Eleusinian Mysteries, in which initiates celebrated Dêmêter, Persephonê, and Dionysos.

EPAPHOS: son of Zeus and Io; ancestor of Thebans and Phoenicians through the line of Agenor.

ERINYËS: Furies; goddesses of vengeance within a bloodline.

EROS: god of love.

ETEOKLÊS: king of Thebes; brother of Polyneikês; son of Oedipus and Iokastê.

EUBOIA: island in the west Aegean Sea; second largest island in the Greek archipelago.

EUMENIDES: the kindly ones; originally the Erinyës; avengers of crime against kindred.

EUMOLPOS: king of the Eleusinians; slain in battle by Erectheus, king of Athens.

EURIPOS: channel between Boiotia and the island of Euboia; location of Aulis.

EUROTAS: river of Sparta.

FURIES: the three terrible female spirits with snaky hair who punish the doers of unavenged crimes; spirits of vengeance; see Erinyës

GANYMEDE: Trojan youth beloved of Zeus; swept up by Zeus's eagle to Olympos; served as cupbearer of the gods.

GIANTS: sons of Uranus and Earth; revolted against the Olympian gods.

GORGON: Medusa; killed by Perseus; to look at her was to be turned to stone.

GRACES: three goddesses of loveliness and grace.

HADES: underworld abode of the souls of the dead; lord of the kingdom bearing his name; son of Kronos and Rhea; brother of Zeus, Dêmêter, and Poseidon; husband of Persephonê.

HAIMON: son of Kreon; betrothed to Antigonê.

HARMONIA: daughter of Arês and Aphroditê; wife of Kadmos of Thebes.

HEKATE: a primitive goddess of the underworld later associated with Artemis; connected with sorcery and black magic.

HÊKTOR: son of Priam and Hêkabê; husband of Andromachê; father of Astyanax; killed by Achilleus.

HELEN: daughter of Zeus and Lêda; wife of Menelaos of Sparta; eloped with Paris to Troy and caused the Trojan War.

HEPHAISTOS: son of Zeus and Hera; god of fire and the forge.

HERA: goddess; daughter of Kronos; sister and wife of Zeus.

HERMÊS: Olympian god; son of Zeus and Maia; messenger and herald of the gods; associated with commerce, cunning, theft, travelers, and rascals.

HERMIONÊ: daughter of Menelaos and Helen; wife of Neoptolemos.

HIPPOMEDON: Argive; one of the Seven against Thebes.

IAKKHOS: name that became associated with Dionysos.

IDA: mountain and range southeast of Troy; favored seat of Zeus.

ILION: another name for Troy.

INACHOS: son of Ocean; a river near Argos.

INO: daughter of Kadmos; sister of Agavê; aunt to Pentheus.

IO: daughter of Inachos; loved by Zeus; changed to a cow by a jealous Hera.

IOKASTÊ: mother and wife of Oedipus; sister of Helen; mother of Antigonê, Ismênê, Eteoklês and Polyneikês.

IPHIGENEIA: daughter of Agamemnon and Klytaimnêstra; sacrificed by Agamemnon at Aulis so that the Greek ships could embark for Troy.

ISMÊNÊ: daughter of Oedipus and Iokastê; sister of Antigonê, Eteoklês, and Polyneikês.

ISMÊNOS: one of the rivers at Thebes.

IXION: king of Thessaly; for an attempted rape of Hera he was bound to a wheel that spins eternally.

KADMOS: legendary founder of Thebes.

KALKAS: Greek prophet of Agamemnon's army.

KAPANEUS: an Argive; one of the Seven Against Thebes; struck by Zeus's lightning bolt as he boasted upon scaling the walls of Thebes.

KASSANDRA: daughter of Priam and Hêkabê; prophetess whose prophecies were never believed; taken as mistress by Agamemnon; killed by Klytaimnêstra.

KASTOR: twin brother of Polydeukês; sons of Zeus (or Tyndareos) by Lêda; deified by Zeus; the Dioskouroi.

KILIKIA: kingdom in Asia Minor; a Trojan ally.

KITHAIRON: mountain range between Boiotia and Attika.

KLYTAIMNÊSTRA: wife of Agamemnon who killed him on his return from Troy.

KOLONOS: a small town north of Athens where Oedipus died.

KOROIBOS: Trojan commander; killed at Troy.

KORYBANTES: companions of Kybêlê.

KORYKIAN PEAKS: a sacred area on Mount Parnassos; home of the Korykian nymphs; associated with Dionysos.

KREON: brother of Iokastê; brother-in law of Oedipus; uncle to Eteoklês, Polyneikês, Ismênê and Antigonê.

KRETE: large island south of Greece; birthplace of Zeus.

KRONOS: father of Zeus and Rhea; ruler of the generation of gods before the Olympians; Zeus overthrew him.

KYBÊLÊ: Phrygian Earth Mother goddess; identified with Rhea; her worship is ecstatic, resembling that of Dionysos.

KYPRIAN: having to do with Kypris; also known as Aphroditê.

KYPRIS: goddess of love; also known as Aphroditê.

LABDAKOS: father of Laïos; grandfather of Oedipus.

LAËRTES: father of Odysseus.

LERNA: city to the south of Argos where Heraklês killed the hydra.

LÊDA: mother of Helen, Klytaimnêstra, and the Dioskouroi.

LÊTO: mother by Zeus of Apollo and Artemis.

LOXIAS: cult name of Apollo.

LYDIA: region on the west coast of Asia Minor; Greek source of slaves.

LYDIAN: pertaining to anything of Lydia.

LYDIAS: river of Macedonia.

LYKIA: area on the southern coast of Asia Minor; a Trojan ally.

MAENADS: female followers of Dionysos, also known as bakkhants.

MAIA: daughter of Atlas; mother of Hermês.

MENELAOS: brother of Agamemnon; husband of Helen; king of Sparta.

MENOIKEUS: father of Kreon; son of Kreon.

MÊRIONÊS: commander of the Kretans at Troy.

MUSAIOS: poet from Thrace; wrote in Greek; disciple of Orpheus.

MUSES: nine goddesses who presided over literature, the arts and sciences.

MYKENÊ: city in the Peloponnesos near Argos; at one time united with Argos under Eurystheus.

MYRMIDONS: subject to Peleus and Achilleus

MYSIA: a Trojan ally.

NAUPLIA: a coastal town in Argos; its bay was the gathering point for the Greek armada before it set off for Aulis

NEMESIS: goddess of retribution; daughter of Zeus.

NÊRÊIDS: fifty nymphs of the sea; daughters of Nêreus.

NÊREUS: sea god; father of the fifty Nêrêids.

NESTOR: wise old statesman; leader of the Greeks at Troy.

NIOBÊ: queen of Phrygia whose six sons and six daughters were killed by Apollo and Artemis because she boasted they were more beautiful than the two gods.

NIREUS: the handsomest man at Troy according to Homer.

NYSA: mountain sacred to Dionysos.

ODYSSEUS: son of Laërtes; king of Ithaka; known for his wily and cunning nature.

OEDIPUS: son of Laïos; son and husband of Iokastê; father and brother of Antigonê, Ismênê, Eteoklês and Polyneikês.

OÏLEUS: father of the lesser Aias.

OINONE: ancient name of the island of Aigina.

OLYMPOS: mountain in northeastern Thessaly; seat of the Olympian gods.

ORESTÊS: son of Agamemnon and Klytaimnêstra; smuggled to Phokis as a child for safekeeping during the Trojan War; kills his mother in revenge for her murder of Agamemnon.

ORPHEUS: mythic poet and musician who charmed trees, rocks, and wild beasts with the beauty of his music.

PAIONIA: land to the northwest of Thebes.

PALAMÊDES: son of Nauplios son of Poseidon; reputedly invented checkers.

PALLAS: another name for Athêna.

PANGAION: mountain in southwestern Thrace.

PARIS: son of Priam and Hêkabê; abducted Helen from Sparta.

PARTHENOPAIOS: Arcadian; son of Atalanta; one of the Seven Against Thebes.

PELASGIA: ancient name for Argos.

PELEUS: king of Thessaly; mortal married to the Nêrêid Thetis; father of Achilleus.

PELION: mountain in Thessaly.

PELOPS: king of Argos; father of Atreus; grandfather of Agamemnon and Menelaos; gave his name to the Peloponnesos.

PERGAMON: a city near Troy.

PERIKLYMENOS: Theban; defeats Parthenopaios in battle.

PERSEPHONÊ: daughter of Dêmêter; queen of the underworld; also known as Korê.

PERSEUS: ancestor of Heraklês and Alkmênê; killed the Gorgon Medusa.

PHERÊS: father of Admêtos.

PHOIBÊ: sister of Klytaimnêstra and Helen.

PHOIBOS: epithet of Apollo; means bright.

PHOKIS: region of Greece near Delphi; kingdom of Strophios.

PHRYGIA: general region in which Troy was situated.

PLEIADES: seven-star constellation; daughters of Atlas placed in the heavens by Zeus.

POLYBOS: king of Korinth; adopted Oedipus as an infant.

POLYDEUKÊS: twin brother of Kastor; sons of Zeus (or Tyndareos) by Lêda; deified by Zeus; the Dioskouroi.

POLYDOROS: young son of Priam and Hêkabê; murdered by Polymêstor for his wealth.

POLYNEIKÊS: brother of Eteoklês, Antigonê and Ismênê; son of Oedipus and Iokastê.

POSEIDON: god of the sea; brother to Zeus.

PRIAM: king of Troy; husband of Hêkabê; killed by Achilleus's son Neoptolemos at Troy.

PROMÊTHEUS: A Titan god who fought on the side of Zeus and the Olympians against his brother Titans.

PROTESILAOS: Greek hero at Troy.

PYLADÊS: son of Strophios; friend-lover of Orestês; husband of Êlektra.

PYTHIAN: relating to the temple of Apollo at Delphi.

RHEA: wife of Kronos; ancient goddess; mother of Zeus and Hera; frequently confused with Kybêlê.

RHESOS: king of Thrace; son of a Muse.

SALAMIS: island off the coast of Athens in the Saronic Gulf.

SARDIS: important city of Lydia.

SCYTHIANS: tribes whose district covered the area between the Danube and the Don.

SELANAIA: the moon; Artemis.

SEMELÊ: daughter of Kadmos; mother of Dionysos by Zeus.

SIDON: city in Syria on the Mediterranean coast.

SIMOÏS: river at Troy.

SIRIUS: the dog star who pursues the Pleiades at night.

SISYPHOS: a king of Korinth; trickster; condemned for various crimes; in Hades his punishment is to roll a large rock to the top of a hill only to have it roll again to the bottom to have the process repeated eternally.

SOWN MEN: men sprung from the dragon's teeth sown by Kadmos at Thebes.

SPARTA: principal city in the southern Peloponnesos

SPHINX: fabulous monster, with human head and body of a lion; originated in Egypt; came to Greece from the Near East; usually female.

STROPHIOS: king of Phokis; father of Pyladês; brother-in-law of Agamemnon.

STRYMON: river between Greece and Thrace in ancient times; also a river god.

TANTALOS: father of Pelops; founder of the House of Atreus.

TALTHYBIOS: Greek herald.

TARTAROS: the lowest level beneath the earth; beneath Hades; reserved for evildoers.

TEIRESIAS: blind Theban prophet.

TELAMON: king of Salamis; father of Aias and Teükros; exiled with Peleus from Aigina by Aiakos for killing Phokos.

THAMYRIS: Thracian musician; grandson of Apollo.

THEBES: major city in Boiotia; founded by Kadmos; populated it with the Sown Men; birthplace of Dionysos.

THÊSEUS: father of Hippolytos, husband of Phaidra; mythical king of Athens.

THESPROTIA: hill beyond the walls of Thebes from which position an Argive attack was launched.

THESSALY: a savage province in northern Greece.

THESTIOS: king of Aitolia.

THETIS: sea-nymph; mother of Achilleus by Peleus.

THRACE: large area situated between Macedon and the Danube; associated by early Greeks with the war god Arês because of its barbarity.

THYESTES: son of Pelops; brother of Atreus.

THYMBRA: town near Troy; cult center of Apollo.

THYRSOS: fennel-stalk wound with ivy at its tip; carried by the Bakkhai in their ecstatic dances.

TMOLOS: mountain in Lydia known for its gold.

TROY: city in northeastern Asia Minor; site of the Trojan War.

TYNDAREOS: king of Sparta; father of Helen and Klytaimnêstra.

TYDEUS: one of the Seven Against Thebes.

ZÊTHOS: brother of Amphion.

ZEUS: chief god of the Olympians.

SELECT BIBLIOGRAPHY

Aristotle. *The Poetics.* Translated by Gerald Else. Ann Arbor: University of Michigan Press, 1967.

Arnott, Peter. *Public and Performance in the Greek Theatre.* London: Routledge, 1989.

―――. *Greek Scenic Conventions in the Fifth Century BC.* Oxford: Oxford University Press, 1962.

Bieber, Margarete. *The History of the Greek and Roman Theater.* 2nd ed. Princeton: Princeton University Press, 1961.

Blundell, Sue. *Women in Ancient Greece.* London: British Museum Press, 1995.

Burian, Peter. *New Directions in Euripidean Criticism.* Durham, NC: Duke University Press, 1985.

Burkert, Walter. *Greek Religion.* Cambridge, MA: Harvard University Press, 1985.

Burnett, Anne Pippin. *Catastrophe Survived: Euripides' Plays of Mixed Reversal.* Oxford: Clarendon Press, 1971.

Bury, J. B., and Russell Meiggs. *A History of Greece to the Death of Alexander the Great.* 4th ed. New York: St. Martin's Press, 1991.

Buxton, R. G. *Persuasion in Greek Tragedy.* Cambridge: Cambridge University Press, 1982.

Collard, Christopher. *Euripides: Iphigenia in Aulis.* Warminster, UK: Aris and Phillips, Ltd. (forthcoming).

Conacher, D. J. *Euripidean Drama: Myth, Theme and Structure.* Toronto: University of Toronto Press, 1967.

Craik, E. *Euripides: Phoenician Women.* Warminster, UK: Aris and Phillips, Ltd., 1988.

Csapo, Eric, and William J. Slater. *The Context of Ancient Drama.* Ann Arbor: University of Michigan Press, 1995.

Dodds, E. R. *Euripides: Bacchae.* 2nd ed. Oxford: Oxford University Press, 1960.

Dunn, Francis M. *Tragedy's End: Closure and Innovation in Euripidean Drama.* New York and Oxford: Oxford University Press, 1996.

Easterling, P. E., ed. *The Cambridge Companion to Greek Tragedy.* Cambridge: Cambridge University Press, 1997.

Else, Gerald F. *The Origin and Early Form of Greek Tragedy.* Martin Classical Lectures, Vol. 20. Cambridge, MA: Harvard University Press, 1965.

Goldhill, Simon. *Reading Greek Tragedy.* Cambridge: Cambridge University Press, 1986.

Grube, G. M. A. *The Drama of Euripides.* London: Methuen, 1941.

Günther, H. C. *Euripides: Iphigenia in Aulis.* New York: Arno Press, 1979.

Hall, Edith. *The Rhesus Attributed to Euripides.* Warminster, UK: Aris and Phillips, Ltd. (forthcoming).

Halleran, Michael. *Stagecraft in Euripides.* London and Sydney: Croom Helm, 1985.

Hornblower, Simon, and Antony Spawforth, eds. *The Oxford Classical Dictionary.* 3rd ed. Oxford: Oxford University Press, 1996.

Hornby, Richard. *Script into Performance.* Austin: University of Texas Press, 1977.

Jones, John. *On Aristotle and Greek Tragedy.* Stanford, CA: Stanford University Press, 1980.

Just, Roger. *Women in Athenian Law and Life.* London and New York: Routledge, 1991.

Kitto, H. D. F. *Form and Meaning in Drama: A Study of Six Greek Plays and of Hamlet.* 2nd ed. London: Methuen, 1964; New York: Barnes and Noble, 1968.

———. *Greek Tragedy: A Literary Study.* 2nd ed. New York: Doubleday, 1964; 3rd ed. London: Methuen, 1966.

———. *Word and Action: Essays on the Ancient Theater.* Baltimore and London: Johns Hopkins University Press, 1979.

Knox, B. M. W. *Word and Action.* Baltimore: Johns Hopkins University Press, 1979.

Kott, Jan. *The Eating of the Gods: An Interpretation of Greek Tragedy.* New York: Random House, 1973.

Lattimore, Richmond. *The Poetry of Greek Tragedy.* Baltimore: Johns Hopkins University Press, 1958.

———. *The Story-Patterns in Greek Tragedy.* Ann Arbor: University of Michigan Press, 1964.

Lesky, Albin. *Greek Tragedy.* London: Ernest Benn, Ltd., 1978.

Lloyd-Jones, Hugh. *The Justice of Zeus.* Sather Gate Lectures, Vol. 41. Berkeley and Los Angeles: University of California Press, 1971.

Mastronarde, D. J. *Euripides: Phoenissae.* Cambridge: Cambridge University Press, 1994.

———. *Contact and Disunity: Some Conventions of Speech and Action on the Greek Tragic Stage.* Berkeley and Los Angeles: University of California Press, 1979.

Michelini, Ann Norris. *Euripides and the Tragic Tradition.* Madison: University of Wisconsin Press, 1987.

Murray, Gilbert. *Euripides and His Age.* London: Oxford University Press, 1946.

Neils, Jenifer. *Goddess and Polis: The Panathenaic Festival in Ancient Athens.* Princeton: Princeton University Press, 1992.

Pickard-Cambridge, A. W. *The Dramatic Festivals of Athens.* 2nd ed. Oxford: Clarendon Press, 1968.

———. *The Theatre of Dionysus in Athens.* Oxford: Clarendon Press, 1946.

Porter, W. H. *The Rhesus of Euripides.* 2nd ed. Cambridge: Cambridge University Press, 1929.

Powell, Anton, ed. *Euripides, Women, and Sexuality.* London and New York: Routledge, 1990.

Rehm, Rush. *The Greek Tragic Theatre.* London and New York: Routledge, 1992.

Seaford, Richard. *Euripides: Cyclops.* Oxford: Oxford University Press, 1984.

Segal, Charles. *Interpreting Greek Tragedy: Myth, Poetry, Text.* Ithaca, NY: Cornell University Press, 1986.

Segal, Erich. *Oxford Essays in Greek Tragedy.* Oxford: Oxford University Press, 1984.

————, ed. *Euripides: A Collection of Critical Essays.* Englewood Cliffs, NJ: Prentice-Hall, 1968.

Steiner, George. *The Death of Tragedy.* New York: Alfred A. Knopf; London: Faber and Faber, 1961.

Taplin, Oliver. *Greek Tragedy in Action.* Berkeley and Los Angeles: University of California Press; London: Methuen, 1978.

Thucydides. *The Peloponnesian Wars.* Translated by Rex Warner. Harmondsworth, UK: Penguin Classics, 1972.

Vernant, Jean-Pierre, and Pierre Vidal-Naquet, eds. *Myth and Tragedy in Ancient Greece.* New York: Zone Books, 1990.

Vickers, Brian. *Towards Greek Tragedy.* London: Longman, 1973.

Walcot, Peter. *Greek Drama in Its Theatrical and Social Context.* Cardiff, UK: University of Wales Press, 1976.

Walton, J. Michael. *The Greek Sense of Theatre: Tragedy Reviewed.* London and New York: Methuen, 1984.

————. *Greek Theatre Practice.* Westport, CT, and London: Greenwood Press, 1980.

Webster, T. B. L. *The Tragedies of Euripides.* London: Methuen, 1967.

West, M. L. *Euripides: Orestes.* Warminster, UK: Aris and Phillips, Ltd., 1987.

Whitman, Cedric. *Euripides and the Full Circle of Myth.* Cambridge, MA: Harvard University Press, 1974.

Wiles, David. *Tragedy in Athens.* Cambridge and New York: Cambridge University Press, 1997.

Willink, C. W. *Euripides: Orestes.* Oxford: Oxford University Press, 1986.

Winkler, John, and Froma I. Zeitlin, eds. *Nothing to Do with Dionysus.* Princeton: Princeton University Press, 1990.

Zuntz, G. *The Political Plays of Euripides.* Manchester, UK: Manchester University Press, 1963.

CARL R. MUELLER has since 1967 been professor in the Department of Theater at the University of California, Los Angeles, where he has taught theater history, criticism, dramatic literature, and playwriting, as well as having directed. He was educated at Northwestern University, where he received a B.S. in English. After work in graduate English at the University of California, Berkeley, he received his M.A. in playwriting at UCLA, where he also completed his Ph.D. in theater history and criticism. In addition, he was a Fulbright Scholar in Berlin in 1960–1961. A translator for more than forty years, he has translated and published works by Büchner, Brecht, Wedekind, Hauptmann, Hofmannsthal, and Hebbel, to name a few. His published translation of von Horváth's *Tales from the Vienna Woods* was given its London West End premiere in July 1999. For Smith and Kraus, he has translated volumes of plays by Schnitzler, Strindberg, Pirandello, Kleist, and Wedekind, as well as Goethe's *Faust, Parts I and II*. In addition to translating the complete plays of Euripides and Aeschylus for Smith and Kraus, he has also cotranslated the plays of Sophokles. His translations have been performed in every English-speaking country and have appeared on BBC-TV.